Ultimate Figma for UI/UX Design

Transform Your UI/UX Design, Craft User-Centric Interfaces, and Create Stunning Experiences with Ease

Aditi Sharma

www.orangeava.com

First Published: February 2025

Published By: Orange Education Pvt Ltd, AVA®

Address: 9, Daryaganj, Delhi, 110002, India

275 New North Road Islington Suite 1314 London,

N1 7AA, United Kingdom

ISBN (PBK): 978-93-48107-79-4

ISBN (E-BOOK): 978-93-48107-35-0

Scan the QR code to explore our entire catalogue

www.orangeava.com

Dedicated To

This Book is Dedicated to My Mother, Indu, Whose Unwavering Love and Encouragement has Been the Bedrock of My Journey, and to My Daughter, Radha, Whose Arrival has Brought Boundless Joy and Inspiration to My Life. Her Presence in My World Makes Everything More Meaningful

About the Author

Aditi Sharma is an award-winning design executive passionate about inclusive, ethical, sustainable, and human-centered innovation. She is the recipient of the prestigious Dr. Sarojini Naidu Award from the Government of India, the '40 under 40' award from Business Elite, the 'Woman Who Builds' award from Globant, and was named an inspirational woman in STEM by *Authority Magazine.*

As a lecturer at Pratt, Aditi curated one of the top ten UX programs offered in the United States. A published design practitioner, she is regularly invited to share her thought leadership through print, keynotes, and podcasts for CampaignLive, Business Insider, AI & Data Analytics Network, Interaction Design Association, Brave UX, Authority Magazine, Inclusive Design Association, Customer Experience Network, Finance Magnates, South by Southwest (SXSW), and Product-Led Alliance (PLA), among others.

Currently, as the Head of Design and Research at Amazon, Aditi manages a global team shaping customer experience for over 30 Fintech products, helping track revenue, usage, costs, and forecasts for AWS. Previously, as the Head of Payments Design/Executive Director of Digital Experience Design at J.P. Morgan Chase, she set up a global design practice to build intelligent enterprise Fintech platforms. Prior to that, at Accenture Interactive, she strategized and executed customer-centric design strategies for clients such as Walmart, DuPont, and Cargill. She continues to explore the dynamism of creativity to deliver customer outcomes at the intersection of human excellence, business profitability, and technical innovation.

About the Technical Reviewer

Rakesh Mondal has over 10 years of experience in SaaS product design, specializing in creating outstanding user experiences and user-friendly interfaces for software-as-a-service products. His skillset is comprehensive, spanning the entire design process. He excels in user research, employing various methodologies to understand user needs, behaviors, and pain points, which inform his design decisions. He is proficient in wireframing, creating detailed blueprints that define layout, functionality, and information hierarchy. Furthermore, he is skilled in prototyping, developing interactive models that allow for user testing and iterative refinement before development begins.

He leverages industry-standard tools like Figma and Miro to bring his design visions to life, using them for everything from creating low-fidelity wireframes to high-fidelity interactive prototypes. His primary focus is on creating user-friendly designs that directly contribute to the success of the product. This involves a strong understanding of fundamental design principles, including usability, accessibility, visual hierarchy, and interaction design. He possesses a keen understanding of how to effectively structure information and interactions, ensuring that users can easily navigate the interface, find the information they need, and accomplish their tasks efficiently.

Acknowledgements

Writing *Ultimate Figma for UI/UX Design* has been an incredible journey, one that would not have been possible without the unwavering support and encouragement of many special people in my life. First and foremost, I express my deepest gratitude to my parents. Their constant encouragement and belief in my abilities have been my guiding light. I thank them for always pushing me to reach my fullest potential and for being my greatest cheerleaders.

To my daughter, Radha, who brought immense joy and perspective to my life. Her presence has reminded me of the importance of perseverance and dedication. I thank her for being my inspiration every day.

A special thanks to Erica Burroughs for contributing a case study to the book. Her insights and expertise have enriched the content, providing invaluable real-world context for readers.

Finally, I extend my heartfelt thanks to my publishers at AVA Books. Their expertise, guidance, and patience have been invaluable throughout this process. Their belief in this vision has been instrumental in bringing this book to life.

This book is a testament to the incredible support system I am blessed with, and I am profoundly grateful to each individual involved. Hope this book brings readers as much learning, joy, and fun as it brought me. Enjoy reading!

Preface

Welcome to *Ultimate Figma for UI/UX Design*. In the rapidly evolving landscape of design, where collaboration, efficiency, and innovation are paramount, mastering the right tools is essential for success. Figma stands at the forefront of this evolution, empowering designers and design teams worldwide with its cloud-based design and collaboration platform.

By understanding the significance of Figma in modern design workflows and the transformative impact it can have on your professional endeavors, you will be motivated to delve deeper into the subsequent chapters of this book. This book is crafted for designers, from beginners to seasoned professionals, seeking to harness the full potential of Figma in their design workflows. Whether you are a UI/UX designer, product designer, or graphic designer, *Ultimate Figma for UI/UX Design* provides you with the knowledge, skills, and insights needed to excel in today's competitive design industry.

This comprehensive guide is curated to help you navigate the complexities of Figma with confidence. From the fundamentals of setting up a Figma account to advanced techniques for prototyping and collaboration, each chapter is designed to equip you with practical skills and actionable insights that you can apply immediately to your design projects. Through step-by-step tutorials, real-world examples, and expert tips, you will learn how to leverage Figma's powerful features, streamline your design workflow, and collaborate seamlessly with your team. Whether you are working on a solo project or collaborating with a global team, Figma empowers you to bring your design ideas to life, iterate rapidly, and deliver exceptional user experiences.

Let us embark on this journey to explore the depths of Figma and unlock its full potential. Whether you are a newcomer to Figma or a seasoned user looking to deepen your expertise, *Ultimate Figma for UI/UX Design* is your definitive guide to mastering modern design and collaboration in the digital age. Let us dive in and elevate your design practice to new heights with Figma. This book is divided into 10 chapters and its details are listed as follows:

Chapter 1 introduces Figma, a powerful design and collaboration tool used by professionals worldwide. It begins with an overview of Figma's significance in modern design workflows, highlighting its accessibility, real-time collaboration features, and cross-platform compatibility. Readers are guided through account setup and interface navigation, learning key elements including toolbar, layers panel, and properties panel. This interface familiarization establishes a foundation for efficient Figma use. This chapter provides a solid understanding of Figma's capabilities and navigation, preparing readers for subsequent chapters

Chapter 2 explores core design principles—composition, hierarchy, color theory, typography, and whitespace—within Figma. Through examples and exercises, readers learn to work with shapes, colors, and typography using Figma's tools. Emphasizing design consistency and coherence, the chapter helps readers create visually appealing and user-friendly interfaces. By applying these principles in Figma, readers build a strong foundation for compelling, effective designs. This chapter is crucial for enhancing design skills and creating professional-quality work in Figma.

Chapter 3 provides a comprehensive overview of the Figma interface, covering key components like the toolbar, layers panel, and properties panel. Readers learn to customize the interface for optimal workflow and discover practical tips for increased efficiency. Essential navigation techniques, such as zooming, panning, and frame navigation, are also covered. Hands-on exercises provide practical experience, enabling confident and efficient platform use. Mastering the Figma interface empowers designers to focus on creative work and achieve more impactful results.

Chapter 4 explores UI element design in Figma, emphasizing its importance in creating intuitive digital experiences. Readers learn to create UI components such as buttons, forms, navigation bars, and icons using Figma's tools, with attention to spacing, alignment, and consistency. The chapter covers best practices for maintaining consistency using design systems, component libraries, and style guides. Hands-on exercises and real-world examples solidify understanding of UI design principles within Figma, equipping designers to build user-friendly and cohesive interfaces.

Chapter 5 focuses on Figma's prototyping capabilities, introducing the concept and its importance in design. Readers learn to create interactive prototypes with transitions, animations, and hotspots, using step-by-step guides for linking frames, defining interactions, and simulating user flows. The chapter also covers prototype testing, previewing, sharing, and gathering feedback. Hands-on exercises and case studies deepen understanding of Figma prototyping for creating engaging user experiences and effectively communicating design visions to stakeholders.

Chapter 6 delves into advanced Figma design techniques, including blending modes, effects, and advanced typography. Readers learn to use blending modes for stunning effects, apply effects like shadows and blurs for depth, and master typography techniques like kerning and leading. Hands-on exercises and examples demonstrate how to apply these techniques creatively. Mastering these skills allows users to elevate the quality and visual impact of their Figma designs.

Chapter 7 focuses on Figma's collaborative features and best practices for teamwork. It highlights Figma's real-time collaboration capabilities, including commenting, sharing, and version control, for streamlined communication and workflow. Practical examples show how teams can collaborate simultaneously, providing feedback and tracking changes. The chapter also covers strategies for managing design iterations, organizing files, creating design systems, and maintaining consistency. Case studies illustrate effective team collaboration on complex projects. Mastering these workflows empowers readers to work more efficiently and achieve better design outcomes

Chapter 8 focuses on extending the functionality of Figma through the integration of plugins and external tools. It overviews the Figma plugin ecosystem, showing how to browse, install, and manage plugins to customize workflows. Practical examples demonstrate how plugins streamline tasks like color management, content generation, and accessibility testing. The chapter also covers integrating third-party tools for seamless use of external resources, such as design handoff tools for developers and design systems for project consistency.

Chapter 9 focuses on designing responsive interfaces in Figma for various devices. It explains the importance of responsive design in today's multi-device world and introduces key concepts such as fluid layouts, flexible grids, and media queries. Practical techniques for designing responsive components and layouts, including Figma's auto-layout feature, are demonstrated. Examples and case studies highlight best practices for optimizing designs for responsiveness and ensuring consistent user experiences. It also covers testing and previewing designs within Figma, empowering readers to identify and address any responsive design issues effectively.

Chapter 10 covers practical Figma application through real-world projects and case studies, demonstrating its use in professional design contexts. Showcasing successful Figma designs, the chapter analyzes the design process from concept to execution. It also offers practical tips for building a professional design portfolio using Figma projects, teaching readers how to effectively showcase their skills. Exploring these real-world examples helps readers understand how Figma solves design challenges and inspires them to apply their skills and build a strong portfolio.

Get a Free eBook

We hope you are enjoying your recently purchased book! Your feedback is incredibly valuable to us, and to all other readers looking for great books.

If you found this book helpful or enjoyable, we would truly appreciate it, if you could take a moment to leave a short review with a 5 star rating on Amazon. It helps us grow, and lets other readers discover our books.

As a thank you, we would love to send you a free digital copy of this book, and a **30%** discount code on your next cart value on our official websites:

www.orangeava.com

www.orangeava.in (For Indian Subcontinent)

☑ **Here's how:**

Leave a review for the book on Amazon.

Take a screenshot of your review, and send an email to **info@orangeava.com** (it can be just the confirmation screen).

Once, we receive your screenshot, we will send you the digital file, within 24 hours.

Thank you so much for your support – it means a lot to us!

Colored Images

Please follow the links or scan the QR codes to download the ***Images*** of the book:

You can find code bundles of our books on our official Github Repository. Go to the following link to and QR code to explore the further:

https://github.com/orgs/ava-orange-education/repositories

Please follow the link to download the Colored Images of the book:
https://rebrand.ly/kau76ne

In case there's an update to the code, it will be updated on the existing GitHub repository.

Errata

We take immense pride in our work at **Orange Education Pvt Ltd,** and follow best practices to ensure the accuracy of our content to provide an indulging reading experience to our subscribers. Our readers are our mirrors, and we use their inputs to reflect and improve upon human errors, if any, that may have occurred during the publishing processes involved. To let us maintain the quality and help us reach out to any readers who might be having difficulties due to any unforeseen errors, please write to us at :

errata@orangeava.com

Your support, suggestions, and feedback are highly appreciated.

DID YOU KNOW

Did you know that Orange Education Pvt Ltd offers eBook versions of every book published, with PDF and ePub files available? You can upgrade to the eBook version at **www.orangeava.com** and as a print book customer, you are entitled to a discount on the eBook copy. Get in touch with us at: **info@orangeava.com** for more details.

At **www.orangeava.com**, you can also read a collection of free technical articles, sign up for a range of free newsletters, and receive exclusive discounts and offers on AVA® Books and eBooks.

PIRACY

If you come across any illegal copies of our works in any form on the internet, we would be grateful if you would provide us with the location address or website name. Please contact us at **info@orangeava.com** with a link to the material.

ARE YOU INTERESTED IN AUTHORING WITH US?

If there is a topic that you have expertise in, and you are interested in either writing or contributing to a book, please write to us at **business@orangeava.com**. We are on a journey to help developers and tech professionals to gain insights on the present technological advancements and innovations happening across the globe and build a community that believes Knowledge is best acquired by sharing and learning with others. Please reach out to us to learn what our audience demands and how you can be part of this educational reform. We also welcome ideas from tech experts and help them build learning and development content for their domains.

REVIEWS

Please leave a review. Once you have read and used this book, why not leave a review on the site that you purchased it from? Potential readers can then see and use your unbiased opinion to make purchase decisions. We at Orange Education would love to know what you think about our products, and our authors can learn from your feedback. Thank you!

For more information about Orange Education, please visit **www.orangeava.com**.

Table of Contents

Chapter 1
Introduction to Figma

Introduction

The first chapter covers the evolution of design tools, the role of Figma in contemporary design practices, that is, core features and benefits of using Figma, and basic navigation techniques in Figma. From understanding the fundamentals of Figma's interface to mastering advanced design techniques and collaboration workflows, readers can expect a comprehensive exploration of Figma's features and functionalities.

Figma has emerged as a leading platform in digital design and collaboration, revolutionizing the way designers create, iterate, and share their work. As such, it is imperative for designers at all levels to familiarize themselves with Figma's capabilities and harness its potential to enhance their workflow and productivity.

We start by setting the stage for the readers' exploration of Figma by providing a comprehensive overview of what you can expect to learn about this versatile design tool. This chapter also introduces frames and components as fundamental building blocks in Figma and provides a step-by-step guide to setting up a Figma account.

By the end of this introduction, you should feel inspired and motivated to embark on your journey of learning and mastering Figma, equipped with the knowledge and confidence to tackle the challenges and opportunities that await you in the world of design.

Structure

In this chapter, the following topics will be covered:

- Evolution of Design Tools
- An Overview of Figma
- Getting Started with Figma
- Navigating Figma

Evolution of Design Tools

How design tools have evolved from traditional software to cloud-based platforms:

The evolution of design tools from traditional software to cloud-based platforms has been a transformative journey driven by advancements in technology, changing design practices, and the growing demand for collaboration and accessibility. Here is how this evolution has unfolded over time:

- **Traditional software era:** In the early days of digital design, designers relied on desktop software installed on individual computers to create graphics and layouts. Examples of traditional design software include Adobe Photoshop, Adobe Illustrator, and CorelDRAW. Designers worked in isolation, creating and saving files locally on their computers. Collaboration was limited, with designers often sharing files via email or physical storage devices.
- **Introduction of web-based tools:** With the rise of web technologies, web-based design tools began to emerge. These tools allowed designers to create and collaborate on designs directly within web browsers, eliminating the need for desktop software. Web-based design tools offer advantages such as accessibility from a variety of devices, real-time collaboration features, and automatic syncing of files to the cloud.
- **Transition to cloud-based platforms:** Cloud-based design platforms took the concept of web-based tools a step further by offering a comprehensive suite of design and collaboration features entirely in the cloud. Cloud-based platforms such as Figma, Adobe XD, Sketch Cloud, and InVision revolutionized the way designers work by providing effortless collaboration, real-time syncing of files, and access to the latest updates and/or upgrades without needing manual installations or updates.

Overall, the transition from traditional software to cloud-based platforms has democratized design, making it more accessible, collaborative, and efficient than ever before. Cloud-based design platforms have become indispensable tools for designers and design teams, empowering them to create, collaborate, and iterate on designs seamlessly in the contemporary fast-paced digital landscape.

Traits of an Ideal UX design and Prototyping Platform

As an ideal design prototyping tool, Figma offers a range of features to help designers create interactive mockups of interfaces and user experiences. Here are some of its notable features:

- **Ease of use:** A user-friendly interface with drag-and-drop functionality for designers to focus on creativity rather than wrestling with operating complex software.

- **Interactivity:** Figma enables the creation of clickable elements and simulated user interactions. This lets users experience the flow and functionality of a design before development begins.
- **Collaboration:** Features such as real-time co-editing and sharing functionalities are crucial for fostering teamwork and gathering feedback on prototypes.
- **Responsiveness:** The ability to design prototypes that adapt to different screen sizes and devices is essential in today's multi-device landscape.
- **Integration:** Compatibility with other design and development tools that allows for a smooth workflow from prototyping to development. This might involve exporting code snippets or design assets for developers.
- **High-fidelity prototyping:** It helps create high-fidelity prototypes that closely resemble the final product in terms of look and feel. This can be helpful for user testing and getting stakeholder buy-in.
- **Animation capabilities:** The ability to add animations and micro-interactions to enhance the user experience of prototypes and make them feel more polished and engaging.
- **Version control:** It enables tracking changes made to prototypes, especially in collaborative environments to allow designers to revert to previous iterations if needed.
- **Asset management:** It helps storing and managing design assets such as icons, buttons, and color palettes within the prototyping tool to streamline the design process and ensure consistency.

The Role of Figma in the Context of Contemporary Design Practices

In the context of contemporary design practices, Figma holds significant importance due to several key factors:

- **Cloud-based real-time collaboration:** Figma's web-based nature facilitates real-time collaboration among designers. This is a game-changer for modern design teams, many of whom are geographically dispersed or work remotely. Multiple designers can edit and iterate on the same project simultaneously, fostering faster development cycles and smoother communication.
- **Accessibility and ease of use:** Figma boasts of a user-friendly interface that makes it accessible to designers of all experience levels. The cloud-based nature eliminates the need for complex installations or software updates, making it ideal for both individuals and design teams of all sizes.

- **Growing community and resources:** Figma has cultivated a large and active community of designers. This translates to a wealth of online resources, tutorials, and plugins that extend Figma's functionality and empower users to tackle complex design challenges.
- **Constant innovation:** The Figma team constantly innovates and keeps adding new features. This ensures Figma stays at the forefront of design technology and adapts to the ever-evolving needs of contemporary designers.

History of Figma

Figma, founded in 2012 by Dylan Field and Evan Wallace, emerged as a pioneer amongst cloud-based collaborative design tools. The platform was conceived as a response to the limitations and inefficiencies of traditional design software, which often required manual file transfers and lacked real-time collaboration features.

In its early stages, Figma attracted attention for its ambitious vision of bringing design collaboration to the cloud. The founders aimed to create a platform that would enable designers to work together seamlessly, regardless of their location or the devices they were using. For their product launch, Figma gained traction with designers and design teams by offering a free beta version of its product, allowing users to experience the benefits of cloud-based design firsthand. As Figma continued to refine its platform and add new features, it quickly gained a loyal following within the design community.

One of Figma's defining features is its robust real-time collaboration capabilities, which allow multiple users to work on the same design file simultaneously. This feature set Figma apart from its competitors and positioned it as a leader in the rapidly evolving design tools landscape. Over the years, Figma has continued to innovate and expand its platform, introducing features such as prototyping, design systems management, and developer handoff. The company has also cultivated a vibrant community of designers, developers, and enthusiasts who contribute to its ecosystem through plugins, templates, and resources.

In 2020, Figma raised $50 million in a Series D funding round, valuing the company at $2 billion. This milestone underscored Figma's growing influence and solidified its position as a key player in the design industry. In September 2022, Adobe announced a $20 billion acquisition of Figma. Subsequently, in December 2023, Adobe was forced to abandon the deal due to regulatory hurdles, particularly in Europe. This came after Adobe put its competing design software XD on hold due to the acquisition.

As of today, Figma remains an independent company, and is widely recognized as one of the most innovative and influential design tools in the market, empowering designers, and design teams to collaborate, iterate, and create impactful design solutions in the cloud. With its commitment to user-centric design, continuous innovation, and community engagement, Figma is poised to shape the future of design for years to come.

An Overview of Figma

Figma is a cloud-based prototyping and design tool that enables collaboration amongst multiple users with a platform for creating, sharing, and collaborating on digital designs in real-time. As a cloud-based tool, Figma operates entirely within a web browser or desktop application, allowing users to access their design files from anywhere with an internet connection.

Figma's significance in contemporary design practices lies in its ability to empower designers and design teams to collaborate effectively, iterate rapidly, maintain consistency, and deliver user-centric solutions in the contemporary fast-paced and dynamic digital landscape. As a versatile and adaptable tool, Figma continues to shape the future of design by embracing emerging trends, technologies, and methodologies, while addressing the evolving needs and challenges of contemporary design practices.

Figma's Core Features

Figma boasts of several key features that make it a powerful and versatile design tool. Let us examine each of these features in detail:

- **Real-time collaboration**: Figma's real-time collaboration feature allows multiple collaborators to work on the same design file simultaneously, regardless of location. This feature is key for distributed teams, remote work setups, and collaborative design projects where designers need to work together in real time to iterate on designs, share feedback, and make decisions collectively.
- **Cloud-based platform**: Figma operates entirely in the cloud, which means that design files are stored securely online and accessible from multiple device types. This cloud-based approach eliminates the need for manual file transfers, ensures automatic file syncing, and enables seamless collaboration across devices and platforms. Cloud-based storage also offers advantages such as version history, automatic backups, and scalability, making it an ideal solution for designers who value accessibility, flexibility, and data security.
- **Design and prototyping tools**: Figma provides a comprehensive set of design and prototyping tools that enable designers to create a wide range of digital designs, from wireframes and mockups to high-fidelity prototypes. Design tools include vector drawing tools, layout grids, typography controls, and image editing features. Prototyping tools allow designers to create interactive prototypes with transitions, animations, and hotspots directly within the platform. These tools empower designers to develop tangible ideas in Figma, explore different design concepts, and communicate their vision effectively to stakeholders and team members.
- **Design system management**: Figma offers robust features for creating and

managing design systems, component libraries, and style guides within the platform. Designers can create reusable components, styles, and assets, ensuring project consistency and scalability. This promotes efficiency, maintains brand coherence, and streamlines workflow, particularly in large-scale design projects or organizations with multiple teams and stakeholders.

- **Version control and collaboration features**: Figma provides advanced version control features allowing designers to track changes, revert to previous versions, and comment on specific design elements. Collaboration features include commenting, sharing, and real-time notifications, enabling frictionless communication and collaboration among team members throughout the design process. These features promote transparency, facilitate feedback loops, and ensure team alignment, contributing to more efficient and effective collaboration.
- **Integration with external tools**: Figma integrates seamlessly with a wide range of external tools and services, including developer handoff platforms, project management tools, and design collaboration platforms. This interoperability enables designers to streamline their workflow, collaborate with stakeholders, and act as a conduit between design and development teams, enhancing productivity, efficiency, and collaboration across the entire design ecosystem.

Overall, the key features of Figma make it a multi-faceted and indispensable tool for designers and design teams, empowering them to collaborate effectively, iterate rapidly, maintain consistency, and deliver high-quality design solutions in the contemporary digital landscape.

Benefits of Using Figma

Learning and mastering Figma offers a plethora of benefits for designers, teams, and organizations, contributing to improved efficiency, collaboration, and overall design quality. There are several compelling reasons to learn Figma, even if you are not a professional designer:

- **Boost communication and feedback**: Prototypes are powerful communication tools since they bridge the gap between abstract ideas and concrete experiences. By creating a clickable prototype, you can effectively communicate your ideas to stakeholders, clients, or even team members who might not have a design background. This can lead to clearer understanding, quick feedback, and fewer revisions down the line.
- **Validate ideas quickly and easily**: Prototyping allows you to test the usability and functionality of your design concepts before investing significant time and resources in development. With a prototype, you can identify potential issues early on and iterate on your design based on user feedback. This "fail fast" approach can save time and money in the long run.

- **Improve problem-solving skills**: The process of creating prototypes encourages you to think critically about user needs and ways in which your design addresses them. It forces you to consider different scenarios and potential user interactions. This problem-solving mindset can be valuable in various other aspects of your work, not simply in design.
- **Increased employability**: Design prototyping skills are becoming increasingly sought-after in many fields, apart from the field of design itself. If you are involved in marketing, product management, or any role where clear communication and user-centric thinking are important, then having design prototyping skills can give you a competitive edge.
- **Enhanced creativity and design thinking**: Prototyping allows you to experiment with different design ideas and explore various possibilities. This fosters creativity and encourages you to think outside the box. It is a great way to bring your ideas to life and see them in action.

Even if you do not consider yourself a creative professional, learning a design prototyping software can equip you with valuable skills for communication, problem-solving, and execution of your ideas in real-life.

Figma Addresses Key Pain Points in the Design Process

Figma addresses several common pain points and challenges in the design process by offering innovative features and capabilities that streamline workflow, enhance collaboration, and promote efficiency. Figma addresses these challenges in the following ways:

- **Real-time collaboration:**
  - **Pain Point**: Collaboration among team members can be challenging, particularly in distributed teams or remote work setups. Designers often need help coordinating and communicating effectively, leading to delays and inefficiencies in the design process.
  - **Figma Solution**: Figma's real-time collaboration feature allows multiple collaborators to work on the same design file, regardless of location. Changes made by one user are visible to others, fostering seamless communication, teamwork, and alignment among team members.
- **Version control and iterative design:**
  - **Pain Point**: Managing version control and tracking changes in design files can be cumbersome and error-prone, especially in complex projects with multiple contributors. Designers may need help to keep track of iterations, reverting to previous versions, and incorporating feedback effectively.

    - **Figma Solution**: Figma offers robust version control features that enable designers to track changes, revert to previous versions, and leave comments on specific design elements. This promotes an iterative design process, facilitates effective feedback loops, and ensures that everyone involved in the project is aligned and informed throughout the design process.

- **Cross-functional collaboration:**
    - **Pain Point**: Collaboration between design and development teams can be challenging due to communication barriers, misaligned workflows, and differing priorities. Designers may need help in communicating design intent effectively, resulting in discrepancies between design and implementation.
    - **Figma Solution**: Figma integrates seamlessly with developer handoff platforms, project management tools, and design collaboration platforms, facilitating communication and collaboration between design and development teams. Designers can share design specs, assets, and prototypes with developers, ensuring that design intent is accurately translated into code and fostering a collaborative and iterative approach to design and development.
- **Maintaining consistency and design systems:**
    - **Pain Point**: Ensuring consistency across design projects and maintaining design systems can be challenging, particularly in large-scale projects or organizations with multiple teams and stakeholders. Designers may need help in enforcing brand guidelines, reusing components, and scaling designs effectively.
    - **Figma Solution**: Figma provides robust features for creating and managing design systems, component libraries, and style guides within the platform. Designers can create reusable components, styles, and assets, ensuring project consistency and scalability. This promotes efficiency, maintains brand coherence, and streamlines workflow, particularly in large-scale design projects or organizations with multiple teams and stakeholders.
- **Remote work and accessibility:**
    - **Pain Point**: Designers may face challenges working remotely or accessing design files from different devices and platforms. Traditional desktop-based design tools may lack accessibility and flexibility, hindering productivity and collaboration.
    - **Figma Solution**: Figma's cloud-based nature and platform agnosticism make it accessible from any device. Designers can work remotely, collaborate across time zones, and access their projects on the go, empowering them to stay productive and connected regardless of location or device.

Comparing Figma to Other Modern Design Tools

When comparing Figma with other design tools, such as Adobe XD, Sketch, and InVision, several factors come into play, including features, advantages, and target audience. While the exact market share numbers can be elusive, Figma's growth, as compared with other design tools, has been impressive. Here are some key statistics gathered from these sources:[1]

User base growth:

- **2015**: Figma launched in closed beta.
- **2016**: Public launch, attracting early adopters primarily from the design community.
- **2018**: Figma reached 1 million users.
- **2021**: Figma reported over 4 million users globally, including many from large organizations.
- **2022**: The user base continued to expand rapidly, driven by the rise of remote work and collaboration needs.

Valuation and funding:

- **2018**: Figma raised $25 million in a Series B funding round, valuing the company at $400 million.
- **2019**: Raised $40 million in Series C funding, reaching a valuation of $440 million.
- **2020**: Figma raised $50 million in Series D funding, doubling its valuation to $2 billion.
- **2021**: A Series E funding round brought in $200 million, pushing Figma's valuation to $10 billion.

---

[1]For references, please visit: *TechCrunch* article, "Figma reaches 1 million users " (2018); Figma Blog, "Our community reaches 4 million designers worldwide " (2021); *The Verge*, "Figma sees massive growth during the pandemic " (2022); *TechCrunch*, "Figma raises $25M in Series B funding " (2018); *Forbes*, "Figma's valuation hits $2 billion after Series D funding " (2020); *Business Insider*, "Figma's $10 billion valuation in Series E round " (2021); *The New York Times*, "Adobe's $20 billion acquisition of Figma " (2022); Figma Careers Page, "Team growth and open positions " (2021); *Bloomberg*, "Figma continues global expansion with growing team " (2022); Figma Blog, "Enterprise customers using Figma " (2021); *TechCrunch*, "Figma's growth in education and freelance markets " (2022) ; Figma Blog, "Introducing Figma Jam " (2021); Figma Community, "Plugins and resources for designers " (2022); *Wired*, "How Figma became the go-to tool for UX/UI design " (2021); *The Verge*, "Figma's global reach and impact " (2022).

- **2022**: By the time Adobe announced its acquisition of Figma, the company's valuation had soared to $20 billion.

Team growth:

- **2016**: Figma started with a small team of around 20 employees.
- **2021**: The company grew to over 300 employees, reflecting its expanding operations and product development.
- **2022**: Figma's team size continued to grow as they scaled their operations globally, adding more staff in engineering, design, customer support, and sales.

Market penetration:

By 2021, Figma had become the design tool of choice for many major companies, including Microsoft, Uber, Google, and Dropbox, due to its robust collaboration features. Figma also saw widespread adoption among students, educators, and freelance designers, offering free or discounted plans to lower the barrier to entry.

Product expansion:

- **Figma Jam**: Introduced in 2021, Figma Jam, a collaborative whiteboarding tool, quickly gained traction, further solidifying Figma's place in the collaborative design and ideation space.
- **Community and Plugins**: Figma's community feature, launched in 2019, allowed users to share templates, plugins, and resources. By 2022, the community had grown substantially, with thousands of plugins and resources available.

Competitive position:

- **Market Leadership**: By 2021, Figma had overtaken many traditional design tools in popularity, particularly in the UX/UI design space, due to its cloud-based, collaborative nature.
- **Global Reach**: Figma's user base spans across the globe, with significant growth in markets including Europe, Asia, and North America.

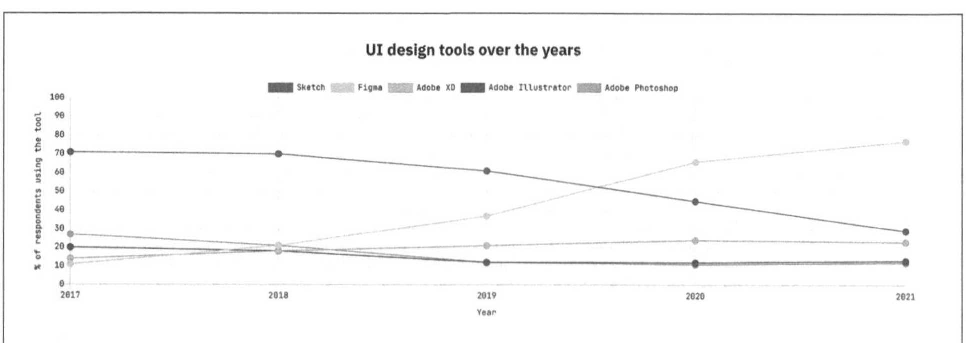

Figure 1.1: *UI design tools comparison over the years (source:https://uxdesign.cc/figma-continues-to-skyrocket-63-reported-it-was-their-primary-ui-design-tool-in-2021-bb9390a8b96b)*

While Figma is a major player, it is not the only design tool available. Established competitors like Adobe XD and Sketch also have a loyal following. However, it is clear that Figma has made a significant headway in the design industry.

Here is a comparison with other design tools based on certain features:

Collaboration:

- **Figma**: Figma is known for its robust real-time collaboration features, allowing multiple users to work on the same design file simultaneously. Changes made by one user are instantly visible to others, fostering seamless teamwork.
- **Adobe XD**: Adobe XD also offers collaboration features, but they are not as comprehensive as those offered by Figma. Users can share prototypes and design specs with stakeholders, but real-time collaboration is limited.
- **Sketch**: Sketch lacks built-in collaboration features and relies on third-party plugins, which may offer a different level of seamless interaction as compared with Figma.
- **InVision**: InVision is primarily focused on prototyping and collaboration, offering tools for sharing designs, gathering feedback, and collaborating with stakeholders, but it may not provide the same level of real-time collaboration as Figma.

Platform compatibility:

- **Figma**: Figma is a web-based tool that works seamlessly on all major operating systems, including Windows, macOS, and Linux. It also offers desktop applications for offline access.
- **Adobe XD**: Adobe XD is available for both macOS and Windows, offering native desktop applications for each platform.
- **Sketch**: Sketch is exclusive to macOS, which limits its accessibility for designers using other operating systems.
- **InVision**: InVision is a web-based platform that can be accessed through web browsers on any operating system, making it platform-agnostic.

Prototyping and interaction design:

- **Figma**: Figma offers robust prototyping and interaction design features, allowing users to create interactive prototypes with transitions, animations, and hotspots directly within the platform.
- **Adobe XD**: Adobe XD is known for its powerful prototyping capabilities, offering features for creating interactive prototypes and user flows.
- **Sketch**: Sketch focuses primarily on design and lacks advanced prototyping features. Users often rely on third-party plugins or integrations with other tools for prototyping.

- **InVision**: InVision is renowned for its prototyping tools, offering features for creating interactive prototypes, user testing, and gathering feedback from stakeholders.

Design system management:

- **Figma**: Figma excels in design system management, offering robust features for creating and maintaining design systems, component libraries, and style guides within the platform.
- **Adobe XD**: Adobe XD provides essential support for design systems and component libraries, but it may offer a different level of flexibility and customization than Figma.
- **Sketch**: Sketch offers extensive support for design systems and component libraries, making it a popular choice for organizations with complex design requirements.
- **InVision**: InVision offers limited support for design systems and component libraries as compared to Figma and Sketch.

Figma's Role in Securing a UX Design Job

Understanding Figma is essential in modern design workflows due to its collaborative nature, accessibility, efficiency, version control capabilities, design system management features, prototyping capabilities, and seamless integration with external tools. According to the 2020 UX tools survey, 77% of designers use Figma for UI design, as opposed to 66% in 2020, and 37% in 2019. Most respondents also use Figma for UI design and continue to stick with it for handoff. By mastering Figma, designers can optimize their workflow, enhance collaboration, and deliver high-quality design solutions that evolve with an ever-changing job landscape.

Learning Figma empowers modern-day designers to adapt to the evolving demands of the design industry. Figma has become an industry-standard design tool widely used by design professionals and organizations of all sizes. Figma's user base spans across various industries, including technology, finance, healthcare, education, and more. Many design teams, agencies, and organizations have adopted Figma for its collaborative features, ease of use, and robust design capabilities. There are more than 1 million teams across the globe using Figma in their collaborative workflows. Figma users spend about two-and-a-half hours on the tool every day with its user base expanding by 100% since 2018.

Figma offers a wealth of resources, tutorials, and community support, empowering designers to expand their skills, stay updated with industry trends, and grow as design practitioners. Acquiring proficiency in Figma enhances a designer's marketability and ensures alignment with industry trends and expectations. Following are the reasons for the relevance of Figma in UX:

- **Prototyping and User Flows**: Figma excels at creating interactive prototypes, allowing UX designers to visualize user journeys and test design concepts.
- **Collaboration**: Figma's cloud-based nature fosters seamless collaboration between UX designers, developers, and other stakeholders within a project.
- **User Interface (UI) Design**: Figma bridges the gap between UX and UI design, enabling designers to create user interfaces that align with user needs defined during the UX process.

It is because of this synergy that Figma proficiency is a highly sought-after skill in UX jobs. Here are some examples of UX roles where Figma is commonly used:

- UX Designer
- UI/UX Designer
- Product Designer
- User Interface Designer (UI Designer) with UX knowledge
- UX Researcher (may use Figma for prototyping based on research)

If you are interested in UX jobs, learning Figma is a great investment. Having Figma skills on your resume can open a broader range of job opportunities and increase your competitiveness in the job market. Mastering Figma demonstrates a designer's commitment to continuous learning and professional development. Many online resources and tutorials can help you develop your Figma skills. Additionally, employers often list Figma proficiency as a requirement or preferred skill in UX job postings [ZipRecruiter, LinkedIn].

Getting Started with Figma

Setting up a Figma account is a straightforward process. Here is a step-by-step guide to the process:

1. **Go to the Figma Website**: Open your web browser and navigate to the Figma website at www.figma.com.
2. **Sign Up**: On the Figma homepage, locate the "`Sign Up`" button and click it. This will take you to the sign-up page.

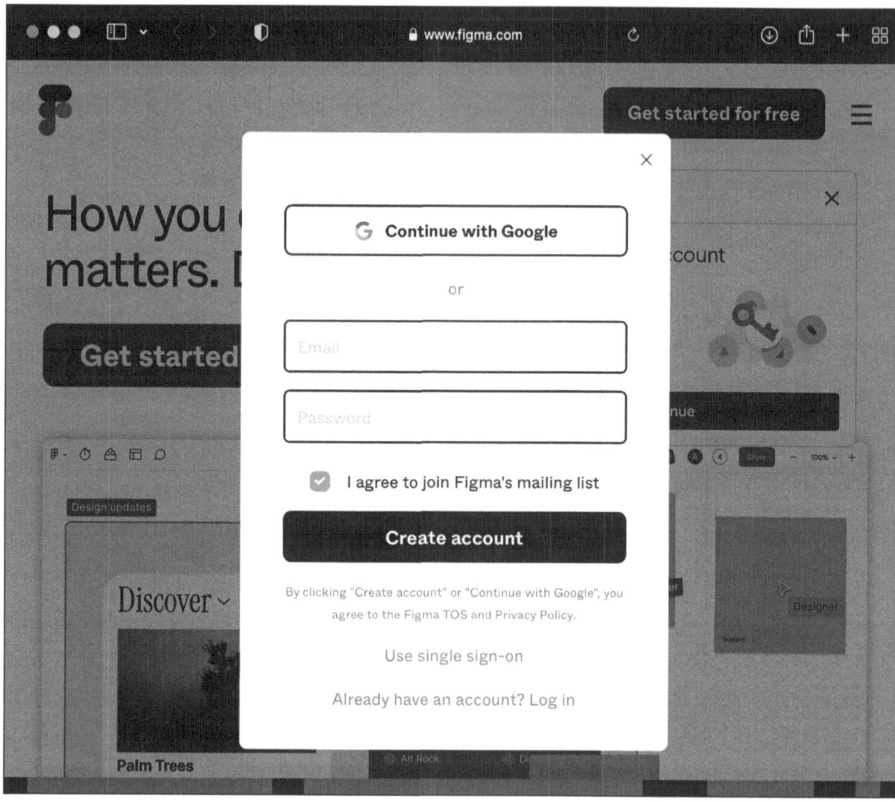

***Figure 1.2**: Getting started with Figma*

3. **Enter your email address**: You will be prompted to enter an email address on the sign-up page. Input the email address that you want to use for your Figma account.

4. **Create a password**: Create a secure password for your Figma account after entering your email address. Use a combination of uppercase or lowercase letters, numbers, and symbols for added security.

5. **Verify your email**: Once you have entered your email address and created a password, you will receive a verification email to the email address you provided for setting up your Figma account. Go to your email inbox and look for the verification email from Figma.

6. **Click the verification link**: Open the verification email from Figma and click the verification link inside. This will verify your email address and activate your Figma account.

7. **Complete your profile**: After verifying your email address, you will be redirected to the Figma website. Follow the prompts to complete your profile by providing additional information, such as your name and preferred username.

8. **Agree to terms of service**: Read through Figma's Terms of Service and Privacy Policy, then check the box to indicate that you agree to these terms.
9. **Choose your plan (if applicable)**: Depending on your needs, you may be prompted to choose a plan for your Figma account. Figma offers both free and paid plans with varying features and limitations. Select the plan that best suits your requirements.
10. **Start using Figma**: Once you have completed the sign-up process and chosen your plan (if applicable), you can start using Figma immediately. You will be taken to the Figma dashboard to create new design files, join teams, and explore the platform's features.

Congratulations! You have successfully set up your Figma account and are ready to start designing and collaborating with others.

Troubleshooting Onboarding

To help new users onboard to Figma, here are additional steps and tips for troubleshooting login issues, enhancing account security, and ensuring a seamless experience:

1. Enabling Two-Factor Authentication (2FA)

a. **Why it is Important:** Two-Factor Authentication adds an extra layer of security to your account by requiring a second form of verification in addition to your password.

b. **How to Enable:**

   i. Log in to your Figma account.

   ii. Go to your Account Settings.

   iii. Navigate to the `Security` tab.

   iv. Select "`Enable Two-Factor Authentication`."

   v. Follow the prompts to set up 2FA using an authenticator app such as Google Authenticator or Authy.

c. **Troubleshooting:**

   i. **Authenticator App not Working:** Ensure that the time on your device is synchronized automatically. If issues persist, try using a different authenticator app or resync the app with Figma.

   ii. **Backup Codes:** Store backup codes provided during setup in a secure place. These can be used if you lose access to your authenticator app.

2. Creating a Strong Password

a. **Why it is Important:** A strong password is the first defense against unauthorized access.

b. **Password Guidelines:**

  i. Use at least 12 characters, including a mix of uppercase and lowercase letters, numbers, and special characters.

  ii. Avoid common phrases, names, or sequential patterns.

  iii. Use a passphrase or a password manager to generate and store complex passwords.

c. **Troubleshooting:**

  i. **Forgotten Password:** Use the "Forgot Password" link on the login page to reset your password. Ensure you have access to the email associated with your Figma account.

  ii. **Password not Accepted:** Ensure that Caps Lock is off and you are entering the correct password. If you recently changed your password, try the new one.

3. Troubleshooting Account Verification Issues

- **Email Verification:**

  a. **Why it is Important:** Verifying your email ensures you can recover your account and receive important notifications.

  b. **Steps to Verify:**

    i. After registering, check your email for a verification message from Figma.

    ii. Click the verification link in the email.

  c. **Troubleshooting:**

    i. **Did not Receive the Email:** Check your spam/junk folder. If you still don't see it, ensure you entered the correct email address and request a new verification email.

    ii. **Link not Working:** If the verification link has expired, request a new one from the Figma login page.

- **Mobile Number Verification (if applicable):**

  a. **Why it is Important:** Adds an additional recovery option for account security.

b. **Steps to Verify:**

   i. Enter your mobile number when prompted during sign-up or in your account settings.

   ii. Receive a code via SMS.

   iii. Enter the code in Figma to verify.

c. **Troubleshooting:**

   i. **Did not Receive SMS:** Ensure your mobile number is entered correctly and your device has network coverage. You can also request the code again.

4. General Troubleshooting Tips

a. **Clear Browser Cache:** If you experience issues logging in via a web browser, clearing the browser cache and cookies can resolve some common problems.

b. **Update the Figma App:** Ensure you are using the latest version of the Figma desktop app or mobile app. Outdated versions can cause login issues.

c. **Check Network Connection:** Ensure you have a stable internet connection. Login issues may arise from intermittent connectivity.

d. **Contact Figma Support:** If all else fails, contact Figma support with detailed information about the issue. They can assist with specific problems that might not be covered in general troubleshooting guides.

5. Preparing for Onboarding

a. **Pre-Onboarding Checklist:** Ensure that new users have access to the required email accounts, mobile devices for 2FA, and any necessary permissions from their organization before beginning the onboarding process.

b. **Walkthrough Guides:** Provide step-by-step walkthroughs for setting up accounts, navigating Figma's interface, and accessing shared projects to ease the learning curve.

Accessing Figma through Web and Desktop Apps

Web Browser:

- **Step 1: Open web browser**

  Launch your preferred web browser (Microsoft Edge, Google Chrome, Mozilla Firefox, or Safari).

- **Step 2: Navigate to Figma website**

  In the browser address bar, type in the URL for the Figma website: www.figma.com.

- **Step 3: Sign In or Sign Up**
  - If you already have a Figma account, click the "**`Sign In`**" button and enter your credentials to log in.
  - If you do not have a Figma account yet, click the "**`Sign Up`**" button and follow the steps outlined in the previous response to create a new account.

- **Step 4: Access Figma dashboard**

  Once you have signed in or signed up, you will be taken to the Figma dashboard, where you can access your design files, collaborate with team members, and explore Figma's features.

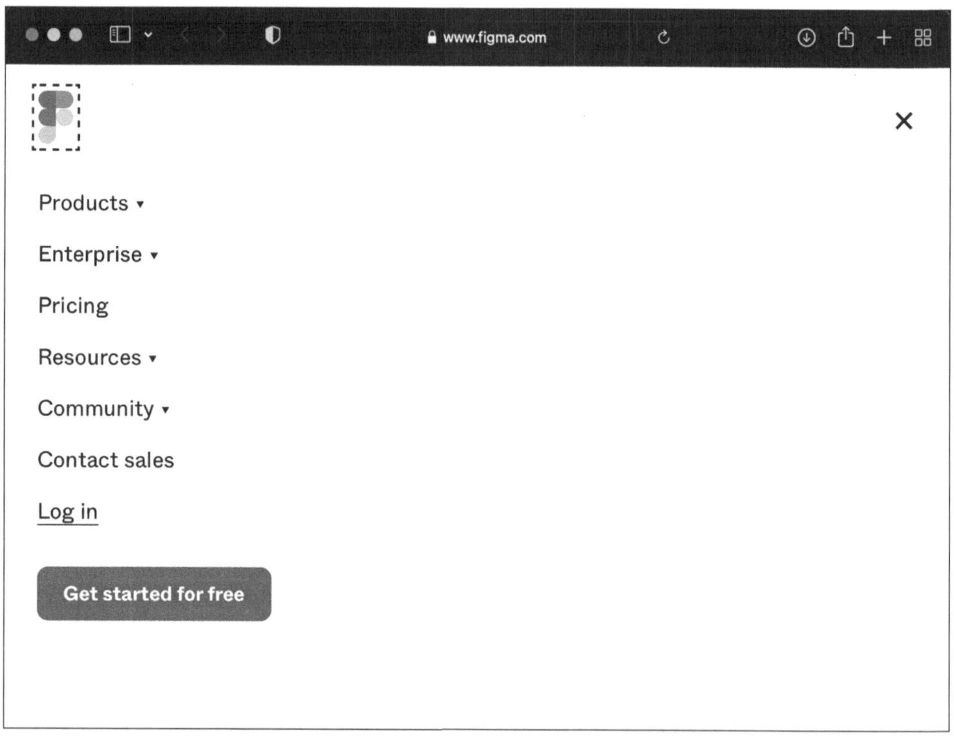

***Figure 1.3**: Accessing Figma from a web browser*

Desktop Application:

- **Step 1: Download the Figma desktop app**
  - Figma offers desktop applications for both Windows and macOS operating systems. To download the desktop app, visit the Figma website and navigate to the "**`Downloads`**" section.

  - Alternatively, you can download the Figma desktop app directly from the App Store (macOS) or Microsoft Store (Windows).

- **Step 2: Install and launch the app**

  Once the download is complete, open the installer file and follow the on-screen instructions to install the Figma desktop app on your computer.

- **Step 3: Sign in to your account:**
  - After installing the app, launch it from your desktop or applications folder. You will be prompted to sign in to your Figma account.
  - Enter your email address and password, then click the "**`Sign In`**" button to access your Figma account through the desktop app.

- **Step 4: Access Figma dashboard**

  Once you have signed in, you will be taken to the Figma dashboard within the desktop app, where you can access your design files, collaborate with team members, and utilize Figma's features.

***Figure 1.4**: Accessing Figma from the desktop app*

By accessing Figma through both web browsers and desktop applications, users can choose the method that best suits their preferences and workflow. Whether working online or offline, Figma provides a seamless experience for designing, prototyping, and collaborating on projects.

Overview of the Figma Interface

The Figma interface is designed to provide users with a streamlined and intuitive experience for creating, editing, and collaborating on design projects. Here is an overview of the main components of the Figma interface:

- **Toolbar**: The Toolbar is located at the top of the Figma interface and contains a set of tools and controls for creating and editing design elements. Common tools found in the Toolbar include selection tools (for example, Move, Scale, Rotate), shape tools (for example, Rectangle, Ellipse), text tools, pen tools, and various other drawing and editing tools. The Toolbar also includes controls for navigating the canvas, zooming in and out, and accessing additional features such as prototyping and commenting.

Figure 1.5: *The Figma toolbar*

- **Canvas**: The Canvas is the main working area where users create and arrange design elements. It occupies the central portion of the Figma interface and serves as the visual representation of the design project and allows the user to drag and drop elements onto the canvas, arrange them in layers, and manipulate them using the tools and controls available in the Toolbar. The Canvas provides a real-time preview of the design, allowing users to see how changes affect the overall layout and composition. In Figma, the maximum canvas size is defined using pixels. The canvas extends from -65,000 pixels to +65,000 pixels along both the X and Y axes. This means the total dimensions of the canvas are 130,000 pixels by 130,000 pixels.

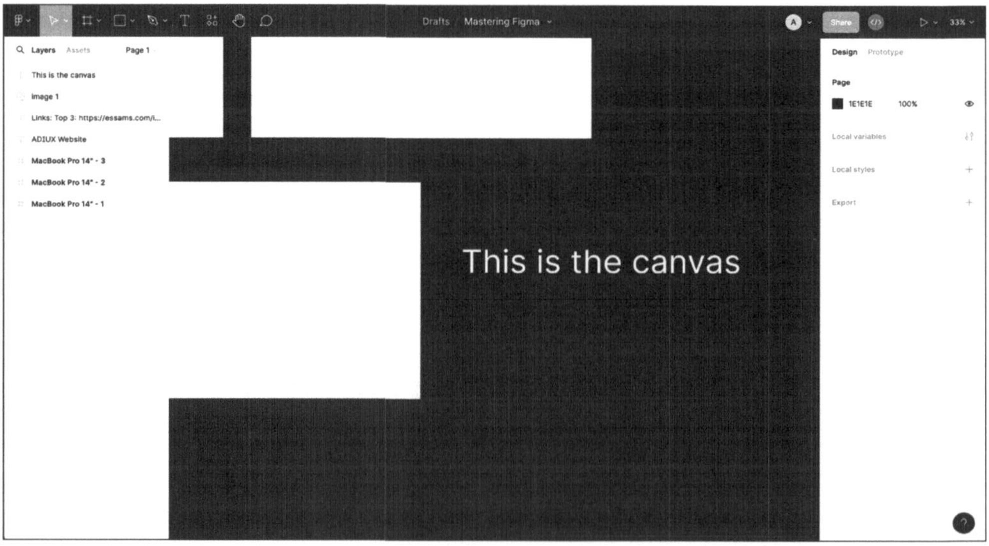

Figure 1.6: *Canvas*

- **Layers Panel**: The Layers Panel is located on the far left of the Figma interface and displays a hierarchical list of all the layers and objects present on the canvas. Users can use the Layers Panel to select, rearrange, and organize layers, as well as control their visibility, opacity, and other properties. The `Layers` Panel also provides options for grouping layers, creating masks, and applying effects such as shadows and blurs.

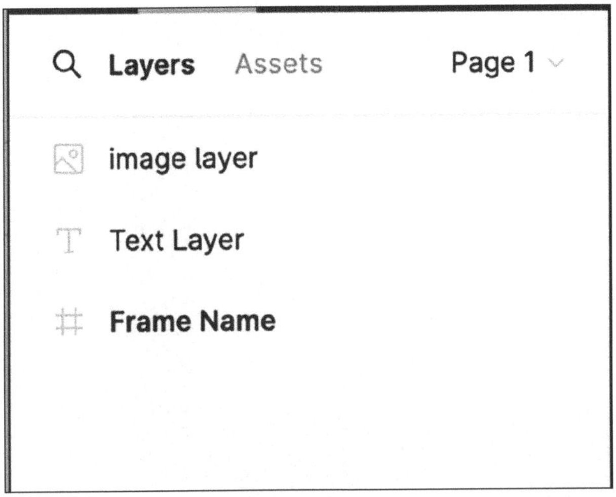

***Figure 1.7**: Figma layers*

- **Properties Panel**: The Properties Panel is located on the right side of the Figma interface and displays contextual properties and settings for the selected object or layer. Depending on the selected element, the Properties Panel may contain options for adjusting fill and stroke colors, typography settings, alignment and distribution, and other properties specific to that element. The Properties Panel also provides additional features and settings related to prototyping, collaboration, and design system management.

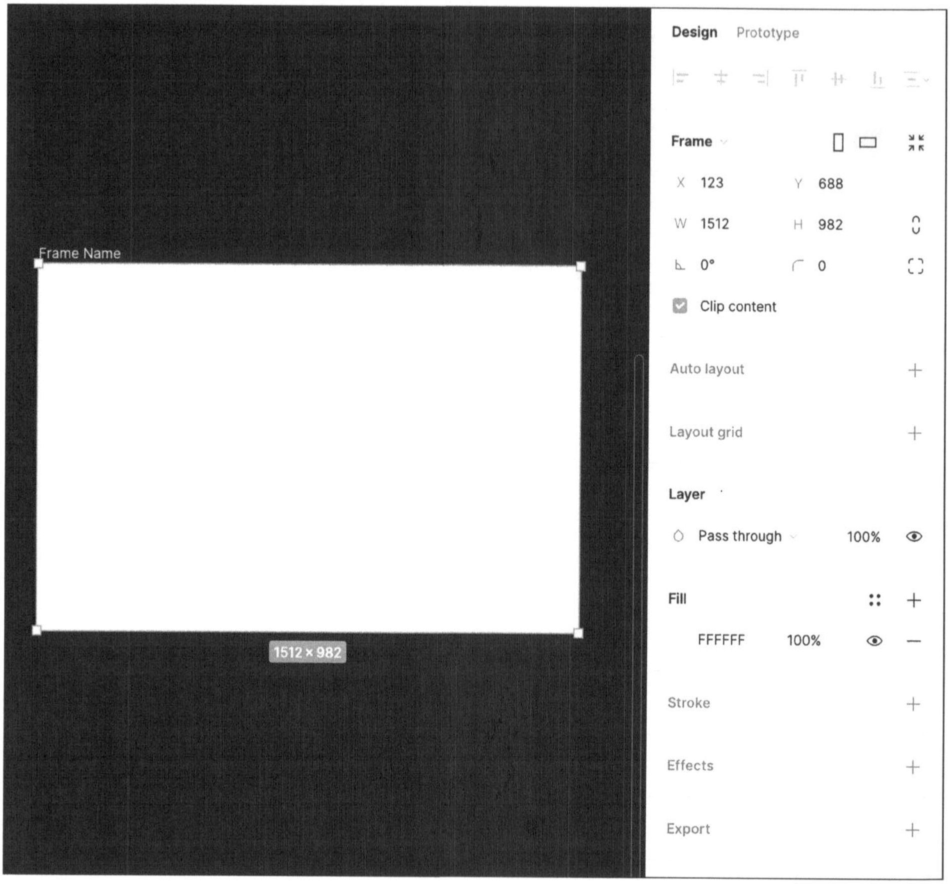

***Figure 1.8**: Property panel*

- **Prototype Mode**: Figma includes a dedicated Prototype Mode that allows users to create interactive prototypes and simulate user interactions. In Prototype Mode, users can define interactions such as clicks, taps, and swipes, as well as transitions, animations, and hotspots between different screens or components. Users can switch between Design Mode and Prototype Mode using the tabs at the top of the Figma interface, enabling a seamless transition between designing and prototyping.

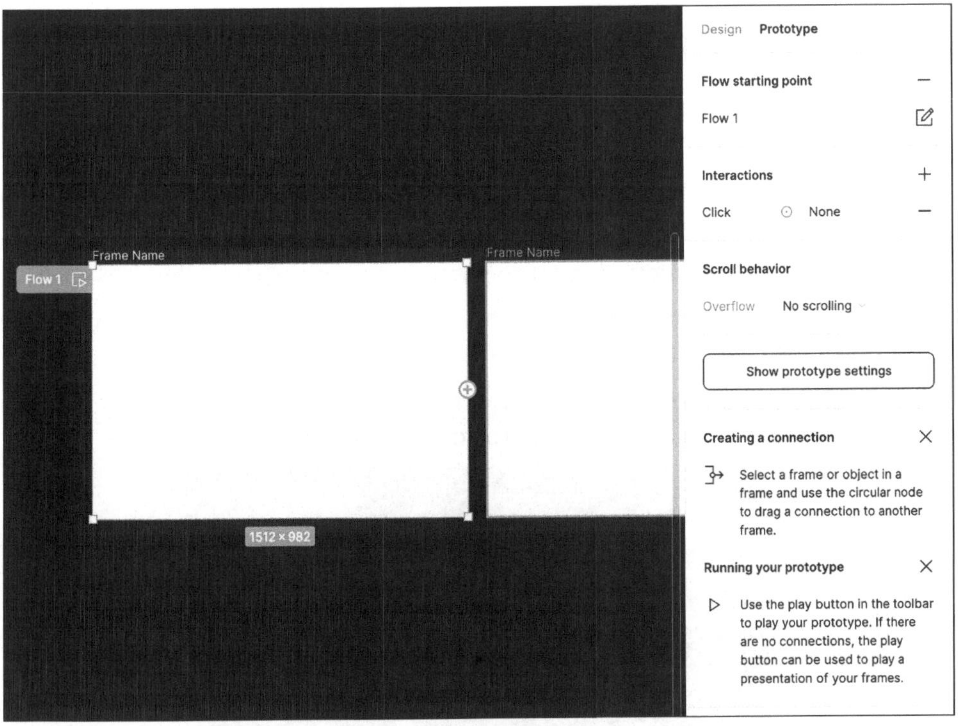

Figure 1.9: *Prototype mode*

- **Comments and collaboration**: Figma includes features for commenting and collaboration, allowing users to leave feedback, annotations, and suggestions directly on the design project. Comments can be added to specific elements or areas of the canvas, and users can reply to comments, resolve threads, and track changes made by collaborators in real time.

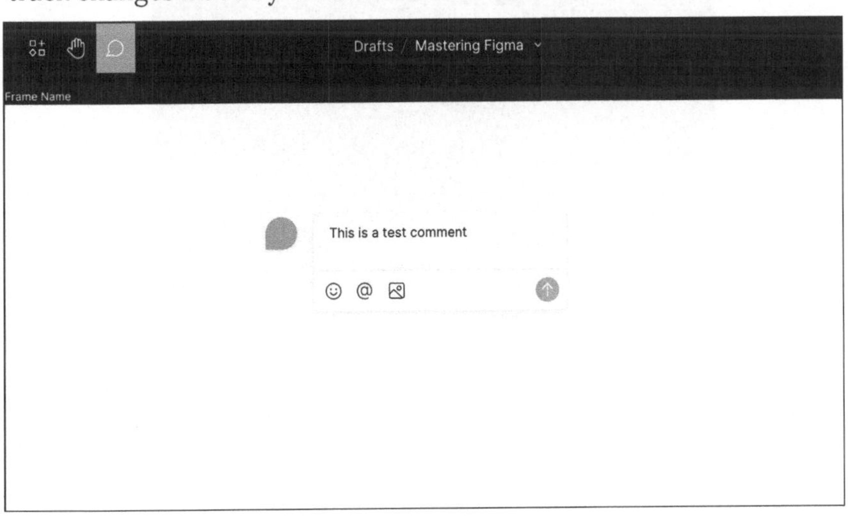

Figure 1.10: *Commenting mode*

Navigating Figma

In Figma, mastering basic navigation techniques is essential for efficiently navigating your design projects. Here are some basic navigation techniques:

- **Zooming**: To zoom in or out on the canvas, you can use the following methods:
    - **Zoom Slider**: Located at the bottom left corner of the interface, you can drag the slider left or right to zoom in or out respectively.
    - **Keyboard Shortcuts**: Use keyboard shortcuts such as *Cmd/Ctrl* + to zoom in and *Cmd/Ctrl* - to zoom out.
    - **Mouse/Trackpad**: Hold down the *Cmd/Ctrl* key and scroll up or down with the mouse or trackpad to zoom in or out.

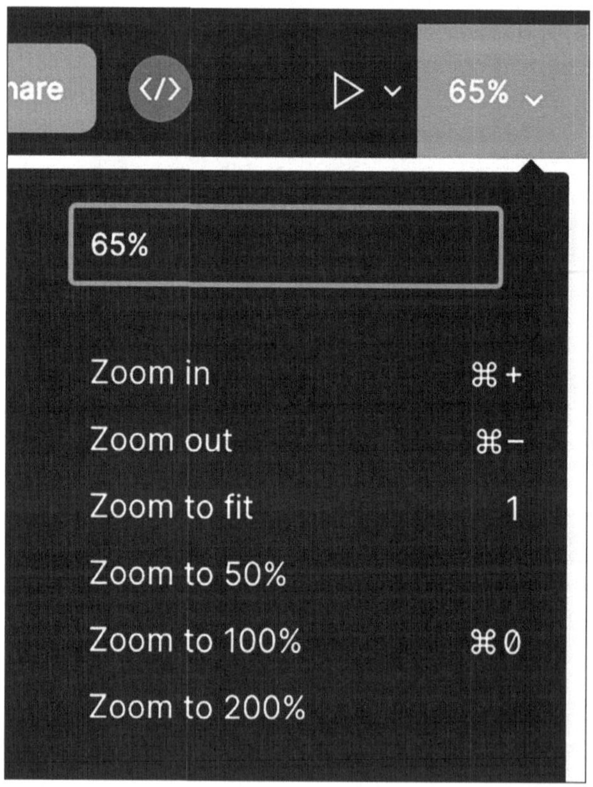

***Figure 1.11**: Zoom slider*

- **Panning**: To pan across the canvas and view different areas of your design:
    - **Click and Drag**: Click and drag the canvas using your mouse cursor. This allows you to move around and explore different parts of your design.
    - **Spacebar Shortcut**: Hold down the spacebar, then click and drag the canvas to pan around.

- **Navigating between Frames and Pages**: If your design contains multiple frames or pages, you can navigate between them using the following methods:
    - **Frames and Pages Panel**: Located on the left side of the interface, the Frames and Pages Panel displays a list of all frames and pages in your design. Click a frame or page in the panel to navigate to it.
    - **Keyboard Shortcuts**: Use keyboard shortcuts such as *Cmd/Ctrl* + 1 to navigate to the first frame/page, *Cmd/Ctrl* + 2 for the second, and so on.
    - **Next/Previous Frame Shortcut**: Use the *Tab* key to navigate to the next frame/page in the sequence, and *Shift* + *Tab* to navigate to the previous one.

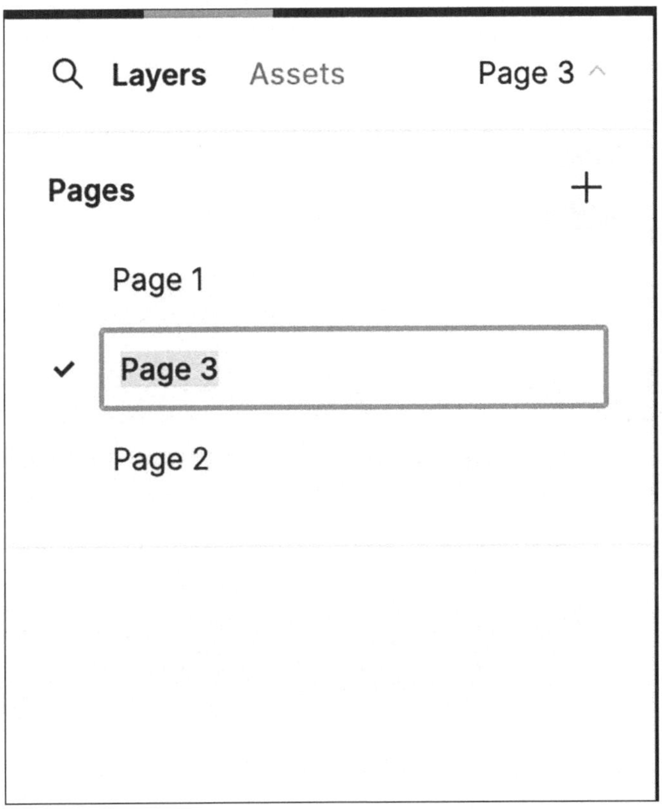

***Figure 1.12**: Frames and pages panel*

By mastering these basic navigation techniques, you can quickly and efficiently navigate your design projects in Figma, zooming in and out, panning across the canvas, and seamlessly moving between frames and pages as needed. These techniques are essential for exploring and working on different parts of your design, collaborating with team members, and ensuring a smooth workflow in Figma.

Introduction to Frames and Components

In Figma, frames and components are fundamental building blocks that enable designers to create, organize, and manage their design projects efficiently. Frames and components are essential concepts in Figma that provide structure, organization, and reusability to your design projects. You will understand how to use frames to contain and arrange design elements to create individual screens or pages, and components to create reusable UI elements. This learning will help you efficiently design, iterate, and collaborate on projects of varying scale or complexity in Figma. Here is an introduction to each of these concepts:

- **Frames**: Frames are containers that hold design elements such as shapes, text, images, and other objects. Think of frames as virtual canvases or bounding boxes where you can place and arrange your design elements. Frames help maintain the spatial relationship between objects, allowing you to group and organize them within a defined area. Frames can be resized, rotated, and manipulated like any other object in Figma, making them versatile for various design purposes. They come in predefined configurations such as Phone, Tablet, Desktop, Watch, Paper, Social Media, and Figma Community.

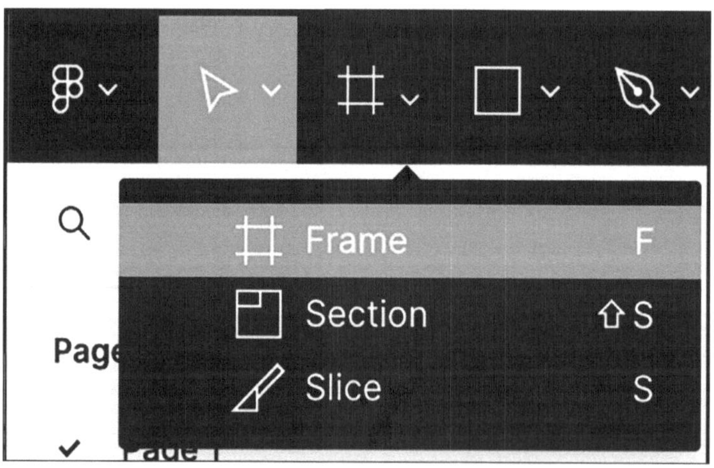

***Figure 1.13**: Accessing frames in Figma*

Figure 1.14 shows the types of frames in Figma:

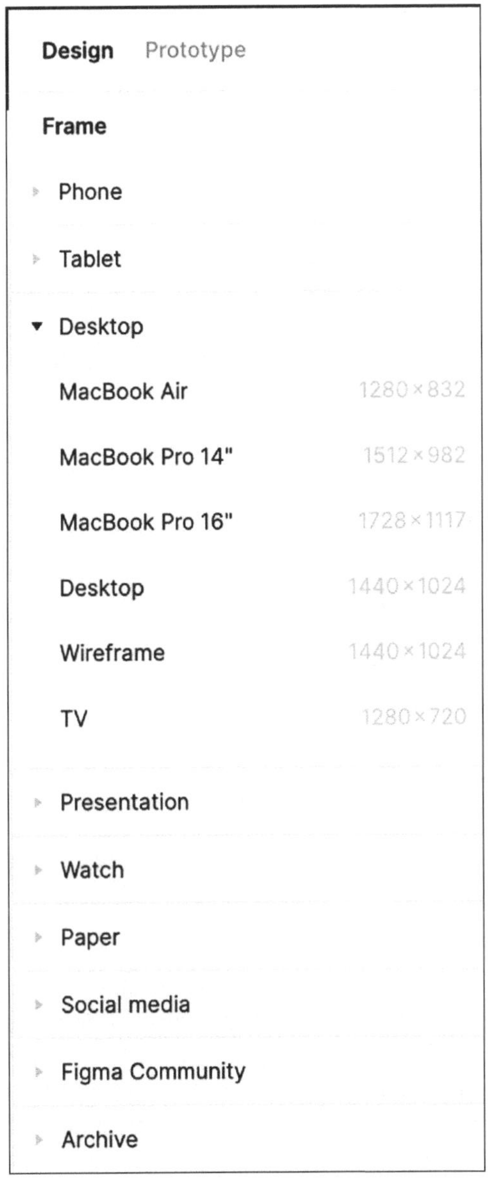

Figure 1.14: *Types of frames in Figma*

****Artboards**: *If you have used earlier variations of a digital design tool such as Sketch, then you will recall the concept of Artboards. In the context of Figma, Artboards are specialized frames used for creating individual screens, pages, or states within a design project.*

- **Components**: Components are reusable design elements that can be used across multiple frames within a design project. Components can include UI elements such as buttons, input fields, navigation bars, icons, and more. By creating components, you can maintain consistency and scalability across your design project, ensuring that similar elements have the same appearance and behavior. Components can be customized and edited individually, and changes made to a component can be propagated to all instances of that component within the project. Components can also have variants, allowing you to create different states or variations of the same component (for example, different button states for hover, active, or disabled).

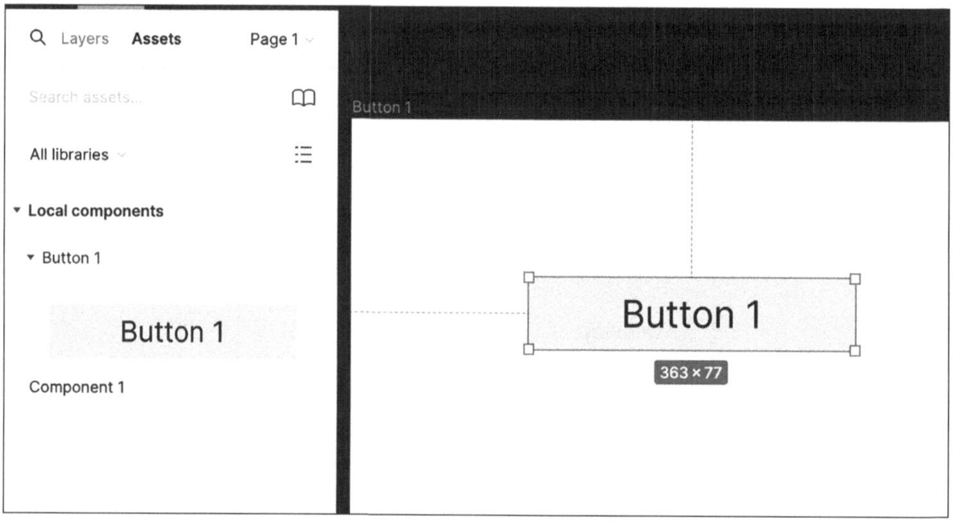

***Figure 1.15**: Components in Figma*

Conclusion

This chapter covers the basics of setting up and navigating Figma, introducing readers to the key features and components of the interface. We hope that with the first chapter you have built a foundational understanding of how to set up a Figma account, navigate the interface, and utilize basic navigation techniques to begin working on design projects. It serves as an introduction to Figma's interface and prepares readers for further exploration and hands-on learning in subsequent chapters.

Transition to the next chapter:

Having gained a foundational understanding of how to set up a Figma account, navigate the interface, and utilize basic navigation techniques in this chapter, it is time to examine in greater detail, the core features and functionalities of Figma. In *Chapter 2, Understanding Design Principles in Figma*, we will explore the essential tools and techniques for creating and editing designs in Figma. From drawing shapes and adding text to manipulating layers and utilizing advanced design features, this chapter will equip you with the skills and knowledge needed to unleash your creativity and bring your design ideas to life in Figma. Get ready to dive into the world of design creation with confidence and discover the endless possibilities that Figma has to offer.

Recap of Key Points

- **The history of Figma**: Understanding the history of modern workday tools for designers and how Figma was founded.
- **What is Figma and its key benefits**: A cloud-based design and collaboration tool that allows creatives to create, prototype, and collaborate on design projects in real time.
- **How to create a Figma account**: The process of setting up a Figma account involves visiting the Figma website, signing up with an email address, creating a password, verifying the email address, and completing the profile setup.
- **Accessing Figma interface**: Figma can be accessed through web browsers or desktop applications. Users can navigate the interface using tools such as the Toolbar, Canvas, Layers Panel, Properties Panel, and Prototype Mode.
- **Basic navigation techniques**: Basic navigation techniques in Figma include zooming, panning, and navigating between frames and pages. Users can zoom in and out using keyboard shortcuts or the Zoom Slider, pan across the canvas by clicking and dragging, and navigate between frames/pages using keyboard shortcuts or the Frames and Pages panels.
- **Overview of interface components**: The Figma interface consists of several key components, including the Toolbar (for accessing tools and controls), Canvas (the main working area for designing), Layers Panel (for organizing and managing layers), Properties Panel (for adjusting properties of selected objects), and Prototype Mode (for creating interactive prototypes).

CHAPTER 2
Understanding Design Principles in Figma

Introduction

This chapter explores in detail the fundamental principles of design within the context of Figma. It begins with elucidating the core principles of design such as composition, hierarchy, color theory, typography, and whitespace utilization. Readers gain insight into how these principles apply specifically within the Figma environment.

Design principles are the fundamental guidelines that govern the creation of visually appealing and effective designs. By understanding its concepts such as balance, hierarchy, contrast, unity, and emphasis, and learning how to leverage Figma's tools and features, you can create designs that resonate with your audience and represent your brand.

Through practical examples and hands-on exercises, readers can learn how to work with shapes, manipulate colors, and apply typography effectively within their designs using Figma's intuitive tools. The chapter emphasizes the importance of maintaining consistency and coherence in design elements to create visually appealing and user-friendly interfaces.

By applying design principles within Figma, readers develop a strong foundation for creating compelling designs that effectively communicate their intended message. This chapter serves as a crucial building block for readers to enhance their design skills and create professional-quality designs using Figma.

Structure

In this chapter, we will cover the following topics:

- Background of Design Principles
- Design Principles in User Interface (UI)
- Applying Design Principles in Figma
- Hands-On Practice

Background of Design Principles with Gestalt

Gestalt principles are a set of psychological laws that explain how humans perceive visual elements and organize them into meaningful wholes. These principles are crucial for understanding how we interpret the world around us, and they have significant implications for various fields, including design, art, and psychology. By understanding how humans naturally perceive visual information, designers can create layouts that are not only aesthetically pleasing but also intuitive and user-friendly. The Gestalt principles continue to be a valuable tool for designers seeking to create clear and effective visual communication. The Gestalt principles of design, with their emphasis on simplifying complexity and organizing visual elements, have become the cornerstone of modern design.

Here are some key reasons why Gestalt principles are important:

- **Understanding Human Perception:**
  - **Organization and Structure**: Gestalt principles help us understand how our brains naturally group and structure visual information. This allows us to quickly identify patterns and relationships within complex scenes.
  - **Illusions and Misperceptions**: By understanding these principles, we can recognize how our perception can sometimes be misleading, thereby giving rise to optical illusions or misinterpretations of visual stimuli.
- **Design and User Experience:**
  - **Effective Communication**: Designers use Gestalt principles to create visually appealing and easy-to-understand designs. By organizing elements in a way that aligns with these principles, designers can ensure that their message is effectively conveyed to the viewer.
  - **User-Friendly Interfaces**: Understanding how users perceive information helps designers create intuitive and user-friendly interfaces. By applying Gestalt principles, designers can guide the user's attention and make navigation more efficient.
- **Art and Creativity:**
  - **Composition and Harmony**: Artists use Gestalt principles to create visually pleasing compositions. By understanding how elements interact and how the human eye perceives them, artists can achieve harmony and balance in their work.
  - **Emotional Impact**: Gestalt principles can be used to evoke specific emotions in viewers. By manipulating the arrangement and relationship between elements, artists can create a desired emotional response.

- **Psychology and Cognitive Science:**
    - **Perception and Cognition**: Gestalt principles provide insights into how our brains process information and form perceptions. This knowledge is valuable for understanding cognitive processes and how we learn and remember.
    - **Problem-Solving and Decision-Making**: By understanding how we perceive patterns and relationships, we can apply Gestalt principles to problem-solving and decision-making tasks.

History and Relevance of Gestalt's Principles

Gestalt psychology emerged in the early 20th century, primarily in Germany and Austria as a reaction against the dominant structuralist schools of thought, which focused on breaking down mental experiences into their smallest components. However, with the rise of the Nazi regime, many Gestalt psychologists, including Wertheimer, Koffka, and Köhler, emigrated to the United States. They continued their work at American universities, spreading the ideas of Gestalt psychology to a wider audience.

- **Birth of a School of Thought (Early 20th Century):**

  Pioneered by psychologists like Max Wertheimer, Kurt Koffka, and Wolfgang Köhler, Gestalt (meaning "unified whole" in German) challenged the prevailing notion that perception is simply the sum of its parts. Instead, they argued that our brains actively organize and interpret sensory information to create a coherent whole.

- ***Prägnanz* – The Driving Force:**

  Central to Gestalt psychology is the concept of *Prägnanz*, a German term roughly translated as "good figure" or "good form". This principle suggests that our brains inherently seek order and simplicity, preferring to perceive visual elements in their most stable and meaningful configuration.

- **From Theory to Design Principles:**

  Gestalt psychologists conducted numerous experiments to understand visual perception. Their findings, particularly regarding how we group and organize visual elements, laid the foundation for the Gestalt principles of design. These principles essentially translate the core tenets of Gestalt psychology into practical guidelines for creating clear and effective visual communication.

Key Figures and Contributions

Figure 2.1: *Max Wertheimer*

Max Wertheimer, a pioneering psychologist, reshaped perception studies with Gestalt principles. Born in 1880, he emphasized holistic experiences over isolated elements. Collaborating with Koffka and Köhler, he identified key principles such as proximity and closure. His work revolutionized psychology, influenced multiple fields from design to artificial intelligence, and left a lasting legacy.

Figure 2.2: *Kurt Koffka*

Kurt Koffka, born in 1886, was a pivotal figure in psychology, renowned for his contributions to Gestalt theory. Alongside Max Wertheimer and Wolfgang Köhler, he challenged reductionist views, emphasizing the importance of holistic perception. Koffka's insights continue to shape our understanding of cognition, perception, and the mind's organization.

Figure 2.3: *Wolfgang Köhler*

Wolfgang Köhler, born in 1887, was a prominent psychologist whose work was central to Gestalt theory. His research, alongside Max Wertheimer and Kurt Koffka, highlighted the mind's tendency to perceive wholes over mere sum of parts. Köhler's work revolutionized psychology, influencing fields from perception to problem-solving and laying foundations for cognitive science.

Understanding Gestalt Principles

Gestalt principles are a set of guidelines that describe how humans tend to perceive and organize visual elements. They stem from Gestalt psychology, which emphasizes that our brains perceive things as unified wholes rather than individual parts.

Here are the six core Gestalt principles:

1. ***Similarity***: Elements that look alike are seen as related. This principle is used in design by grouping similar items together, for example, using the same color for buttons with the same function on a website.

2. ***Proximity***: Elements close together are seen as connected. Imagine a website that groups related menu items in a bar to create a clear hierarchy.

3. ***Closure***: Our brains tend to "fill in the gaps" to create a complete image. Think

of logos that use negative space to form an image, like the FedEx arrow where the negative space creates an arrow between the "E" and "X".

4. ***Continuity***: Elements arranged in a line or curve are perceived as flowing together. Leading lines in photography, which guide the viewer's eye, are a great example of continuity.

5. ***Figure-ground***: The brain distinguishes between a figure (object in focus) and the background. Ensuring high contrast between text and background on a website improves readability by creating a clear distinction between figure and ground.

6. ***Symmetry and order (Prägnanz)***: Our brains favor balanced and organized layouts. Symmetrical website layouts can evoke a sense of formality and stability.

These are the six core principles, but there are additional ones that have emerged in design practices, such as:

7. ***Uniform connectedness***: Elements that are visually linked together are seen as more related. Imagine using outlines to connect elements in a diagram.

8. ***Common regions***: Elements enclosed within the same space are perceived as a group. Grouping information boxes with a border is an example of the same.

9. ***Common fate***: Elements moving in the same direction are seen as connected. Animations where elements move together leverage this principle.

10. ***Focal points***: Elements that stand out visually draw attention. Using a contrasting color for a call-to-action button creates a focal point.

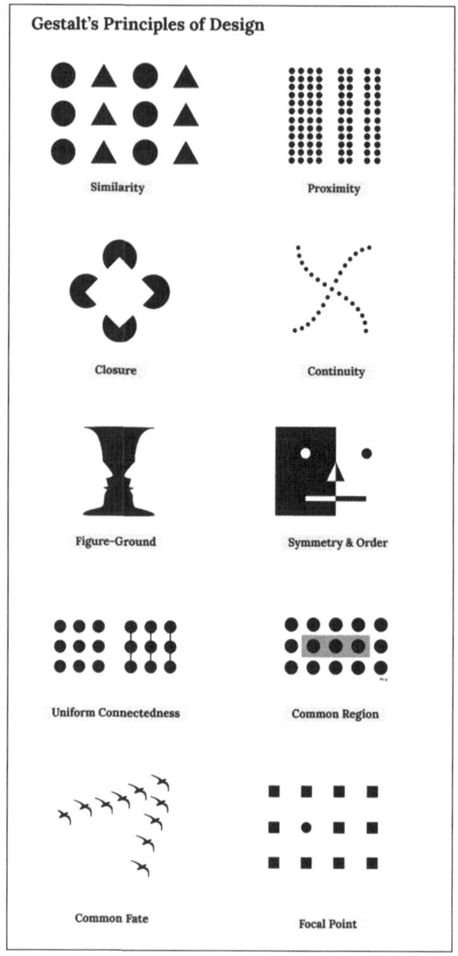

Figure 2.4: *Gestalt's principles of design*

Gestalt's Lasting Impact

The Gestalt principles have transcended the realm of psychology and have become a foundational concept in various design disciplines, such as the following:

- **Graphic Design**: Gestalt principles guide the arrangement of elements in logos, posters, and layouts.
- **Web Design**: They influence website layouts, navigation structures, and information hierarchy.
- **UI Design**: These principles help organize elements on apps and software for clear functionality.
- **Product Design**: Gestalt informs product form and functionality to enhance usability and aesthetics.

Design Principles in User Interface

Design principles serve as the foundation for creating successful digital designs. They provide designers with a framework for making informed decisions about layout, typography, color, and other elements of design to improve aesthetic usability.

The Principles of Design in UI:

- **Balance:** Balance refers to the distribution of visual weight in a design. There are three main types of balance – symmetrical, asymmetrical, and radial. Symmetrical balance occurs when elements are evenly distributed around a central axis, creating a sense of stability and order. Asymmetrical balance involves arranging elements of different sizes and weights in a way that creates equilibrium. Radial balance emanates from a central point, with elements radiating outward in a circular pattern.
- **Hierarchy:** Hierarchy establishes the order of importance within a design. By using variations in size, color, and typography, designers can guide the viewer's eye and convey the relative importance of different elements. Establishing hierarchy helps users understand the structure of a design and navigate it more easily.
- **Contrast:** Contrast involves creating differences between elements to make certain parts of a design stand out. This can be achieved through variations in color, size, shape, texture, or value. Contrast helps create visual interest and draw the viewer's attention to important elements within a design.
- **Unity:** Unity refers to the cohesion and consistency of a design. A unified design feels cohesive and well-integrated, with all elements working together to create a harmonious whole. Consistency in typography, color, and layout helps establish unity and reinforce the overall theme or message of a design.
- **Emphasis:** Emphasis involves highlighting certain elements to make them stand out and draw the viewer's attention. This can be achieved through variations in size, color, or contrast. Emphasizing key elements helps users understand the most important parts of a design and navigate it more effectively.
- **Scale and proportion:** These twin elements are the power couple of design, and influence how we see element size and relationships. Scale is the absolute size of an element in comparison with something else (for example, entire design, another element, or reality). Proportion focuses on how elements compare to each other. Together, they create hierarchy (larger implies more important), balance (matching sizes for order), and emotional impact (think tiny flower for sweetness, giant monster for fear). They are used in many fields, ranging from photography to architecture, and these principles help designers craft visually engaging compositions that guide the viewer's eye and deliver the message.

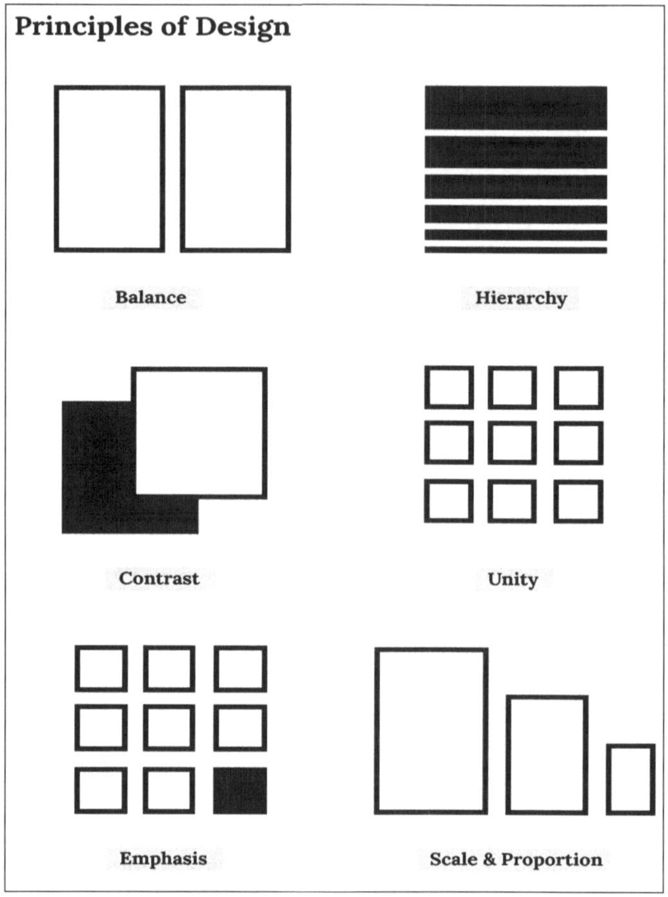

Figure 2.5: *Principles of design in UI*

Applying Design Principles in Figma

Now that we have explored the core principles of design, let us discuss how to apply these principles within the Figma platform. Let us recall how to set up a new design file in Figma. Open Figma and click the "`Create a new file`" button. You may choose a template that Figma offers for different screen sizes and platforms. Finally, create a Frame and start designing.

Layout Composition

Layout Composition is the arrangement and organization of visual elements within a design. In Figma, designers have access to a variety of tools and features for creating balanced and visually appealing layouts. These tools are layout grids, frames, alignment guides, and spacing controls.

Layout Grids:

Figma allows designers to define custom layout grids to establish consistent spacing and alignment throughout their designs. Grids can be configured to match different design systems and screen sizes, ensuring that designs are visually balanced and harmonious. To set up grids in Figma, go to **`View`** > **`Show Layout Grid`**. Adjust grid settings (density, color, and others) to your preference. To create custom grids, use shapes to draw grid lines. Shortcut: *Shift*+G.

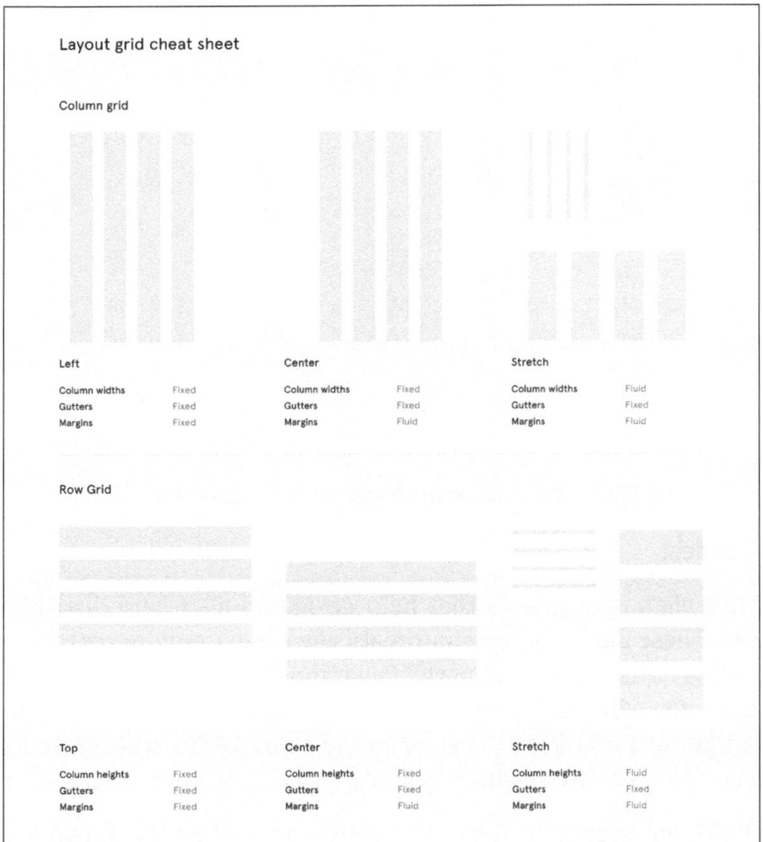

Figure 2.6: *Layout grids in Figma. Image credits: Figma.com*

Frames:

Frames are container elements that hold other design elements and help organize content within a layout. In Figma, designers can create frames of various sizes and shapes and use them to group related elements together. Frames can also be nested within other frames, allowing for complex layout structures. In Figma, click the Frame tool in the toolbar on the left side of the screen. It looks like a rectangle with a plus sign inside. Click and drag your cursor on the canvas to create a frame of the desired size and shape. Shortcut: F.

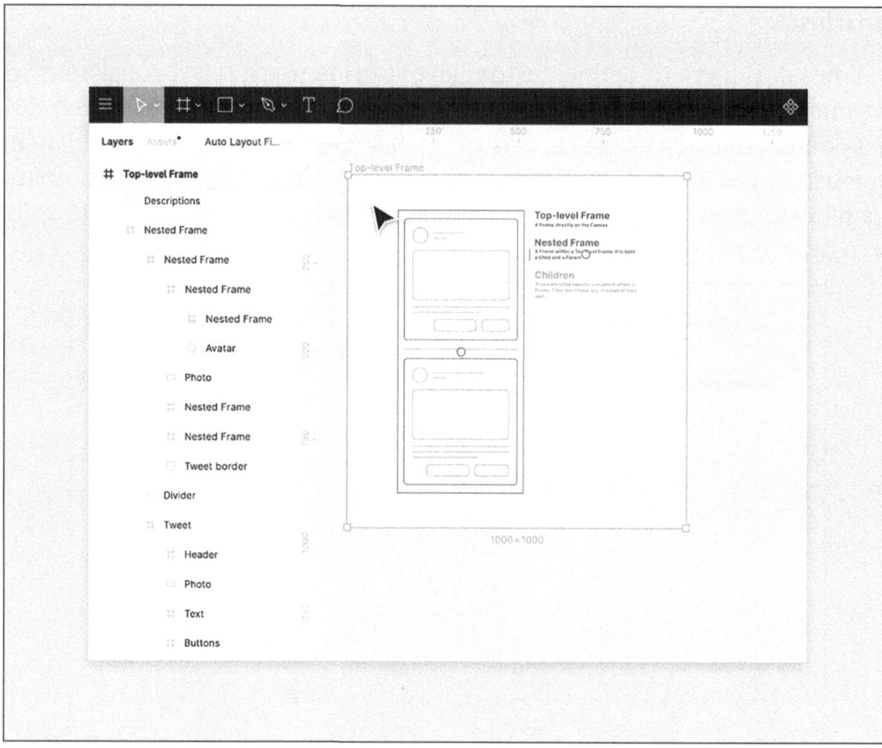

***Figure** 2.7: Frames in Figma. Image credits: Figma*

Alignment Guides:

Figma provides alignment guides that help designers align and distribute elements with precision. These guides appear automatically when dragging, resizing, or aligning elements, making it easy to achieve perfect alignment and spacing. To enable alignment guides in Figma, you will need to first go to view and turn on rulers (Shortcut: *Shift* + R). Then Click and drag a line from the ruler to the canvas. This will create a guide. Hold *Option* (Mac) or *Alt* (Windows) while dragging an existing guide to create a duplicate.

There are additional alignment features, for example, when you move objects, smart guides will appear to help you align them to the edges, centers, and other elements on the canvas. Additionally, Auto Layout allows you to automatically align and space elements within a frame. It is a powerful tool for creating responsive designs.

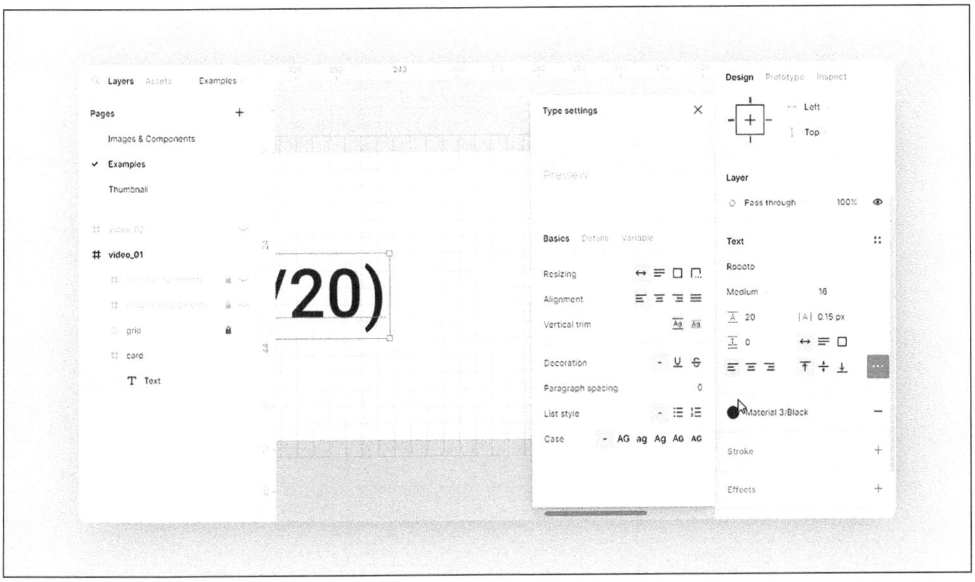

Figure 2.8: *Alignment guides. Image credits: Figma.com*

Spacing Controls:

Figma offers controls for adjusting spacing between elements, including padding, margin, and spacing between columns or rows. Designers can use these controls to create visually balanced and well-proportioned layouts that enhance readability and usability. You can set fixed spacing values or use auto layout to maintain consistent spacing as the content changes. There are also various plugins available in the Figma community online that can help you with spacing, such as *Spacing* and *Layout Grid*.

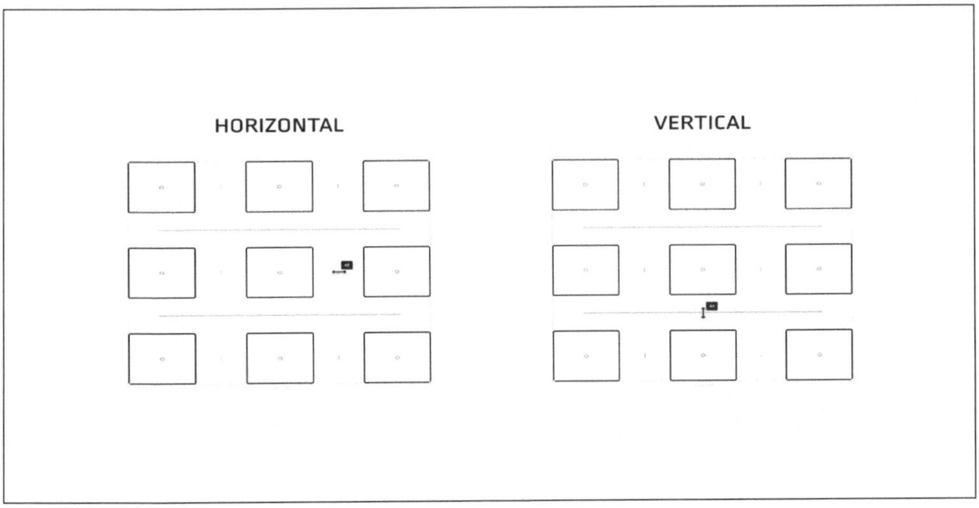

Figure 2.9: *Horizontal and vertical spacing between elements. Image credits: Figma.com*

You can group elements and add spacing in between them.

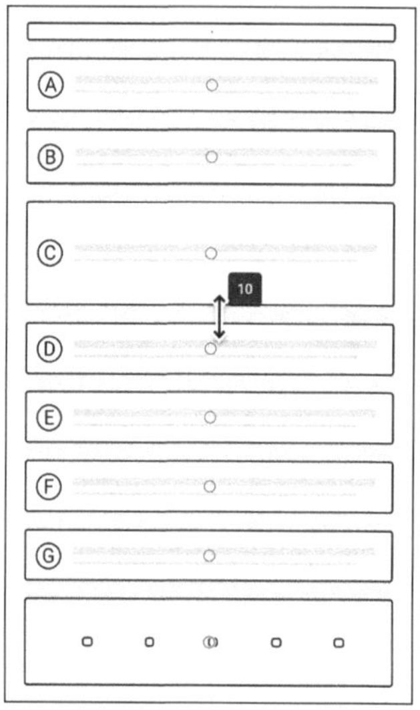

Figure 2.10: *Spacing between rows. Image credits: Figma.com*

You can also edit spacing controls to create visually appealing layouts.

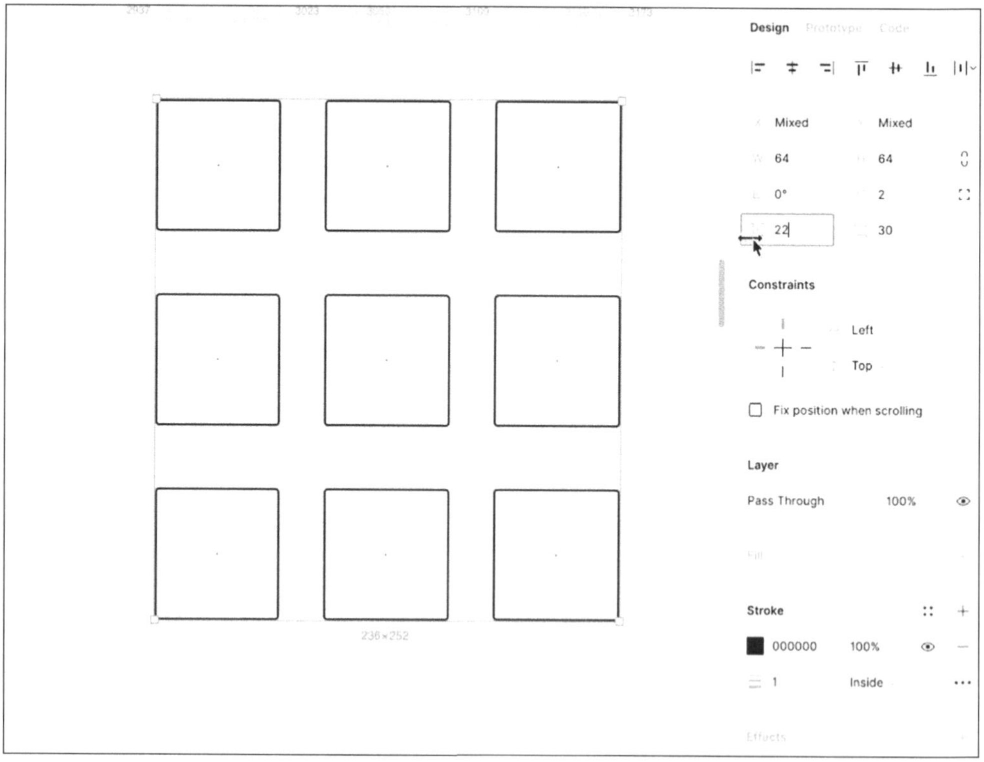

Figure 2.11: *Spacing controls. Image credits: Figma.com*

Typography

Typography plays a crucial role in establishing hierarchy, conveying tone and personality, and enhancing readability in a design. In Figma, designers have access to a wide range of typography tools and features for controlling text appearance and layout.

Text Styles:

Figma allows designers to create and apply text styles to maintain consistency and coherence across their designs. Text styles can include font family, font size, font weight, line height, letter spacing, and text alignment. By defining text styles, designers can ensure that typography is consistent and visually harmonious throughout a design.

To create a text style in Figma, select a text layer with the desired font, size, weight, color, and other properties. Right-click the text layer and select **`Create Style`**. Or, in the Properties panel, click the **+** button next to **`Text Styles`**. Give your style a descriptive name (e.g., "**`Heading 1`**," "**`Body Copy`**"). Select another text layer and apply the style from the **`Text Styles`** panel.

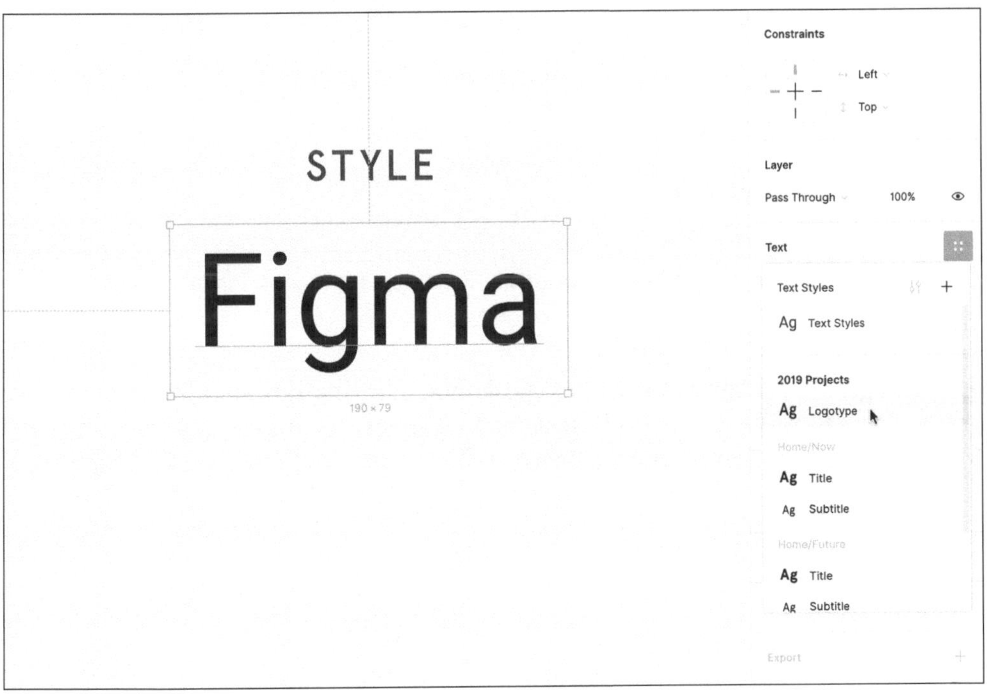

Figure 2.12: *Text style in Figma. Image credits: Figma.com*

Typography Controls:

Figma provides controls for adjusting typography settings directly within the text editor. Designers can customize text appearance, including font size, font weight, font style, line height, letter spacing, text color, and text alignment. These controls allow for precise control over typography and help achieve the desired visual hierarchy and emphasis.

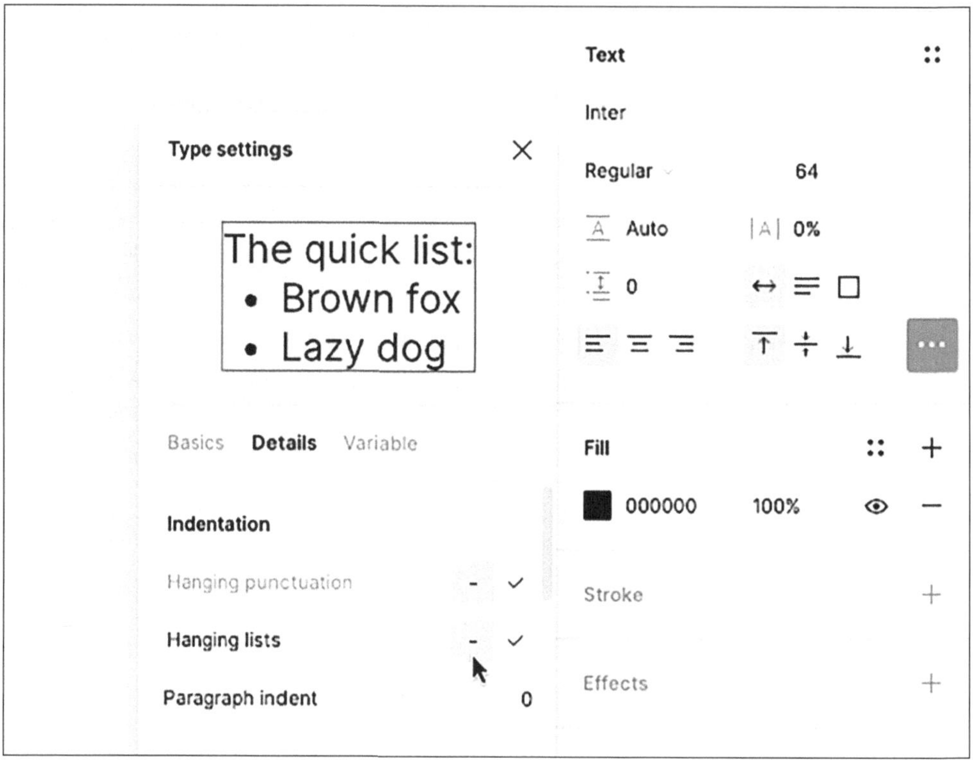

Figure 2.13: Typography controls in Figma. Image credits: Figma.com

Google Fonts Integration:

Figma integrates seamlessly with Google Fonts, allowing designers to access a vast library of web fonts for use in their designs. Designers can browse, preview, and select fonts directly within Figma, making it easy to find the perfect typeface for their project.

Figure 2.14: *Google font pairings on Figma.com*

Color Palette

Color is a powerful design element that can evoke emotions, convey meaning, and create visual interest in a design. In Figma, designers can leverage a variety of tools and features for creating and managing color palettes, applying color to elements, and ensuring color consistency across a design.

In Figma, click the **`Color`** tool in the toolbar. Pick a color using the color picker or enter a hex code. Right-click the color swatch and select **`Add to Document`** Color Palette.

Alternatively, drag and drop the color swatch onto the Color Palette panel. You can click on a color in the palette to select it. Select an element in your design (for example, a shape, text).

Click the **Fill** or **Stroke** color property in the **Properties** panel. Select the desired color from the palette. To edit a color, double-click a color in the palette to open the color picker. You can adjust the hue, saturation, and lightness. Right-click a color and select **Rename**. You can create color sets, by grouping related colors into sets for better. You can also define reusable color tokens with descriptive names to apply colors consistently across your design and communicate effectively with front-end engineers.

Color Picker:

The color picker allows designers to select colors from a spectrum of hues, adjust color saturation and brightness, and enter color values manually. Use the 'I' key shortcut, to sample colors from existing elements and save them to the color palette for future use.

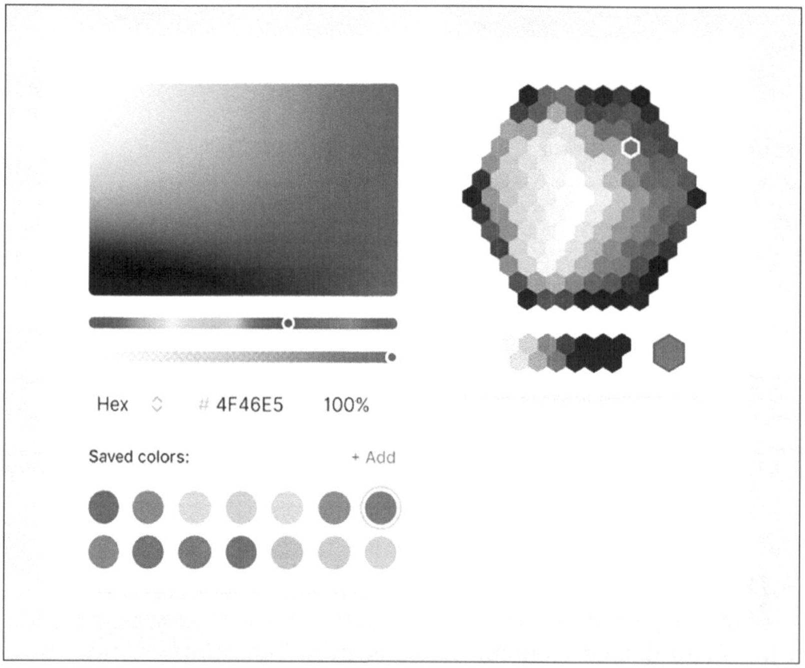

Figure 2.15: *Figma's color picker. Image credits: Figma.com*

Swatches:

Figma allows designers to create custom color swatches and save them to the color palette for easy access. Swatches can be organized into groups, named for easy identification, and shared with team members to maintain consistency across projects.

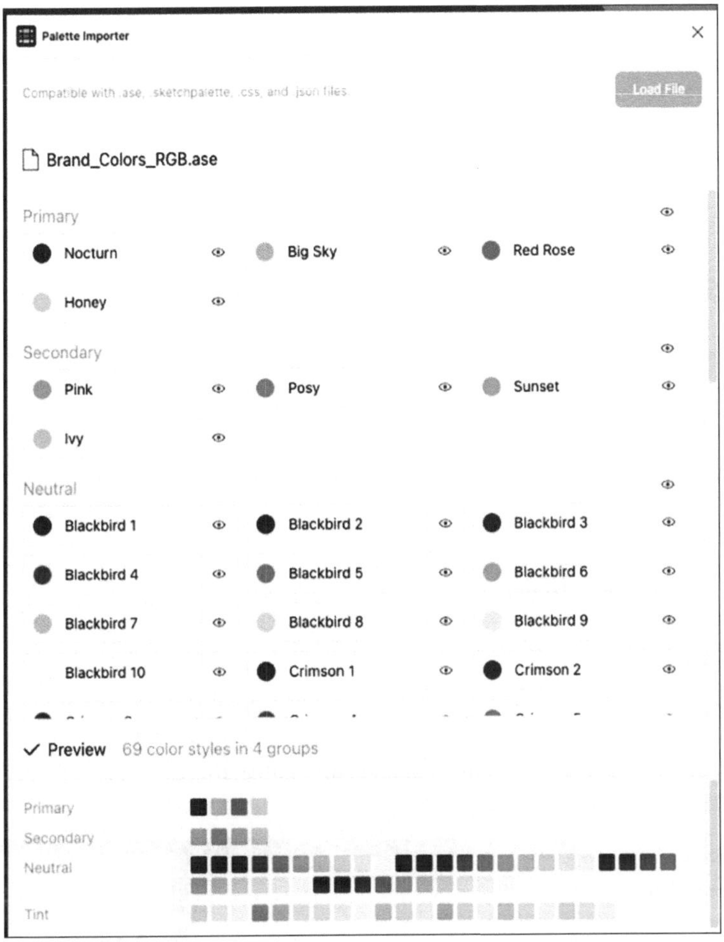

***Figure 2.16:** Figma's color swatches. Image credits: Figma.com*

Color Styles:

Figma's color styles feature allows designers to define and apply color styles to elements within a design. Color styles act as reusable presets that can be applied to multiple elements, ensuring consistency and efficiency in color management.

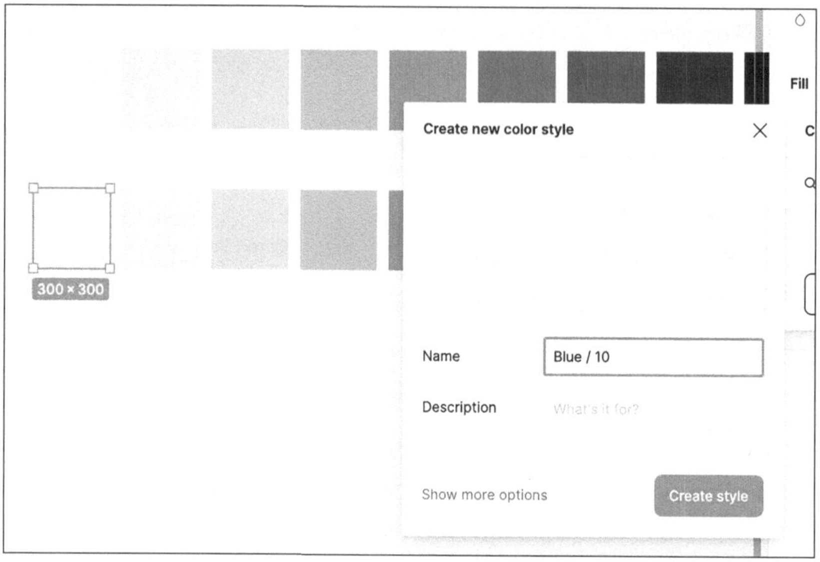

***Figure 2.17:** Figma's color styles. Image credits: Figma.com*

Color Contrast Checker:

Figma includes a built-in color contrast checker that helps designers ensure that the text is legible against background colors. The contrast checker evaluates color combinations based on accessibility guidelines and provides recommendations for improving contrast if necessary.

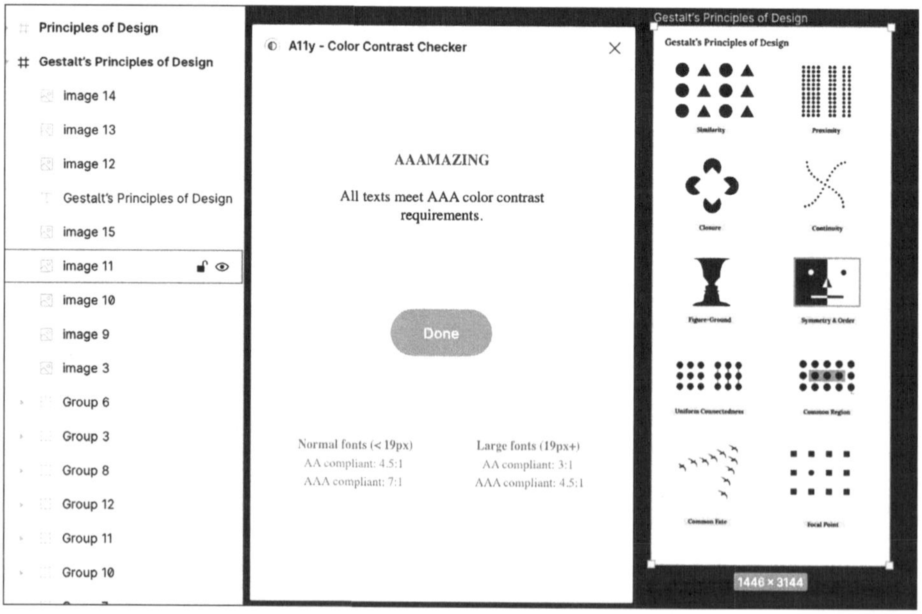

***Figure 2.18:** Figma's color contrast checker. Download the A11Y contrast checker here: https://www.figma.com/community/plugin/733159460536249875/a11y-color-contrast-checker*

Visual Hierarchy

Establishing visual hierarchy is essential for guiding attention and conveying the intended message effectively. In Figma, designers can leverage a combination of layout, typography, color, and contrast to create a clear and compelling visual hierarchy in designs.

Size and Scale:

Designers can use variations in size and scale to establish visual hierarchy and emphasize important elements within a design. Larger elements tend to attract more attention and convey greater importance, while smaller elements recede into the background.

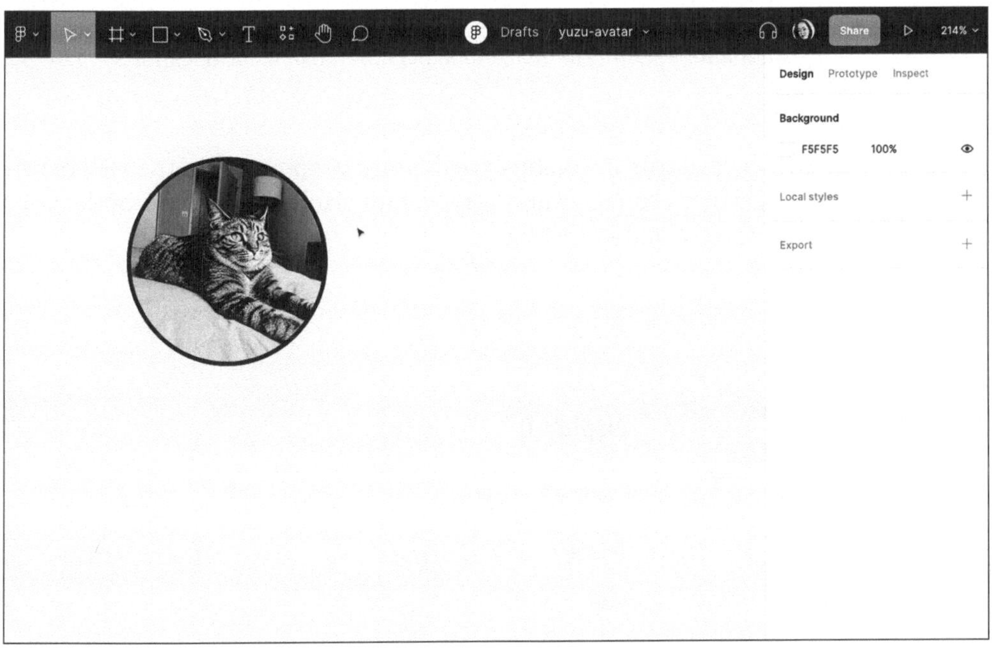

***Figure 2.19:** Figma's scale tool. Image credits: Figma.com*

Color and Contrast:

Contrasting colors can be used to create focal points and draw attention to specific elements within a design. Designers can also vary color intensity, saturation, and brightness to establish visual hierarchy and convey meaning effectively.

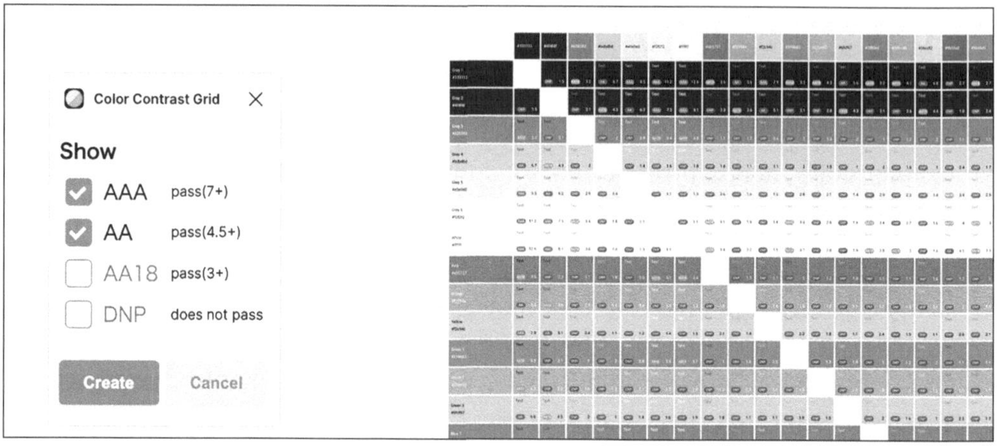

Figure 2.20: *Plug-in on Figma for color contrast checker. Get yours here: https://www.figma.com/community/plugin/1039910246084959068/color-contrast-grid*

Typography:

Typography plays a crucial role in establishing hierarchy and guiding the viewer's eye through a design. Designers can use variations in font size, weight, style, and color to create emphasis, hierarchy, and readability.

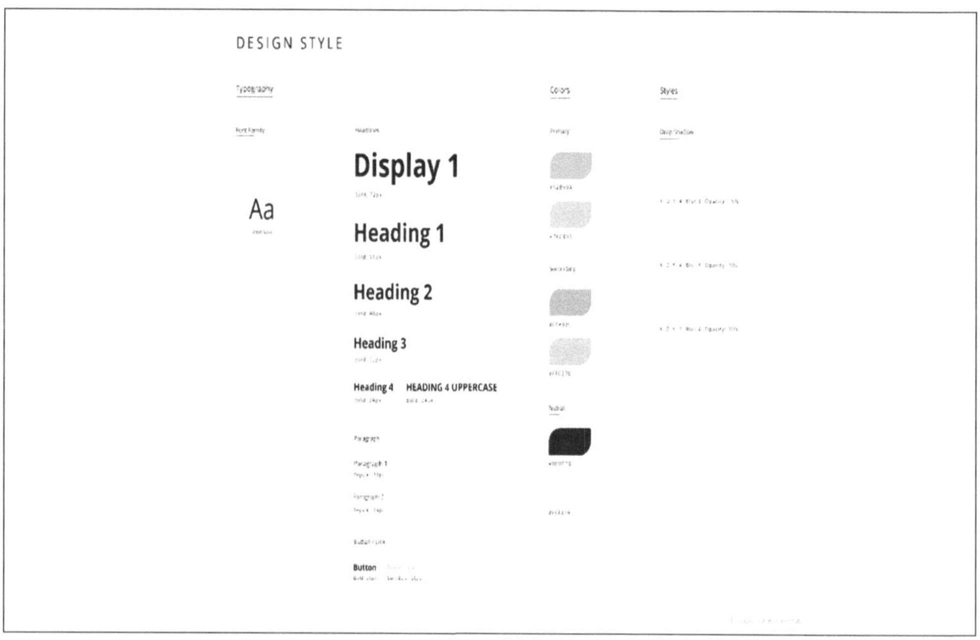

Figure 2.21: *An example of a typography style in Figma*

Spatial Arrangement:

The spatial arrangement of elements within a layout can influence visual hierarchy and flow. Designers can use principles such as proximity, alignment, and spacing to group related elements together and create logical visual relationships.

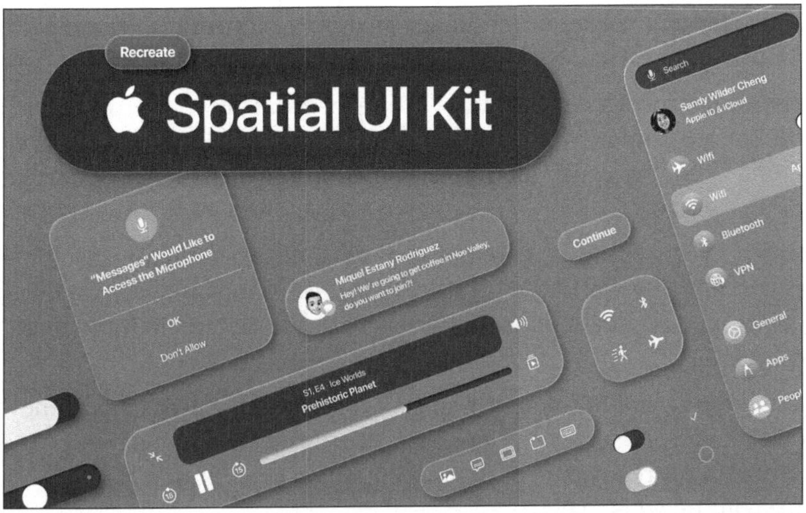

Figure 2.22: *An example of a spatial UI kit in Figma. Find example here: https://www.figma.com/community/file/1248660823114058951*

Getting Started with Figma Templates

Figma UI templates are pre-designed layouts or components that you can use as a foundation for your own designs. These templates are created by designers to help streamline the design process and provide a starting point for building interfaces.

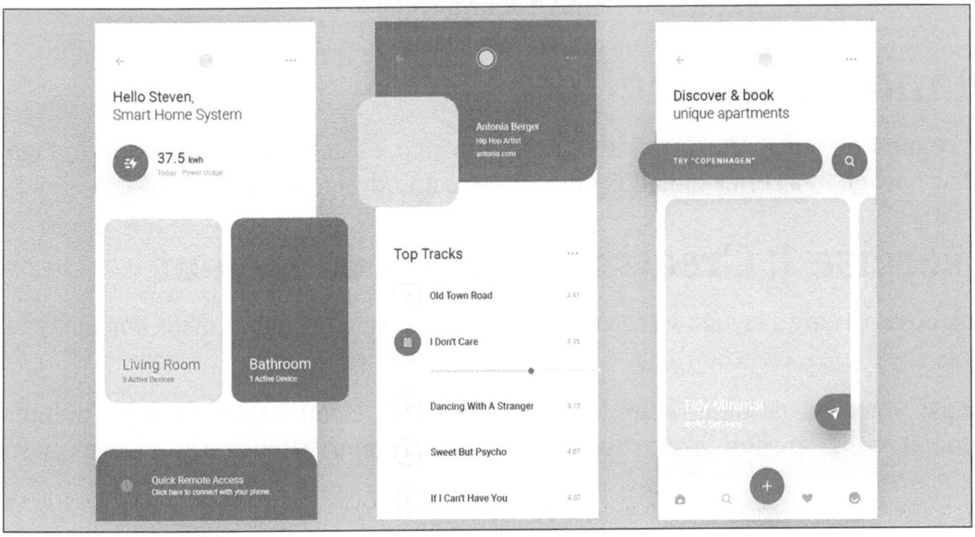

Figure 2.23: *Get started with Figma UI templates. Find templates here: https://elements.envato.com/learn/top-10-ui-templates-for-figma-and-adobe-xd*

Here is how you can use Figma UI templates effectively:

- **Exploration and Inspiration**: Browse through Figma's vast collection of UI templates to explore different design styles, layouts, and components. This can provide inspiration and ideas for your own projects.
- **Customization**: Once you find a UI template that fits your project requirements, you can customize it to suit your needs. Figma allows you to easily modify colors, typography, layout, and components to align with your brand identity and design goals.
- **Rapid Prototyping**: UI templates can be particularly useful for rapid prototyping. By starting with a pre-designed template, you can quickly create a prototype of your application or website and iterate on it based on feedback and testing.
- **Consistency and Efficiency**: Using UI templates ensures consistency in design across different screens or pages of your project. It also saves time and effort by providing ready-made components and layouts that you can easily drop into your designs.
- **Collaboration**: Figma UI templates can facilitate collaboration within design teams. Multiple team members can work on the same template simultaneously, making it easy to share ideas, collaborate on design iterations, and ensure consistency across the project.
- **Learning and Skill Development**: Studying and deconstructing existing UI templates can also be a valuable learning experience for designers. It allows you to analyze design patterns, best practices, and techniques used by other designers, helping you improve your own design skills.

Hands-On Practice

To reinforce your understanding of design principles and their application in Figma, let us engage in a series of hands-on exercises and design challenges.

Exercise 1: Creating a Balanced Layout

Objective: Create a layout with symmetrical balance using Figma's grids and alignment tools.

Steps: Start by defining a grid system for your layout, then arrange elements symmetrically around a central axis. Use alignment guides to ensure precise placement.

Exercise 2: Establishing Hierarchy with Typography

Objective: Design a typographic composition that demonstrates clear visual hierarchy using font size, weight, and style.

Steps: Choose a primary headline and sub headline for your composition, then experiment with different font sizes, weights, and styles to establish hierarchy. Use variations in typography to guide the viewer's eye.

Exercise 3: Applying Color Contrast for Emphasis

Objective: Create a design with contrasting colors to emphasize key elements.

Steps: Select a color palette with complementary or contrasting colors, then apply these colors strategically to highlight important elements within your design. Pay attention to color contrast and readability when combining colors.

Exercise 4: Creating Unity and Consistency in Design

Objective: Design a set of related elements (for example, buttons, icons, cards) that exhibit unity and consistency in style and appearance.

Steps: Define a set of design guidelines for your elements, including color palette, typography, shape, and style. Apply these guidelines consistently across all elements to create a cohesive and unified design system.

Conclusion

This chapter has provided a comprehensive exploration of design principles and their application within the Figma platform. By understanding the fundamental principles of design, including balance, hierarchy, contrast, unity, and emphasis, designers gain the necessary framework to create visually compelling and effective designs.

Through hands-on exercises and practical examples, we have demonstrated how to apply these principles within Figma, leveraging its powerful tools and features to create balanced layouts, establish clear visual hierarchy, utilize color effectively, and maintain consistency and unity in design. By mastering these principles and techniques, designers can create designs that not only look aesthetically pleasing but also effectively communicate their intended message to the audience. In the next chapter, we will delve into advanced design techniques and strategies for prototyping in Figma, further expanding your design repertoire and enhancing your skills as a designer.

Transition to the next chapter

As we conclude *Chapter 2, Understanding Design Principles in Figma*, we have gained a comprehensive understanding of design principles and how to apply them within the Figma platform. Now equipped with the knowledge of balance, hierarchy, contrast, unity, and emphasis, we are ready to delve deeper into the world of design elements and explore advanced techniques for prototyping in Figma. In *Chapter 3, Mastering the Figma Interface*, we will explore how to leverage frames, artboards, and components to streamline our design workflow and create interactive prototypes that bring our designs to life. Join us as we continue the journey towards mastering Figma and elevating design skills to new heights.

Recap of Key Points

- **Design Principles Overview**: We introduced the core principles of design, including balance, hierarchy, contrast, unity, and emphasis. These principles serve as the foundation for creating visually appealing and effective designs.
- **Applying Design Principles in Figma**: We discussed how to apply design principles within the Figma platform, utilizing tools and features such as layout grids, frames, alignment guides, typography controls, color palettes, and visual hierarchy techniques.
- **Layout Composition**: We explored the importance of layout composition and discussed how to create balanced and visually appealing layouts using Figma's layout grids, frames, alignment guides, and spacing controls.
- **Typography**: We learned how typography plays a crucial role in establishing hierarchy and conveying tone and personality in a design. We discussed the use of Figma text styles, typography controls, and Google Fonts integration to create consistent and visually appealing typography.
- **Color Palette**: We explored the power of color in design and discussed how to create and manage color palettes in Figma. We learned how to use Figma's color picker, swatches, color styles, and contrast checker to apply color effectively and ensure visual harmony.
- **Visual Hierarchy**: We discussed the importance of establishing visual hierarchy in design and explored techniques for creating clear and compelling visual hierarchy using size, color, typography, and spatial arrangement within Figma.

CHAPTER 3
Mastering the Figma Interface

Introduction

This chapter provides readers with a comprehensive understanding of the Figma interface. It begins with an overview of the various components of the interface, including the toolbar, layers panel, and properties panel, ensuring that readers are familiar with the layout of the workspace. You will be guided through the customization options, allowing you to tailor the interface to suit your individual preferences and workflow. Practical tips and tricks are provided to help you optimize your workspace for efficiency and productivity.

The chapter also covers essential navigation techniques within Figma, such as zooming, panning, and navigating between frames. Readers learn how to navigate complex projects seamlessly, ensuring smooth and efficient workflow management.

Through hands-on exercises, you will gain practical experience in working with the Figma interface, enabling you to navigate the platform confidently and efficiently. By mastering the interface, designers are empowered to focus more on the creative aspects of their work, ultimately leading to more effective and impactful design outcomes.

Structure

In this chapter, we will cover the following topics:

- Figma Interface at a Glance
- Toolbar
- Canvas
- Properties Panel
- Assets Panel
- Prototype Tab

- Comments and Collaboration
- Hands-On Practice

The Figma Interface at a Glance

The Figma interface serves as your workspace to bring design ideas to life. It consists of several key components that work together seamlessly to facilitate the design process.

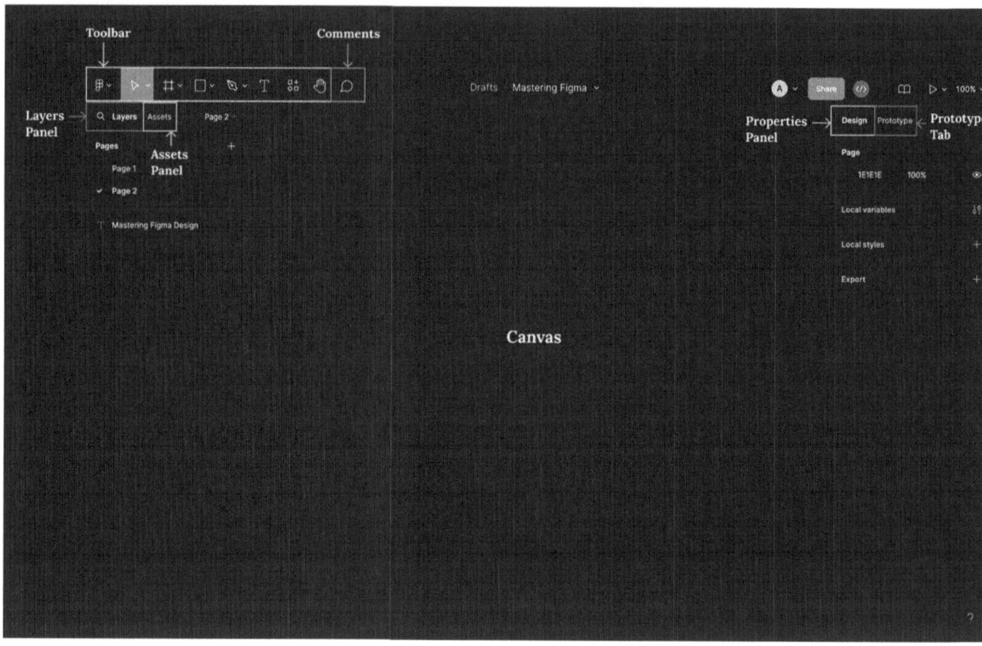

Figure 3.1: *An overview of the Figma interface*

Let us begin by familiarizing ourselves with these components:

- **Toolbar**

  The toolbar is located at the top of the Figma interface and provides quick access to essential tools and commands. Here, you will find tools for creating shapes, text, and lines, as well as options for selecting, editing, and navigating your designs.

- **Canvas**

  The canvas is the central area where you create and manipulate your designs. It serves as a blank slate where you can place and arrange design elements such as frames, shapes, text, and images. The canvas is where your creativity takes shape.

- **Layers Panel**

  The layers panel, located on the left side of the interface, displays a hierarchical list of all the elements in your design. It allows you to easily select, organize, and manipulate individual layers, frames, and objects within your design.

- **Properties Panel**

  The properties panel is located on the right side of the interface and provides context-sensitive options and settings for the currently selected object or element. Depending on what you have selected, the properties panel will display options for editing styles, dimensions, effects, and more.

- **Assets Panel**

  The assets panel, located on the left side of the interface below the layers panel, provides access to your design assets, including components, styles, and libraries. It allows you to easily reuse and manage design elements across multiple projects.

- **Prototype Tab**

  The prototype tab, located at the top of the interface, allows you to create interactive prototypes of your designs. It provides tools for adding links, transitions, and animations to simulate user interactions and flows.

- **Comments and Collaboration**

  Figma offers robust collaboration features that allow you to share your designs with team members and stakeholders, gather feedback, and collaborate in real-time. Comments, annotations, and version history help streamline the collaborative design process.

Navigating the Figma Interface

Navigating the Figma interface is intuitive and streamlined, with a toolbar providing access to essential tools and commands, while the canvas offers ample space for designing and arranging elements seamlessly. With straightforward zooming and panning controls, designers can effortlessly navigate between frames and pages to create cohesive and visually engaging designs.

Toolbar

Each tool serves a specific purpose in the design process essential for creating, editing, and navigating designs. By mastering these tools, you will be able to create complex designs with precision and efficiency.

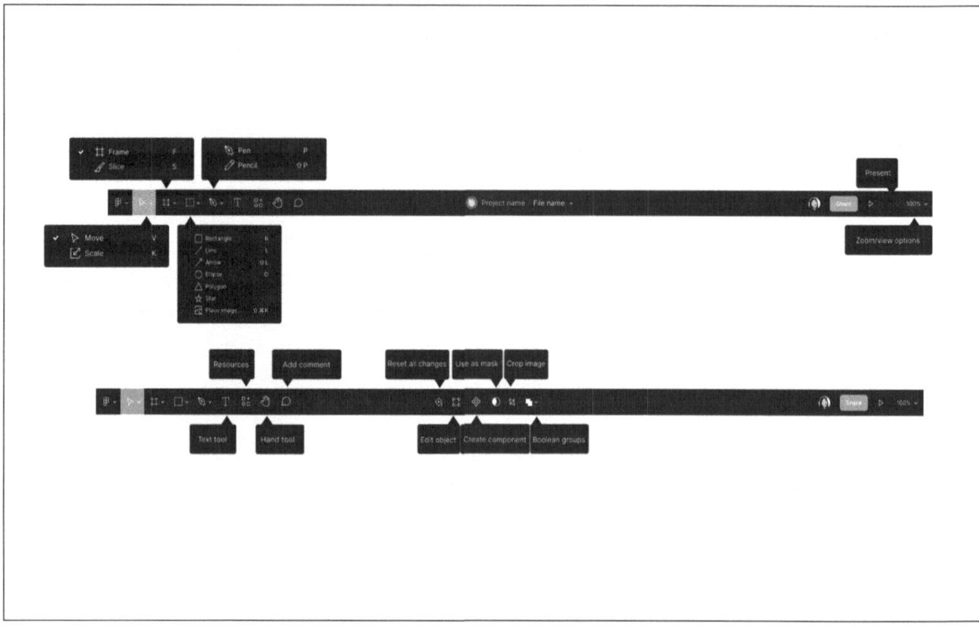

Figure 3.2: *An overview of the Figma toolbar*

Following is the list of these tools and their shortcuts:

- **Selection Tool (V):** The selection tool is used to select and manipulate objects on the canvas. You can move, resize, rotate, and edit selected objects using this tool.
- **Move Tool (Q):** The move tool allows you to move selected objects on the canvas. It provides a quick way to adjust the position of objects without needing to switch to the selection tool.
- **Rectangle Tool (R):** The rectangle tool is used to draw rectangles and squares on the canvas. You can create shapes with solid fills or outlines, adjust corner radii, and customize dimensions.
- **Ellipse Tool (O):** The ellipse tool is used to draw circles and ellipses on the canvas. You can create shapes with solid fills or outlines, adjust dimensions, and customize corner radii.
- **Polygon Tool (Y):** The polygon tool allows you to draw polygons and stars on the canvas. You can adjust the number of sides, inner radius, and rotation to create custom shapes.
- **Line Tool (L):** The line tool is used to draw straight lines and arrows on the canvas. You can adjust the line thickness, style, and arrowhead options.
- **Pen Tool (P):** The pen tool allows you to draw custom paths and shapes on the canvas. You can create freeform shapes, curves, and lines by clicking and dragging to define anchor points.

- **Text Tool (T):** The text tool is used to add text to the canvas. You can create text boxes, adjust font size, style, alignment, and spacing, and apply text effects.
- **Frame Tool (F):** The frame tool is used to create frames on the canvas. Frames are containers for organizing and grouping design elements, such as shapes, text, and images.
- **Slice Tool (S):** The slice tool is used to create slices of your design for exporting. You can define areas of your design to export as individual images or assets.
- **Zoom Tool (Z):** The zoom tool allows you to zoom in and out of the canvas. You can click to zoom in or use the zoom slider to adjust the zoom level.
- **Hand Tool (H):** The hand tool is used to pan around the canvas. You can click and drag to move the canvas view, making it easier to navigate large designs.
- **Vector Tool (V):** The vector tool is used to draw vector shapes and paths on the canvas. You can create custom shapes and paths with smooth curves and adjustable control points.
- **Comment Tool (C):** The comment tool allows you to add comments to specific areas of design. You can leave feedback and annotations for collaborators to review.

Customizing the Toolbar

By customizing the toolbar in Figma to suit your preferences and workflow, you can optimize your design process and work more efficiently. Take the time to identify your most used tools, remove unnecessary clutter, and organize the toolbar in a way that is most useful for you. With a personalized toolbar setup, you will be able to focus on your designs without distractions and access the tools you need with ease.

Here are some tips for customizing the toolbar to suit your preferences and workflow:

- **Identify Your Most Used Tools:** Take some time to identify the tools and commands you use most frequently in your design process. These may include selection tools, shape tools, text tools, and other commonly used commands.
- **Remove Unnecessary Tools:** Figma's default toolbar includes a wide range of tools and commands, but you may not need all of them for your workflow. Consider removing any tools that you rarely use to declutter the toolbar and focus on the essentials.
- **Add Custom Tools:** If there are specific tools or commands that you frequently use but are not available in the default toolbar, you can add them as custom tools. This allows you to access them quickly without navigating through menus.
- **Organize Tools by Functionality:** Group similar tools and commands together

to make them easier to find and access. For example, you could group shape tools, text tools, and drawing tools together in logical sections of the toolbar.

- **Prioritize Frequently Used Tools:** Arrange the toolbar so that your most frequently used tools are easily accessible and located towards the beginning of the toolbar. This minimizes the need for scrolling or searching for tools during your design process.
- **Utilize Keyboard Shortcuts:** In addition to customizing the toolbar, take advantage of keyboard shortcuts to access tools and commands even faster. By memorizing and using keyboard shortcuts, you can streamline your workflow and save valuable time.
- **Experiment and Iterate:** Do not be afraid to experiment with different toolbar configurations to find what works best for you. Your workflow and preferences may evolve over time, so be open to adjusting and iterations to your toolbar setup.
- **Save Custom Toolbar Layouts:** Once you have customized the toolbar to your liking, you can save your custom toolbar layout as a preset. This allows you to easily switch between different toolbar configurations depending on the task at hand.

Canvas

The Figma canvas serves as a dynamic workspace where designers can bring their ideas to life, arranging and organizing elements with precision and flexibility. Its infinite canvas allows for seamless exploration and iteration, empowering designers to craft intricate designs without limitations.

Mastering Navigation Techniques

By mastering navigation and zooming techniques, you will be able to navigate large designs with ease, focus on specific areas of your canvas, and work more efficiently in Figma.

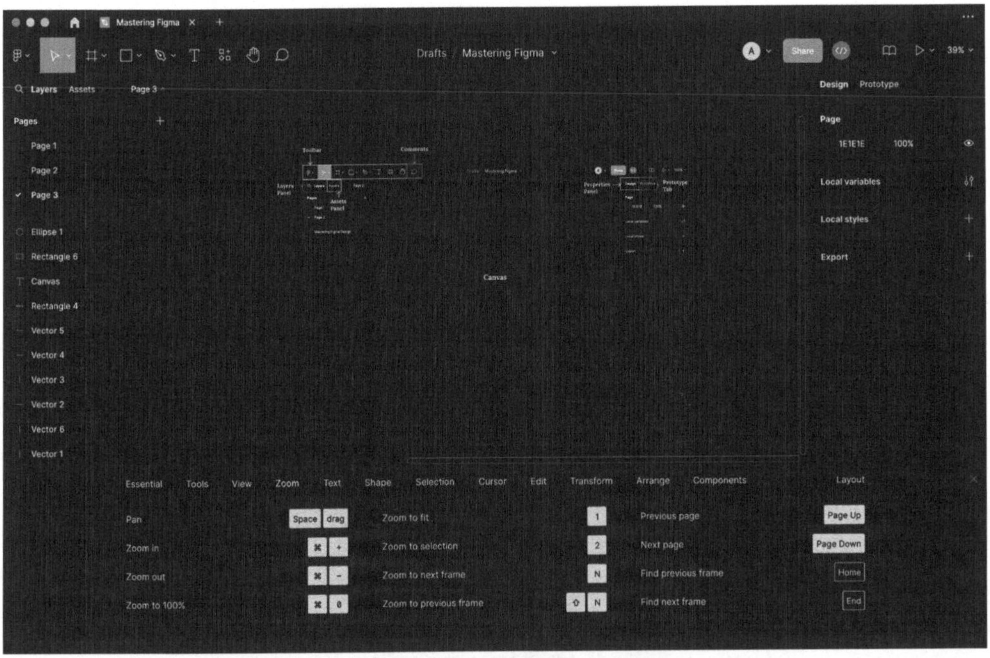

Figure 3.3: *Zoom shortcuts that can be accessed with the question mark at the bottom right of the Figma canvas*

Practice these listed techniques regularly to become proficient:

- **Panning:** To move around the canvas, click and hold the mouse wheel or middle mouse button (if available) and drag the canvas in the desired direction. Alternatively, you can use the Hand tool (shortcut: H) to pan around the canvas.
- **Keyboard Shortcuts:** You can use keyboard shortcuts to navigate the canvas quickly. Press and hold the spacebar to temporarily activate the Hand tool for panning. Release the spacebar to return to the previously selected tool. Additionally, you can use the arrow keys to nudge the canvas in small increments.

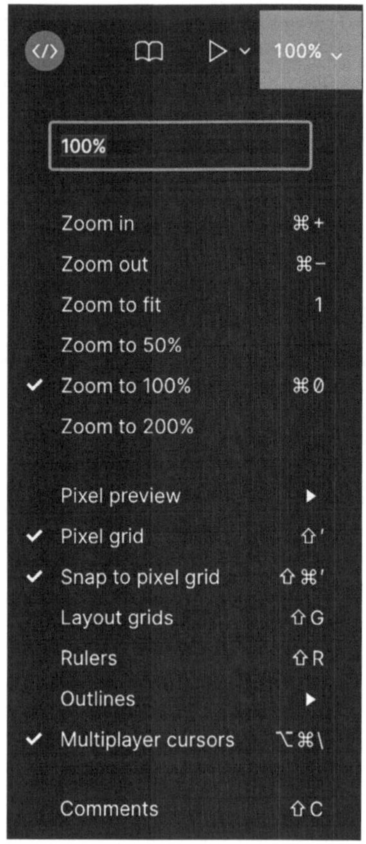

Figure 3.4: *Zoom dropdown options from the toolbar*

- **Zoom:** Use the keyboard shortcuts *Cmd/Ctrl* + Plus (+) to zoom in and *Cmd/Ctrl* + Minus(-) to zoom out. Alternatively, you can use *Cmd/Ctrl* + 0 to fit the canvas to the screen. To zoom to selection, double-click an object to zoom in on it. This action centers the selected object on the canvas and zooms in to fill the screen with the object. Double-click again to return to the previous zoom level. Double-click a frame in the layers panel to zoom in on that frame. This action centers the frame on the canvas and zooms in to fit the frame within the viewport.
- **Mouse Wheel:** You can also zoom in and out of the canvas using the mouse wheel. Scroll the mouse wheel away from you to zoom in and towards you to zoom out. This method provides a quick and intuitive way to adjust the zoom level.

Arranging Design Elements on Figma

Arranging and organizing design elements on the canvas is crucial for creating structured and visually appealing designs in Figma.

Here are some techniques for effectively arranging and organizing your design elements:

Figure 3.5: *Accessing frames from the toolbar with presets for different device types, such as phone, tablet, desktop, TV, presentation, watch, paper, social media*

- **Use Frames:**
  - Frames act as containers for organizing and grouping design elements. Use frames to encapsulate related elements and create logical groupings within your design.
  - To create a frame, select the objects you want to include, right-click, and choose "**`Frame Selection`**" or use the shortcut *Cmd/Ctrl* + *Option/Alt* + G.
  - Frames can be resized, rotated, and manipulated like any other object on the canvas. They also have their own properties, such as constraints and layout grid settings.

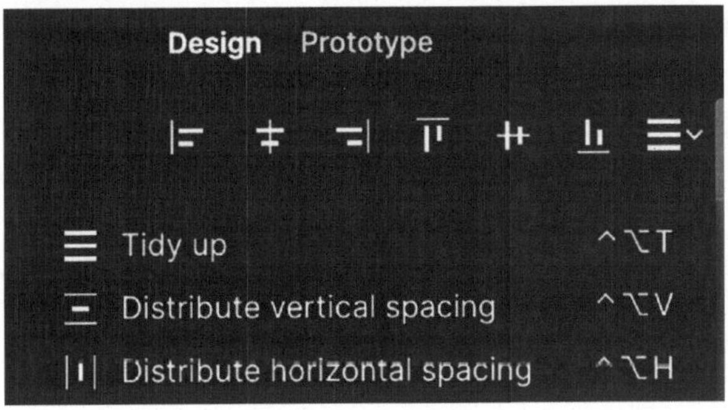

Figure 3.6: *Align and distribute menu in Figma can be activated after you select multiple objects in the canvas*

- **Align and Distribute:**
    - Figma offers alignment and distribution tools to help you arrange elements with precision. Select multiple objects, then use the alignment options in the toolbar or the "`Arrange`" menu to align them horizontally or vertically.
    - You can also distribute objects evenly along a horizontal or vertical axis using the distribution options. This ensures consistent spacing between elements.

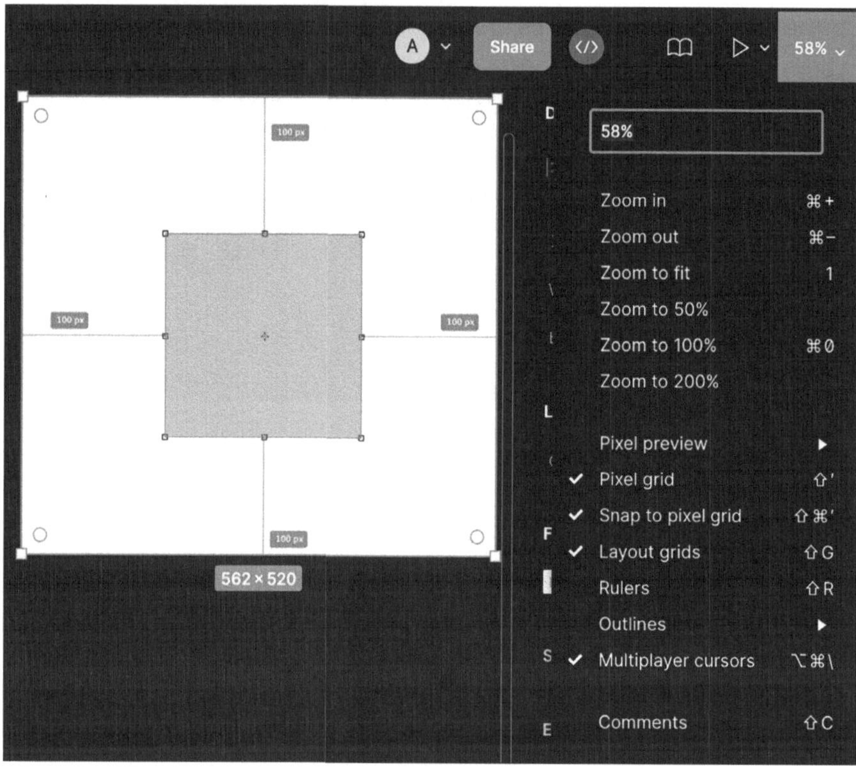

Figure 3.7: *Smart guides*

- **Smart Guides:**
    - Smart guides in Figma provide visual cues to help you align and position objects accurately. When moving or resizing objects, smart guides appear to indicate alignment with nearby objects, edges, or centers.
    - Smart guides also appear when you are placing objects at equal distances from each other or aligning them with the canvas edges.

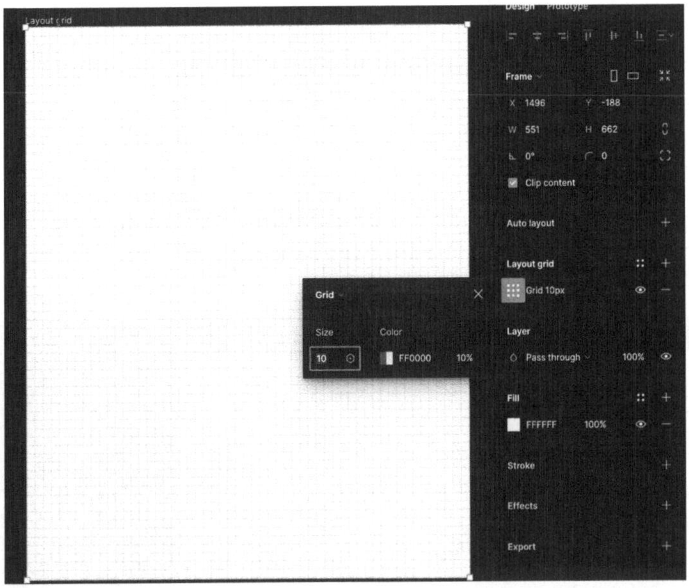

Figure 3.8: *Layout grid settings*

- **Grids and Layout Grids:**
    - Figma allows you to create custom grids and layout grids to assist with alignment and spacing. Grids provide a visual reference for positioning objects, while layout grids help maintain consistency in your design's spacing and proportions.
    - You can customize grid settings such as grid type, grid size, grid color, and grid visibility to suit your design needs. Layout grids can be applied to frames to control the layout of their contents.

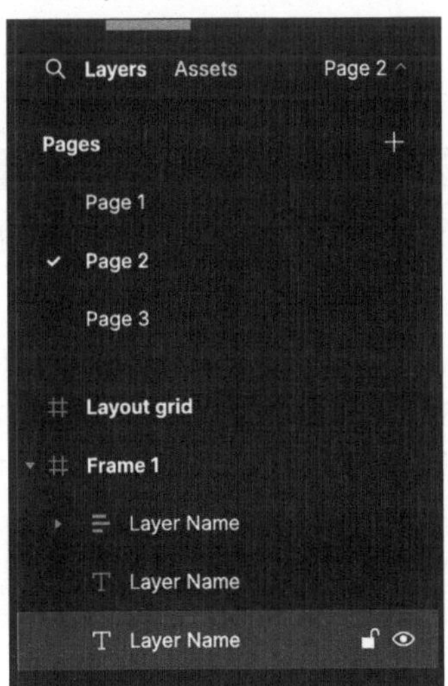

Figure 3.9: *Layers*

- **Layer Organization:**
  - Proper layer organization is essential for maintaining a structured and manageable design file. Use the layers panel to arrange objects hierarchically, grouping related elements together and organizing them into logical layers.
  - Rename layers and use folders to further organize your design elements. This makes it easier to find and manage objects, especially in complex designs with multiple layers.

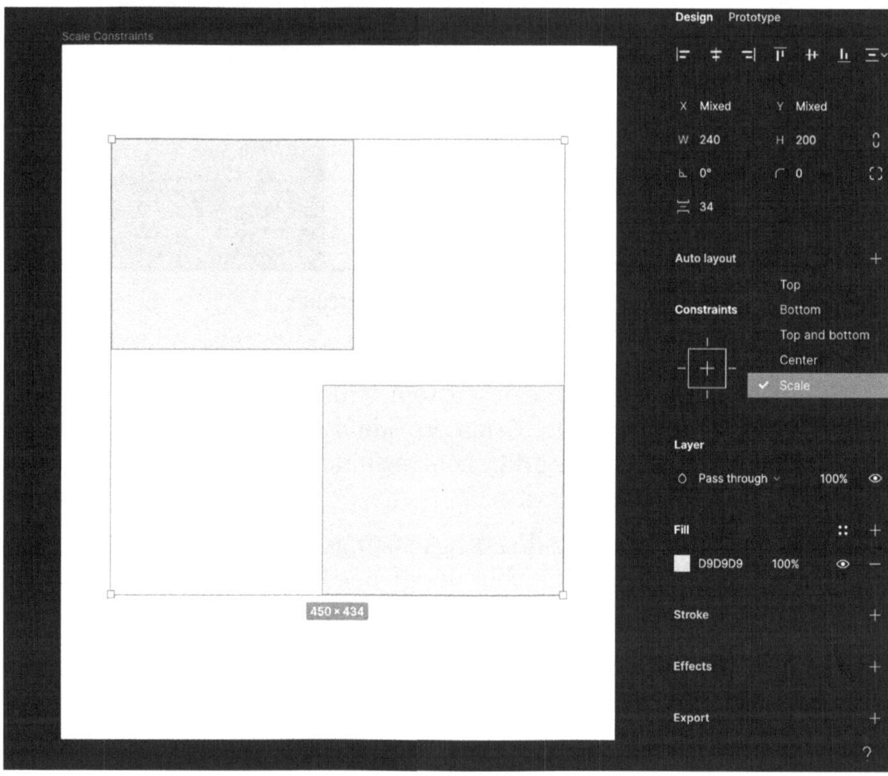

Figure 3.10: *Constraints menu with multiple options*

- **Use Constraints:**
  - Constraints allow you to define how objects behave when their parent frames are resized. By setting constraints on objects within frames, you can create responsive designs that adapt to different screen sizes and orientations.
  - Experiment with different constraint settings, such as "**`Fill`**," "**`Fit`**," "**`Center`**," and "**`Stretch`**," to achieve the desired layout behavior.

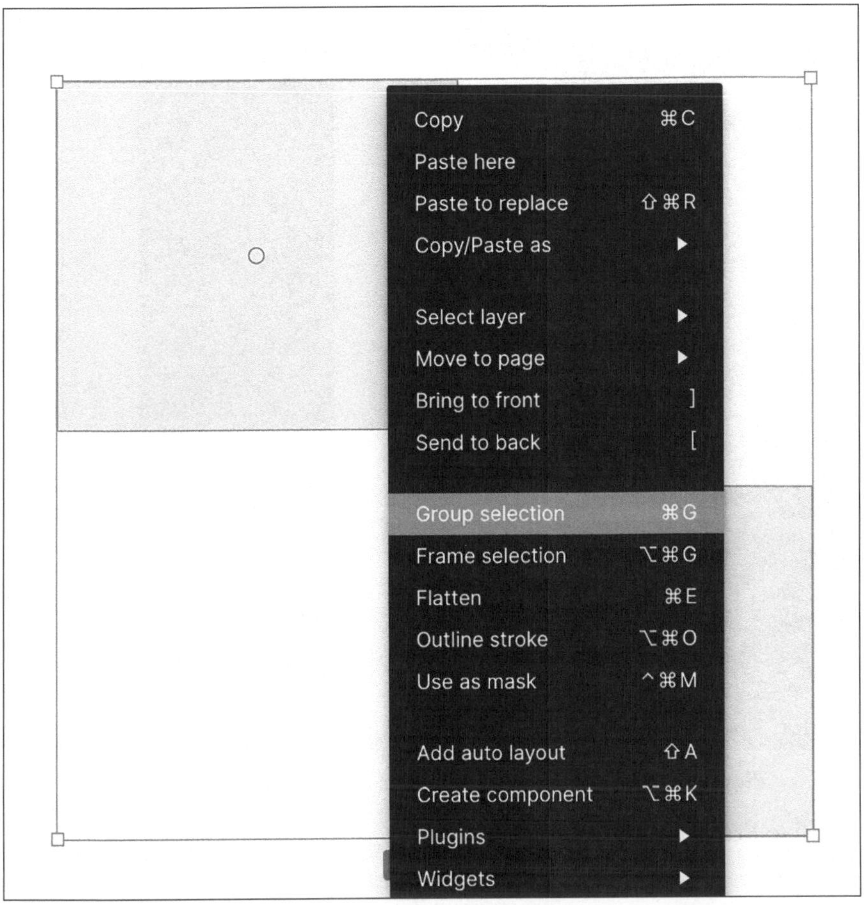

Figure 3.11: *Grouping elements using the right click options*

- **Group and Ungroup:**
  - Grouping objects together is a quick way to organize related elements and manipulate them as a single unit. Select multiple objects, right-click, and choose "**`Group Selection`**" or use the shortcut *Cmd/Ctrl* + G to create a group.
  - You can ungroup objects at any time to revert them to their individual components. Right-click a group and choose "**`Ungroup`**" or use the shortcut *Cmd/Ctrl* + *Shift* + G.

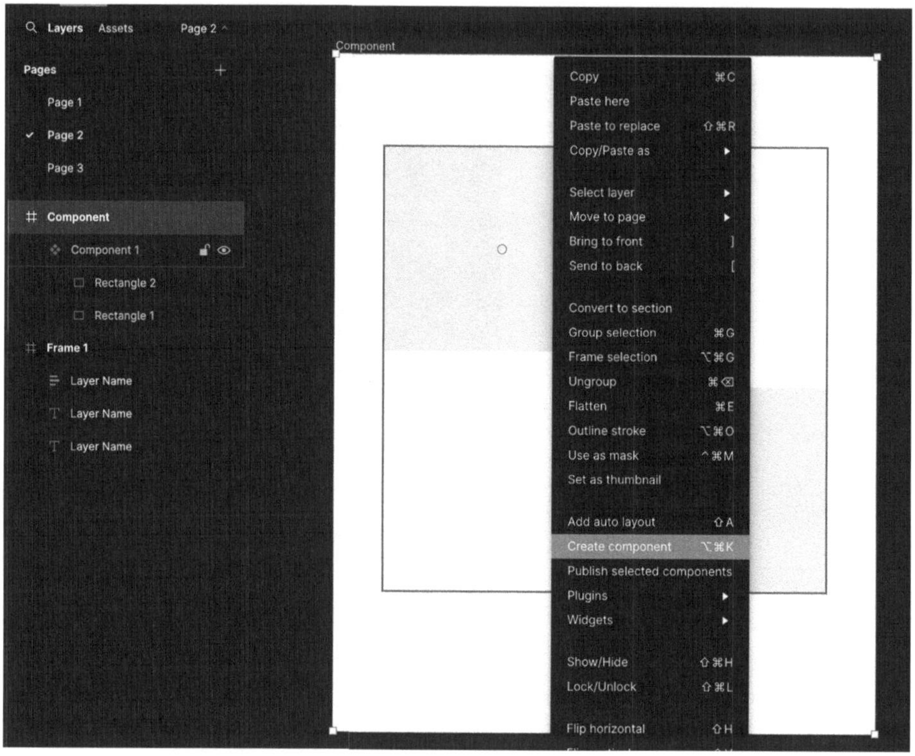

Figure 3.12: *Utilizing the components feature [symbols] in Figma*

- **Utilize Frames as Symbols:**
  - Frames can be turned into components (symbols) in Figma, allowing you to reuse them across multiple instances in your design. Once created, any changes made to the master component are automatically reflected in all instances.
  - Use components for recurring elements such as buttons, icons, headers, and footers to maintain consistency and efficiency in your design workflow.

Auto Layout

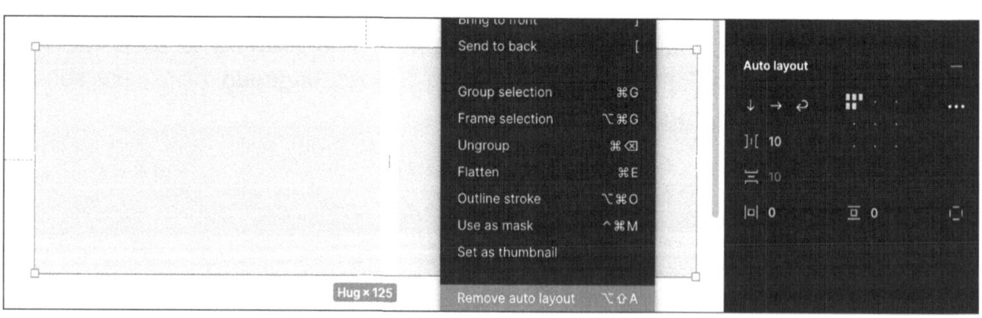

Figure 3.13: *Auto layout in Figma*

Figma's auto layout is a powerful feature that lets you create flexible and responsive UI elements. It basically removes the need for you to manually adjust layouts when resizing elements or changing content. Here is a quick rundown of what auto layout does:

- **Container Adaptability**: You can set up frames and components to automatically resize based on their content. This is useful for buttons with dynamic text or cards with varying amounts of information.
- **Responsive Layouts**: By using auto layout, you can design layouts that adapt to different screen sizes. This is crucial for designing websites and apps that look good on any device.
- **Effortless Alignment**: Auto layout makes it easy to align elements within a frame. You can set properties such as spacing, padding, and margins to ensure everything stays visually balanced.

Steps to set auto layout in Figma:

1. **Select your elements**: Choose the objects you want to group and manage together.
2. **Activate Auto Layout**: Use the shortcut *Shift* + A or click the Auto Layout button in the top toolbar.
3. **Set up your layout**: In the right-hand panel, adjust spacing, padding, and alignment for a balanced look.
4. **Resize and see the magic**: Change the content or element size – Figma automatically adjusts everything to maintain your defined layout.

Canvas Customization

Understanding canvas settings and options for customizing the workspace in Figma is essential for tailoring the environment to your specific needs and preferences. Here is a breakdown of canvas settings and customization options available in Figma:

- **Canvas Color:**

  You can customize the background color of the canvas to suit your preferences or project requirements. To change the canvas color, click the canvas name at the top-left corner of the interface, then select "Canvas Color" and choose a color from the color picker.

- **Grids:**
  - Figma allows you to overlay grids on the canvas to assist with alignment and spacing. You can choose between regular grids, isometric grids, and custom grids.

- Customize grid settings such as grid type, grid size, grid color, and grid visibility to align design elements precisely.

- **Layout Grids:**
  - Layout grids help maintain consistency in spacing and proportions across your design. You can define layout grids for frames to control the layout of their contents.
  - Customize layout grid settings such as grid type, column width, gutter width, and alignment options to create a structured layout for your designs.
- **Pixel Grid Alignment:**
  - Pixel grid alignment ensures that design elements align to whole pixel values, resulting in crisp and clean visuals, especially in raster-based designs.
  - Enable pixel grid alignment in canvas settings to snap objects to the pixel grid and ensure pixel-perfect alignment.
- **Zoom Level:**
  - Adjust the zoom level of the canvas to focus on specific areas of your design or get an overview of the entire canvas.
  - Use the zoom slider at the bottom-right corner of the interface or keyboard shortcuts (*Cmd/Ctrl + Plus/Minus*) to zoom in and out of the canvas.
- **Canvas Size and Orientation:**
  - Figma allows you to customize the size and orientation of the canvas to match your project requirements. You can choose from predefined canvas sizes or create custom canvas dimensions.
  - Select the desired canvas size and orientation (portrait or landscape) when creating a new file or adjust canvas size in document settings.
- **Frame Background:**
  - Frames can have customizable backgrounds, allowing you to add colors, gradients, or images as backgrounds for your designs.
  - Double-click a frame to open its properties panel, then adjust the background settings to add a fill color, gradient, or image background.
- **Frame Constraints:**
  - Constraints define how objects within frames behave when the frame is resized. You can set constraints on objects to control their positioning and scaling relative to the frame boundaries.
  - Experiment with different constraint settings, such as "**`Fill`**," "**`Fit`**," "**`Center`**," and "`Stretch`," to achieve the desired layout behavior for your designs.

Properties Panel

Understanding the context-sensitive options and settings available in the properties panel is essential for efficiently editing styles, dimensions, effects, and other properties of design elements in Figma.

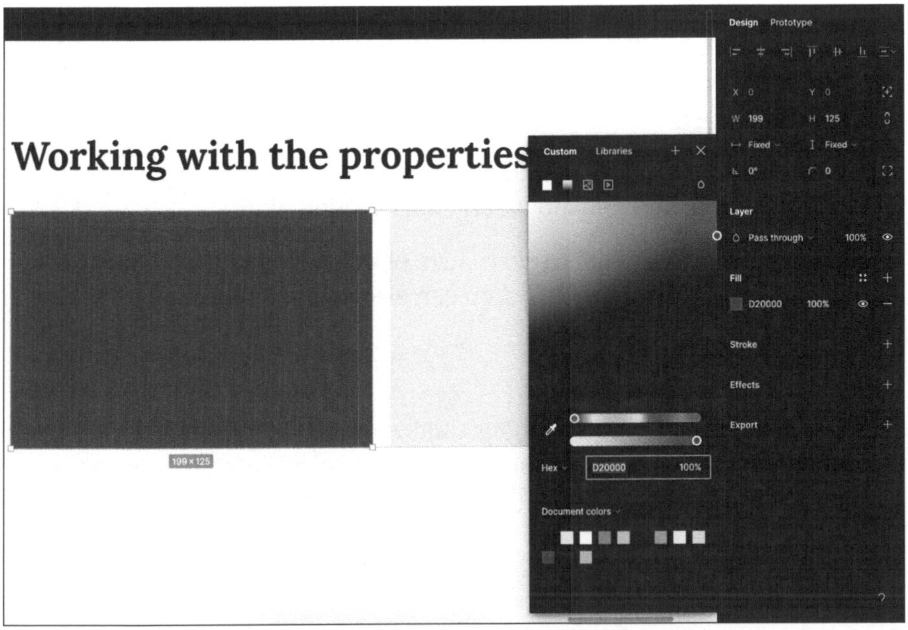

Figure 3.14: *Working with the properties panel*

Here is a comprehensive overview of the properties panel and techniques for using it to streamline your design process and workflow:

- **Context-Sensitive Options:**

  The properties panel in Figma displays context-sensitive options and settings based on the selected object or group of objects.

  Depending on the type of object selected (for example, shape, text, image), the properties panel will present relevant options for editing styles, dimensions, effects, and other properties.

- **Editing Styles:**

  The properties panel allows you to modify various styles of design elements, including fill color, stroke color, border width, corner radius, opacity, and blending modes.

  Use the color picker to select colors from swatches, input specific color values, or sample colors from the canvas. You can also apply gradients and patterns to fills and strokes.

- **Adjusting Dimensions:**

  You can adjust the dimensions of design elements directly in the properties panel by inputting numerical values for width, height, and position (X and Y coordinates).

  Use the "Lock aspect ratio" option to maintain the aspect ratio of objects while resizing. This ensures that objects scale proportionally without distorting their shapes.

- **Applying Effects:**

  Figma offers a variety of effects that you can apply to design elements, such as shadows, blurs, inner shadows, and background blurs.

  Use the properties panel to customize effect settings, including shadow color, blur radius, spread, and angle. You can also adjust opacity and blending modes for effects.

- **Other Properties:**

  In addition to styles, dimensions, and effects, the properties panel provides options for editing other properties of design elements, such as text properties (font, size, alignment, line height), vector paths (points, curves), and constraints.

  Explore the properties panel to discover additional options and settings specific to the type of object you are editing.

Tips for Streamlining Your Workflow:

- **Keyboard Shortcuts**: Learn keyboard shortcuts for accessing common properties and settings in the properties panel. This can significantly speed up your workflow and reduce the need for manual mouse clicks.
- **Panel Organization**: Customize the layout of the properties panel to prioritize the properties and settings you use most frequently. You can collapse sections, rearrange panels, and pin frequently used properties for quick access.
- **Quick Actions**: Take advantage of quick actions available in the properties panel, such as duplicating, grouping, aligning, and distributing objects. These actions allow you to perform common tasks without navigating through menus or using additional tools.
- **Undo and Redo**: Use the undo (*Cmd/Ctrl* + Z) and redo (*Cmd/Ctrl* + *Shift* + Z) shortcuts to revert changes or redo actions in the properties panel. This helps prevent accidental changes and allows you to experiment with different settings confidently.
- **Preview Changes**: Before finalizing changes in the properties panel, preview how they affect your design by keeping an eye on the canvas. Figma provides real-time updates, allowing you to see changes immediately as you make them.

Assets Panel

Learning how to access and manage design assets such as components, styles, and libraries is crucial for maintaining consistency and efficiency in your designs in Figma.

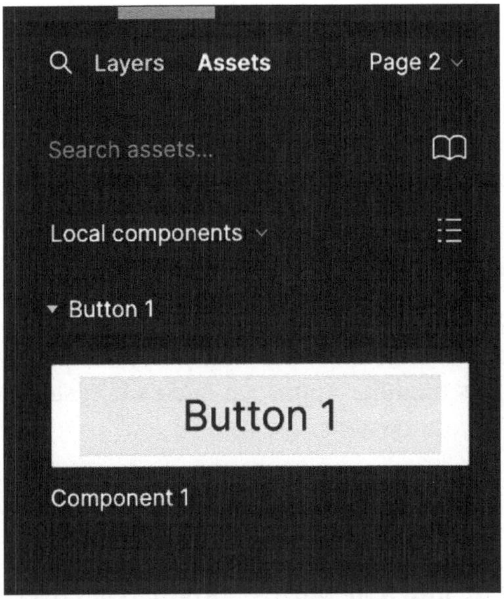

Figure 3.15: *Assets panel with access to the design file's library*

Here is a comprehensive guide to access and manage design assets, along with techniques for creating, organizing, and reusing assets across multiple projects:

Accessing Design Assets:

- The assets panel in Figma provides centralized access to design assets such as components, styles, and libraries.
- You can access the assets panel by clicking the "Assets" tab in the sidebar.

Managing Components:

- Components are reusable building blocks of your designs that can be shared and reused across multiple instances and projects.
- Use the assets panel to create, organize, and manage components. You can create new components, edit existing components, and organize components into libraries for easy access.

Managing Styles:

- Stylcs dcfinc the visual appearance of design elements such as colors, typography, and effects. By using styles, you can ensure consistency in your designs and streamline the editing process.

- Use the assets panel to manage styles by creating and organizing color styles, text styles, effect styles, and grid styles. You can also edit and update styles globally across your designs.

Managing Libraries:

- Libraries are collections of components, styles, and assets that can be shared across multiple projects and teams. Libraries help maintain consistency and streamline collaboration in large design projects.
- Use the assets panel to manage libraries by creating, importing, and updating library files. You can link libraries to your projects to access shared components and styles.

Techniques for Creating and Organizing Assets:

- **Create Atomic Components**: Break down design elements into smaller atomic components that can be reused and combined to create more complex components. This modular approach makes it easier to maintain consistency and flexibility in your designs.
- **Use Naming Conventions**: Establish consistent naming conventions for components, styles, and assets to ensure clarity and organization. Use descriptive names that reflect the purpose and function of each asset.
- **Organize Assets into Categories**: Group related components, styles, and assets into logical categories or folders within the assets panel. This makes it easier to navigate and find assets when working on projects.
- **Create Design Systems**: Develop comprehensive design systems that encompass all aspects of your design, including components, styles, guidelines, and best practices. Design systems serve as a central reference point for maintaining consistency and coherence in your designs.

Tips for Leveraging the Assets Panel:

- **Reuse Components**: Take advantage of reusable components and styles from the assets panel to save time and maintain consistency across your designs. Instead of recreating elements from scratch, reuse existing assets whenever possible.
- **Update Assets Globally:** Use the assets panel to update components and styles globally across your designs. When you make changes to a component or style in the assets panel, those changes will be reflected automatically in all instances throughout your designs.
- **Collaborate with Teams**: Share libraries and assets with team members to facilitate collaboration and ensure consistency. By using shared libraries, team members can access the same components and styles, promoting coherence in design workflows.

- **Version Control**: Keep track of changes to assets using version control features in Figma. Version history allows you to review and revert to previous versions of components, styles, and designs, ensuring accountability and traceability in your design process.

Prototype Tab

The prototype tab in Figma allows you to create interactive prototypes that simulate the behavior and functionality of your designs. You can define user interactions, such as clicking buttons, navigating between screens, and triggering animations, to showcase the user experience and flow of your designs.

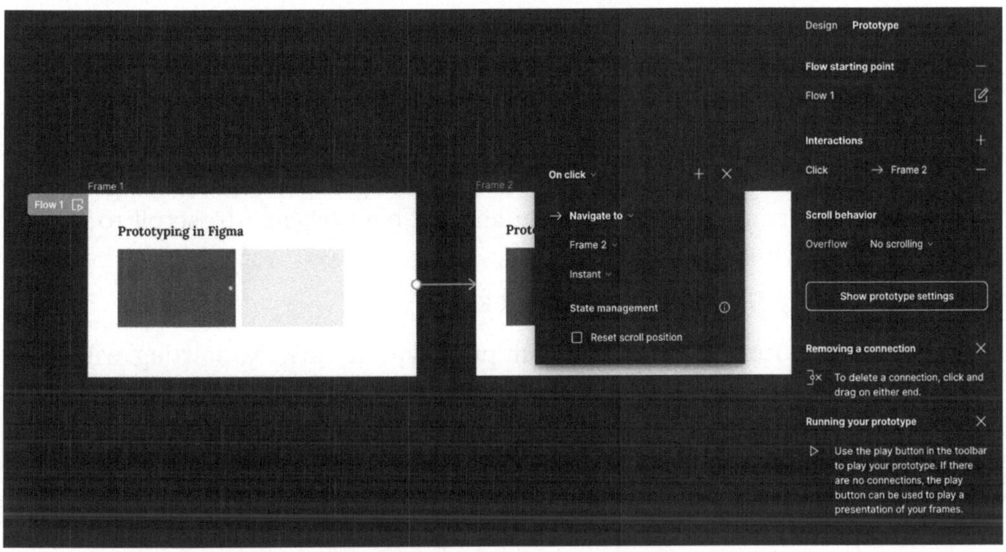

Figure 3.16: *Prototyping tab in Figma*

Here is a comprehensive guide to the prototype tab, along with techniques for creating interactive prototypes with links, transitions, and animations, as well as tips for simulating user interactions and flows to validate and iterate on your designs:

Creating interactive prototypes:

- **Adding Interaction Points**: Start by selecting the elements in your design that you want to make interactive, such as buttons, links, or navigation elements.
- **Defining Interactions**: With the elements selected, switch to the prototype tab and click the interaction points (blue handles) that appear on the selected elements. Drag the handle to the destination frame/screen to create a link.
- **Setting Triggers**: Choose the trigger for the interaction, such as "`On Click`," "`On Hover`," or "`On Drag`," and define the action, such as navigating to another frame, opening an overlay, or scrolling to a specific position.

- **Customizing Transitions**: Customize the transition between frames/screens by choosing from various transition options, such as "`Instant`," "`Dissolve`," "`Slide`," or "`Push`," and adjust the duration and easing curve to control the animation.

Techniques for Interactive Prototypes:

- **Creating Navigation Flows**: Define the navigation flow of your prototype by linking screens together to simulate user interactions and transitions between different states and screens.
- **Adding Animations**: Incorporate animations to enhance the user experience and communicate feedback. Use the "Smart Animate" feature to automatically animate changes between frames based on shared elements.
- **Simulating User Inputs**: Use interactive elements such as input fields, dropdowns, and checkboxes to simulate user inputs and interactions. Define triggers and actions to simulate the response to user inputs.
- **Creating Scrolling Effects**: Simulate scrolling behavior by linking frames/screens vertically or horizontally and defining triggers to scroll to specific positions within a frame/screen.

Tips for Simulating User Interactions and Flows:

- **Prototype Iteratively**: Build your prototype iteratively, starting with basic interactions and gradually adding complexity. Test and refine the prototype as you go to ensure that it accurately reflects the intended user experience.
- **Gather Feedback**: Share your prototype with stakeholders, clients, or users to gather feedback and validate design decisions. Use comments and annotations to capture feedback directly within the prototype.
- **Test Across Devices**: Test your prototype across different devices and screen sizes to ensure responsiveness and compatibility. Use Figma's preview mode to test the prototype on desktop, tablet, and mobile devices.
- **Iterate Based on Feedback**: Use feedback from testing sessions to iterate on your designs and refine the prototype. Make adjustments to interactions, transitions, and animations to improve usability and clarity.

Comments and Collaboration

Learning how to share your designs with team members and stakeholders is crucial for gathering feedback, resolving comments, and collaborating effectively in Figma.

***Figure 3.17:** Commenting tab in Figma*

Here is a comprehensive guide to sharing designs, exploring techniques for gathering feedback, resolving comments, and collaborating in real-time, along with tips for using comments, annotations, and version history to streamline the collaborative design process:

Sharing Your Designs:

- **Share Links**: Use Figma's sharing features to generate shareable links for your designs. You can control access permissions, such as view-only, comment, or edit, to ensure that only authorized users can access and interact with your designs.
- **Invite Collaborators**: Invite team members and stakeholders to collaborate on your designs by sending them invitation links via email or Figma's built-in invitation feature. Collaborators can access the shared files and contribute to the design process in real-time.

Gathering Feedback:

- **Commenting**: Encourage collaborators to leave comments directly on your designs to provide feedback, suggestions, or questions. Comments can be added to specific elements or areas of the design, making it easy to pinpoint issues or discuss specific aspects.
- **Annotations**: Use Figma's annotation tools to add contextual notes,

explanations, or instructions directly on the canvas. Annotations help communicate design decisions and provide additional context to collaborators reviewing the designs.

Resolving Comments and Collaborating in Real-Time:

- **Real-Time Collaboration**: Collaborate with team members and stakeholders in real-time by working on the same design files simultaneously. Changes made by one user are instantly visible to others, allowing for seamless collaboration and coordination.
- **Resolving Comments**: Address comments and feedback by responding directly within the comment thread. Use the "@" mention feature to notify specific collaborators or assign tasks. Once the comment is addressed, mark it as resolved to keep track of progress.

Tips for Streamlining Collaboration:

- **Version History**: Take advantage of Figma's version history feature to track changes and revisions made to your designs over time. Access previous versions of the file to revert changes, compare iterations, or restore deleted elements if needed.
- **Naming Conventions**: Establish clear naming conventions for files, frames, and layers to maintain organization and clarity. Consistent naming makes it easier for collaborators to understand the structure and purpose of each element in the design.
- **Use Templates**: Create design templates or starter files for common projects or design tasks. Templates help maintain consistency and save time by providing a starting point with predefined styles, components, and layouts.
- **Feedback Sessions**: Schedule regular feedback sessions with team members and stakeholders to review designs, discuss progress, and address any questions or concerns. Use screen sharing or presentation mode to walk through designs and gather feedback in real time.

Hands-On Practice

In the practice material that follows, we will cover some hands-on exercises to help you gain practical experience and confidence in navigating and mastering the Figma interface. We implore you to actively engage with the tools and features discussed in this chapter. This will empower you to tackle real-world design projects and collaborate effectively with team members and stakeholders.

Exercise 1: Toolbar Mastery

Objective: Familiarize yourself with the tools and commands available in the Figma toolbar.

Steps:

1. Select the Rectangle tool from the toolbar and draw a rectangle on the canvas.
2. Use the Pen tool to create a custom shape.
3. Experiment with the Text tool to add text to your design.
4. Explore the Vector tool and create a simple vector shape.
5. Try out other tools such as the Line tool, Ellipse tool, and Polygon tool.
6. Use keyboard shortcuts to access tools quickly. For example, press “V” for the Selection tool, “R” for the Rectangle tool, and “T” for the Text tool.
7. Customize the toolbar by right-clicking it and selecting "`Customize Toolbar`." Add your most frequently used tools for easy access.

Exercise 2: Canvas Navigation

Objective: Learn how to navigate and manipulate the canvas in Figma.

Steps:

1. Zoom in and out of the canvas using the zoom controls or keyboard shortcuts (*Cmd/Ctrl + Plus/Minus*).
2. Pan around the canvas by clicking and dragging with the mouse or using the Hand tool.
3. Experiment with the Frame tool to create different-sized frames on the canvas.
4. Arrange frames on the canvas by dragging and dropping them into position.
5. Create a new page by clicking the “+” icon next to the page tabs at the bottom of the canvas.
6. Use the Layout Grid tool to add a grid to your canvas and align objects more precisely.
7. Explore canvas settings by clicking the canvas name at the top-left corner. Adjust settings such as canvas color, grid visibility, and pixel grid alignment.

Exercise 3: Layers Panel Mastery

Objective: Create a design with contrasting colors to emphasize key elements.

Steps:

1. Create multiple shapes and text objects on the canvas.
2. Use the layers panel to select and rearrange objects. Drag objects up or down in the layer hierarchy to change their stacking order.
3. Rename layers by double-clicking their names in the layers panel.
4. Experiment with layer organization by grouping objects together. Select multiple objects, right-click, and choose "`Group Selection`" or press *Cmd/Ctrl* + G.
5. Explore layer properties such as opacity and blending modes. Adjust these properties for selected layers in the properties panel.
6. Hide and show layers by clicking the eye icon next to their names in the layers panel.
7. Lock layers to prevent accidental changes. Click the lock icon next to layer names to lock or unlock them.

Exercise 4: Properties Panel Exploration

Objective: Understand how to use the properties panel to modify object properties.

Steps:

1. Select a shape or text object on the canvas.
2. Use the properties panel to modify properties such as fill color, stroke color, border radius, and opacity.
3. Experiment with text properties such as font size, font weight, alignment, and line spacing.
4. Explore effects such as drop shadows, inner shadows, blurs, and background blurs. Apply these effects to selected objects and adjust their properties in the properties panel.
5. Use the "`Convert to`" option in the properties panel to convert shapes to paths or frames to components.
6. Learn how to apply and manage styles in the properties panel. Create new styles, apply existing styles, and edit style properties.
7. Utilize the "`Constraints`" section in the properties panel to control how objects behave when resized or moved within frames.

Exercise 5: Prototype Tab Practice

Objective: Explore the prototype tab and learn how to create interactive prototypes.

Steps:

1. Create a new frame on the canvas and design a simple user interface with multiple interactive elements such as buttons, links, and input fields.
2. Switch to the prototype tab at the top of the interface.
3. Select an object (for example, a button) and drag a connection handle to another frame to create a link. Choose a trigger (for example, "`On Click`") and select the destination frame.
4. Experiment with different transition types such as "`Instant`," "`Smart Animate`," and "`Dissolve`." Preview the prototype to see how transitions behave.
5. Add interactions to other objects on the canvas, such as hover effects or drag interactions.
6. Explore advanced prototyping features such as overlays, fixed elements, and scrollable frames.
7. Share your prototype with others by generating a shareable link or inviting collaborators directly within Figma.

Exercise 6: Comments and Collaboration

Objective: Practice collaborating with team members and gathering feedback on your designs in Figma.

Steps:

1. Share your design with a team member or collaborator by clicking the "`Share`" button in the top-right corner.
2. Add comments to specific elements of your design by selecting them and clicking the comment icon that appears.
3. Resolve comments by addressing feedback or making changes to your design.
4. Use the version history panel to review previous iterations of your design and revert to earlier versions if needed.
5. Collaborate in real time by inviting team members to edit the design together. See their changes instantly and work together to refine the design.
6. Explore additional collaboration features such as Slack notifications, design handoff, and developer handoff.

7. Iterate on your design based on feedback received from collaborators and continue refining and improving your work.

Conclusion

In this chapter, we have embarked on a comprehensive exploration of the Figma interface, gaining a deep understanding of its various components, tools, and features. By mastering the interface, you will be better equipped to unleash your creativity, streamline your workflow, and collaborate effectively with team members and stakeholders. In the next chapter, we will delve into advanced design techniques and strategies for creating stunning visuals and prototypes in Figma, further expanding your design repertoire, and elevating your skills as a designer.

Transition to the next Chapter

As we conclude our journey through *Chapter 3, Mastering the Figma Interface,* you have gained a comprehensive understanding of the Figma interface and its various components, tools, and features. Armed with this knowledge, you are now ready to dive deeper into advanced design techniques and strategies in *Chapter 4, Designing UI in Figma.* In the next chapter, we will explore how to unleash your creativity and elevate your designs to new heights using Figma's powerful tools and capabilities. From advanced prototyping techniques to sophisticated design strategies, we will equip you with the skills and insights needed to create stunning visuals and prototypes that captivate and engage your audience. Join us as we continue our exploration of Figma and embark on the next phase of our design journey.

Recap of Key Points

- **Introduction to the Figma Interface**: We explored the essential components of the Figma interface, including the toolbar, canvas, layers panel, properties panel, assets panel, prototype tab, and collaboration features.
- **Toolbar Mastery**: Understanding the various tools and commands available in the toolbar, and how to use them for creating, editing, and navigating designs efficiently.
- **Canvas Navigation**: Learning essential techniques for navigating and manipulating the canvas, such as zooming, panning, arranging frames, creating new pages, and using layout grids.
- **Layers Panel Mastery**: Exploring the layers panel to manage and manipulate layers effectively, including renaming layers, grouping objects, adjusting properties, and organizing the layer hierarchy.

- **Properties Panel Exploration**: Understanding how to modify object properties using the properties panel, including fill color, stroke color, opacity, text properties, effects, styles, and constraints.
- **Prototype Tab Practice**: Experimenting with the prototype tab to create interactive prototypes, adding links, transitions, interactions, overlays, fixed elements, and scrollable frames.
- **Comments and Collaboration**: Practicing collaboration features such as comments, version history, real-time collaboration, Slack notifications, design handoff, and developer handoff to streamline the collaborative design process.

CHAPTER 4
Designing UI in Figma

Introduction

This chapter delves deep into the process of crafting UI elements and providing the readers with comprehensive insights into the foundational aspects of UI design. Beginning with an overview of UI elements and their significance in digital experiences, the chapter explores the fundamental principles that govern UI design, including hierarchy, consistency, and feedback. Readers will learn how to plan and sketch UI elements effectively based on user needs and project requirements.

The chapter then deals with the specifics of designing various UI elements, such as buttons, interactive components, navigation bars, form fields, and information display components. Through detailed discussions and practical examples, readers will gain a thorough understanding of the principles and best practices underlying each element of UI design, along with actionable tips for implementation.

Furthermore, the chapter covers the role of icons and illustrations in UI design, highlighting their importance in enhancing visual communication and user engagement. Readers will learn strategies for selecting and designing icons that align with the overall visual language and brand identity, as well as best practices for integrating illustrations to provide context and personality to UI designs.

Finally, the chapter addresses the prototyping and iteration process for UI elements, emphasizing the importance of user testing and feedback in refining designs for optimal usability and effectiveness. By the end of the chapter, readers will be equipped with the knowledge, skills, and resources needed to craft compelling and user-friendly UI elements that elevate the overall user experience.

Structure

In this chapter, we will cover the following topics:

- Introduction to UI Elements
- Understanding UI Design Principles
- Planning and sketching UI Elements

- Designing Buttons and Interactive Elements
- Crafting Navigation Components
- Creating Form Elements and Input Fields
- Designing Information Display Components
- Incorporating Icons and Illustrations
- Prototyping and Iterating UI Elements
- Future of UI design

Introduction to UI Elements Design

UI elements are the foundational components of digital interfaces, serving as the bridge between users and technology. From the moment users interact with an application or website, they encounter UI elements that facilitate navigation, input, and interaction. In this section, we will explore the definition, significance, and common types of UI elements, as well as the importance of consistency, usability, and accessibility in their design.

Definition of UI Elements and Their Significance

UI elements encompass a wide range of interactive components and visual cues that enable users to navigate, interact with, and manipulate digital interfaces. They include buttons, forms, navigation bars, icons, sliders, and various other elements that facilitate user interactions and convey information.

UI elements play a pivotal role in shaping the user experience, influencing how users perceive, interact with, and navigate through digital interfaces. The significance of UI elements in UI design cannot be overstated. They serve as the building blocks of user interfaces, providing users with the means to perform tasks, access information, and accomplish goals within digital environments. Effective UI element design enhances usability, fosters engagement, and promotes user satisfaction, ultimately contributing to the success of digital products and services.

To start working on your wireframes in Figma, create a new Figma file. Use the Frame tool to create a canvas for your wireframe. Choose a suitable size, such as a mobile or desktop screen size. Employ shapes like rectangles, ovals, and lines to represent UI elements. Rectangles can be used for buttons, input fields, and content blocks. Ovals can represent icons or images. Lines can be used for dividers or arrows. Use the Text tool to add labels, headings, and other text elements. Arrange the shapes and text elements to create a basic layout of your design. Focus on the overall structure and information hierarchy.

Overview of Common UI Elements

Let us discuss some common elements of UI:

1. **Buttons**: Buttons are interactive elements that prompt users to perform actions or navigate to different parts of an interface. They come in various shapes, sizes, and styles, including primary, secondary, and tertiary buttons, and often feature labels or icons that indicate their function.

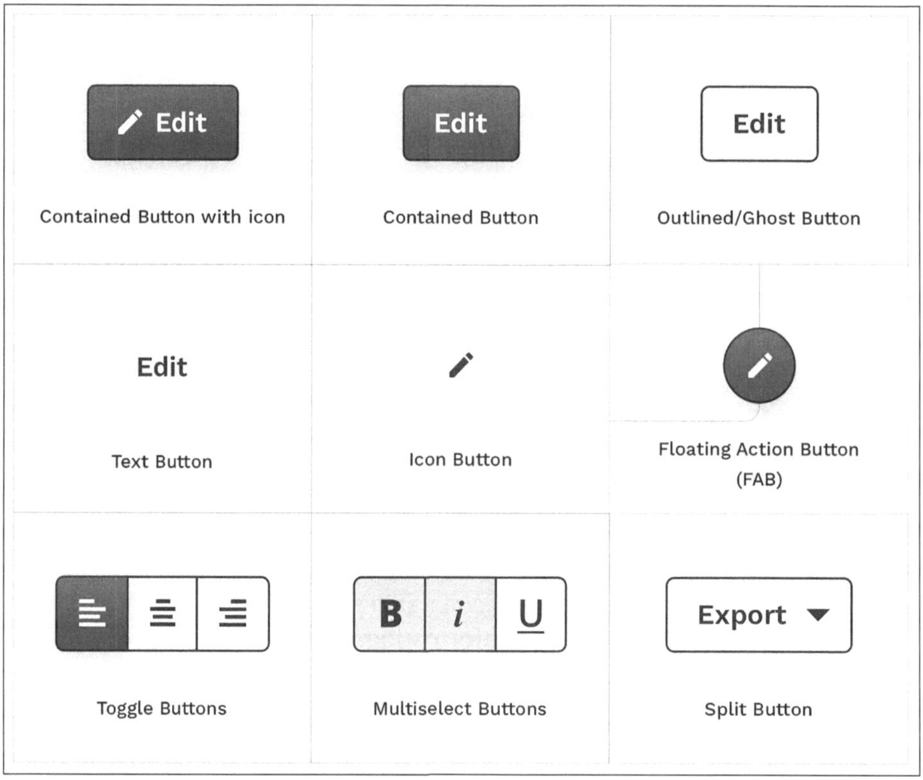

***Figure 4.1**: Different styles of a button*

2. **Forms**: Forms are used to collect user input, such as text, numbers, selections, and uploads. They typically consist of input fields, checkboxes, radio buttons, dropdown menus, and submit buttons, arranged in a structured layout to facilitate data entry and submission.

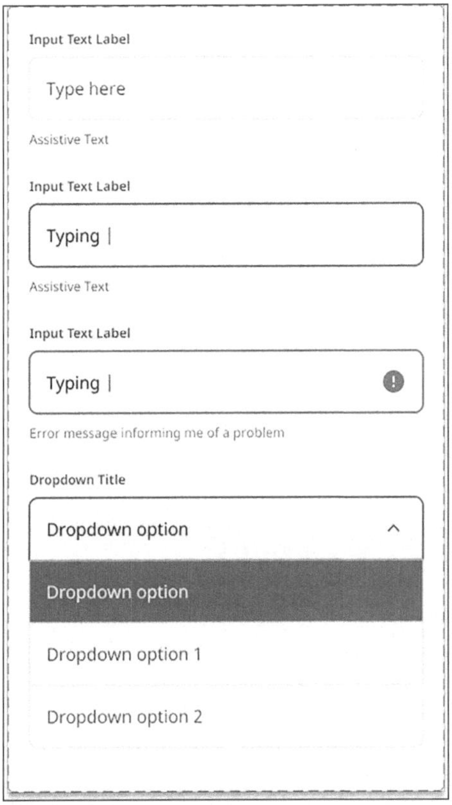

***Figure 4.2**: Styling in a form*

3. **Navigation Bars**: Navigation bars provide users with means to navigate between different sections or pages of a website or application. They often include links or icons representing various destinations, such as home, about, products, and contact, thereby allowing users to quickly access relevant content.

***Figure 4.3**: Responsive navigation bars*

4. **Cards**: Cards are versatile UI elements used to organize and present content in a visually appealing and digestible format. They contain information, images,

and interactive elements, such as buttons or links, and are commonly used in interfaces with a modular or grid-based layout.

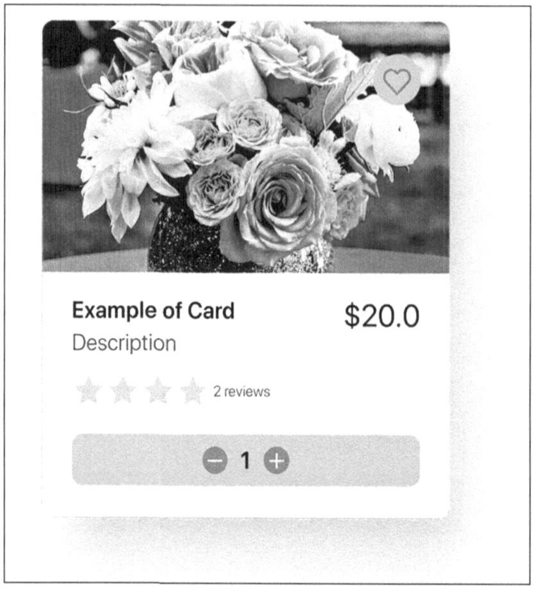

Figure 4.4*: Example of a card*

Understanding UI Design Principles

In this exploration of UI design principles, we will delve into key concepts such as hierarchy, consistency, clarity, and feedback, examining how they shape the design of UI elements. Additionally, we will discuss the principles of affordance and signifiers and their influence on UI element design. Throughout the discussion, we will draw upon case studies to illustrate exemplary UI designs that embody these principles effectively.

Exploration of Key Design Principles:

- **Hierarchy:** Refers to the visual organization of elements within a UI, emphasizing their relative importance and guiding users' attention. A well-defined hierarchy helps users navigate interfaces effortlessly by prioritizing essential content and actions. For instance, headings, colors, sizes, and spatial relationships can be used to establish hierarchy, with primary actions and critical information given prominence.
- **Consistency**: Ensures that UI elements behave predictably and maintain a uniform appearance throughout the interface. Consistent design patterns and conventions enhance usability by reducing cognitive load and allowing users to anticipate how elements will behave. Consistency encompasses visual consistency (for example, typography, color schemes), functional consistency

(for example, navigation patterns), and behavioral consistency (for example, interaction patterns).

- **Clarity:** Entails the clear communication of information and functionality to users, ensuring that interfaces are easy to understand and navigate. UI elements should be self-explanatory and unambiguous, providing clear affordances and signifiers that convey their purpose and function. Clear labeling, descriptive feedback, and intuitive interactions contribute to clarity in UI design.
- **Feedback:** Plays a vital role in user interaction, providing users with information about the outcome of their actions and guiding them through the interface. Effective feedback acknowledges user input promptly, confirming actions, providing status updates, and offering error messages or corrective guidance when necessary. Feedback fosters a sense of control and confidence in users, enhancing their overall experience.
- **Usability**: Focuses on the effectiveness, efficiency, and satisfaction with which users can accomplish tasks within a digital interface. Well-designed UI elements are intuitive, easy to understand, and responsive to user input, facilitating seamless interaction and task completion. To measure the usability of Figma designs, a combination of qualitative and quantitative methods can be employed. User testing, both remote and in-person, allows for direct observation and feedback. Heuristic evaluation involves assessing designs against established usability principles. Analytics tools track user behavior, identifying areas of difficulty. A/B testing enables comparison of different design variations to optimize user experience. By considering metrics like task completion rate, time on task, error rate, user satisfaction, and perceived ease of use, designers can gain valuable insights and make data-driven improvements to their designs.
- **Accessibility**: Ensures that digital interfaces are usable and inclusive for all users, including those with disabilities or impairments. Designers often adhere to accessibility standards like WCAG (Web Content Accessibility Guidelines). These guidelines provide specific criteria for making content accessible, including principles such as perceivable, operable, understandable, and robust design. Web Content Accessibility Guidelines (WCAG) define three levels of compliance: A, AA, and AAA. These levels are designed to address various accessibility needs and situations.
    - Level A: Baseline Accessibility: Level A represents the minimum standard for web accessibility. It focuses on eliminating major barriers that could render a website unusable for people with disabilities. Key requirements include:
        - Keyboard navigation without traps
        - Alternatives for non-text content
        - Captions for video content

        - Avoiding reliance on color, shape, or size alone to convey meaning
        - Failing to meet Level A standards can make a website extremely challenging for users with disabilities.
    - Level AA: Enhanced Accessibility: Level AA is the target standard for most organizations. It encompasses all Level A criteria plus additional requirements. Websites meeting Level AA are generally accessible to most users, regardless of ability. Essential Level AA requirements include:
        - Sufficient color contrast (typically 4.5:1 ratio)
        - Consistent navigation throughout the site
        - Proper labeling of form fields
        - Screen reader compatibility for status updates
        - Logical heading structure
    - Level AAA: Optimal Accessibility: Level AAA represents the highest standard of web accessibility. It includes all Level A and AA criteria, plus further enhancements. Key Level AAA requirements include:
        - Sign language interpretation for audio/video content
        - Higher color contrast (7:1 ratio in most cases)
        - Eliminating time constraints on activities
        - Providing context-sensitive help

While Level AAA offers the best user experience, it may be challenging to implement across an entire website. Organizations often focus on achieving Level AAA for specific content based on their audience's needs. UI elements should be designed with accessibility in mind, incorporating features such as proper contrast, keyboard navigation, and screen reader compatibility to accommodate diverse user needs. Figma offers several accessibility plugins to help designers create inclusive digital experiences such as, Stark, A11y, Alee Comprehensive Accessibility Tool, and Axe. These plugins offer features such as color contrast checking, focus order visualization, color blindness simulation, and more. By utilizing these tools, designers can identify and address accessibility issues early in the design process, ensuring that their designs are accessible to users with disabilities.

Important Concept on Affordance and Signifiers

Affordance refers to the perceived actions or functionalities that an object or element offers to users based on its appearance or design. In UI design, affordances indicate how users can interact with elements and what actions are possible. For example, a button with a raised appearance affords clicking, while a slider affords dragging.

Designing clear and intuitive affordances helps users understand how to interact with UI elements effectively.

Signifiers are cues or indicators that convey information about the functionality or purpose of UI elements. They provide visual or auditory clues that guide user interactions and help them interpret the meaning of elements. Signifiers can take various forms, such as icons, labels, tooltips, hover effects, and animations. Thoughtfully incorporating signifiers into UI designs enhances usability and aids in comprehension.

Figure 4.5: *Example of affordance [door handle] and signifier [push and pull sign]*

Case Studies that Embody Design Principles

We will explore two exemplary UI designs–Google Material Design and Apple's Human Interface Guidelines (HIG)–and examine how they embody key design principles to deliver exceptional user experiences.

Google Material Design

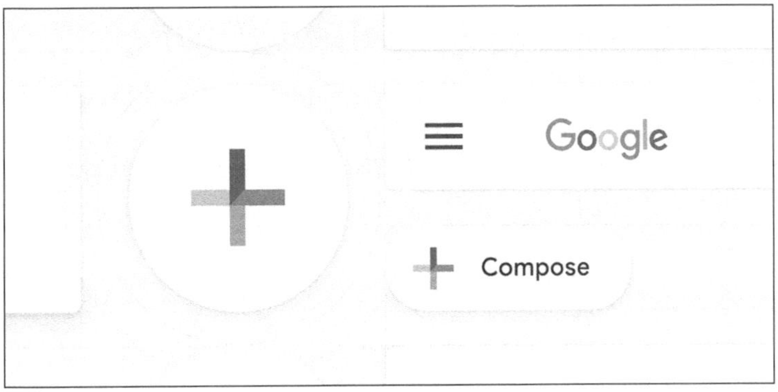

Figure 4.6: *Google's material design. Source: https://material.io/blog/google-material-custom-theme*

Google Material Design is a design language developed by Google in 2014, with the goal of creating a unified visual language for all of Google products and services across platforms and devices. Material Design is characterized by its use of bold colors, responsive animations, and tactile surfaces, creating intuitive interfaces.

Adherence to Design Principles:

- **Hierarchy:** Material Design employs a clear hierarchy of elements, with bold typography, vibrant colors, and spatial relationships guiding user attention. Elevated surfaces and drop shadows create depth and dimensionality, distinguishing primary elements from secondary ones.
- **Consistency:** Material Design maintains consistency across the Google ecosystem, with standardized design patterns, components, and behaviors that users can rely on. Consistent use of colors, typography, and iconography ensures a cohesive and familiar user experience across different applications and platforms.
- **Clarity:** Material Design prioritizes clarity in UI elements, ensuring that they are easily recognizable and understandable. Clear typography, descriptive labels, and intuitive interactions provide users with the information they need to navigate interfaces effectively.
- **Feedback**: Material Design provides immediate and responsive feedback to user actions, confirming interactions with animations, transitions, and visual cues. Feedback is used to indicate the outcome of actions, guide users through processes, and provide status updates, enhancing the overall user experience.

Impact and Success:

Google Material Design has had a significant impact on the design community, influencing countless designers and developers to adopt its principles and guidelines. By providing a comprehensive design language and toolkit, Material Design has enabled designers to create visually appealing and consistent interfaces for users.

Apple's Human Interface Guidelines (HIG)

Human Interface Guidelines (HIG) is a set of design principles and best practices developed by Apple for designing software interfaces across its various platforms, including iOS, macOS, watchOS, and tvOS. The HIG emphasizes simplicity, clarity, and consistency, reflecting Apple's commitment to delivering intuitive and delightful user experiences.

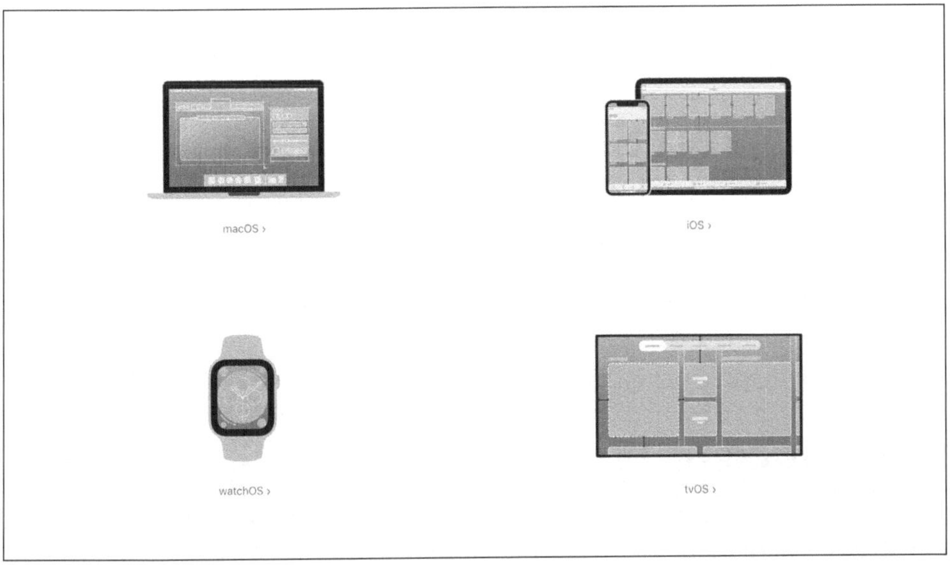

***Figure 4.7:** Apple's human interface guidelines. Source: https://developer.apple.com/design/human-interface-guidelines/*

Adherence to Design Principles:

- **Hierarchy**: The HIG establishes a clear hierarchy of elements, with distinct visual styles and layouts that prioritize essential content and actions. Consistent use of typography, spacing, and alignment helps users navigate interfaces effortlessly and focus on key tasks.
- **Consistency**: Apple's HIG promotes consistency in UI design, with standardized design patterns, interactions, and gestures that users are familiar with. Consistency across Apple's ecosystem ensures that users can seamlessly transition between different devices and platforms without encountering unfamiliar interfaces.
- **Clarity**: The HIG prioritizes clarity in UI design, ensuring that interfaces are easy to understand and navigate. Clear labeling, descriptive icons, and intuitive gestures provide users with the guidance they need to interact with applications effectively.
- **Feedback**: Apple's HIG emphasizes the importance of providing responsive feedback to user actions, confirming interactions with animations, transitions, and sound effects. Feedback is used to reinforce user actions, provide status updates, and guide users through interfaces, enhancing the overall user experience.

Impact and Success:

Apple's HIG has been instrumental in shaping the design landscape, influencing not only Apple's own products but also the broader design community. By promoting simplicity, consistency, and clarity in UI design, the HIG has empowered designers to create intuitive and user-friendly interfaces that resonate with users.

Planning and Sketching UI Elements

In the realm of UI design, the process of planning and sketching UI elements serves as a crucial foundation for creating interfaces that are intuitive, visually appealing, and effective in meeting user needs. In this comprehensive section, we will delve into the importance of wireframing and sketching as initial stages in UI design, explore techniques for planning and sketching UI elements effectively, and provide tips for iterating and refining UI sketches to achieve desired outcomes.

Importance of Wireframing and Sketching

Wireframing and sketching are essential steps in the UI design process, serving as the initial stages where ideas are conceptualized, explored, and refined before moving into more detailed design and development phases. These stages allow designers to visualize layout, structure, and functionality, and to iterate on design concepts in a quick and cost-effective manner.

- **Conceptualization:** Wireframing and sketching enable designers to explore different design concepts and solutions, brainstorming ideas and visualizing potential UI layouts and structures. By sketching out rough wireframes and concepts, designers can quickly iterate on ideas and experiment with different approaches.
- **Communication:** Wireframes and sketches serve as communication tools, allowing designers to convey their ideas and concepts to stakeholders, clients, and team members. These visual representations help stakeholders understand the proposed UI design and provide feedback early in the design process, reducing the risk of misunderstandings or misinterpretations later on.
- **Validation:** Wireframing and sketching enable designers to validate design concepts and ideas before investing time and resources in detailed design and development. By testing and refining concepts early in the process, designers can identify potential usability issues and make informed design decisions.
- **Efficiency:** Wireframing and sketching are efficient ways to explore and iterate on design concepts in quick and cost-effective ways. Unlike detailed design and development phases, which require significant time and resources, wireframing and sketching allow designers to iterate on ideas rapidly, making adjustments and refinements as needed.

Techniques for Planning and Sketching UI Elements

Effective wireframing and sketching require careful consideration of user needs, project requirements, and design objectives. Here are some techniques to help you plan and sketch UI elements effectively:

- **Define User Needs:** Start by understanding the needs, goals, and preferences of your target users. Conduct user research, gather feedback, and create user personas to gain insights into user behaviors, preferences, and pain points.
- **Establish Design Objectives:** Define clear design objectives and goals for your UI project. Determine what you want to achieve with your design, whether it is improving usability, increasing engagement, or driving conversions.
- **Storyboarding:** Use storyboarding techniques to visualize user interactions and workflows. Create sequential sketches or storyboards to illustrate how users will navigate through the interface and accomplish tasks.
- **Iterative Sketching:** Adopt an iterative approach to sketching, starting with rough, low-fidelity sketches and gradually refining them over time. Experiment with different layout, structure, and functionality options, exploring multiple design concepts and variations.
- **Grids and Templates:** Use grids and templates to maintain consistency and alignment. Grids help you organize content and establish visual hierarchy, while templates provide a framework for common UI elements and layouts.
- **Annotation and Documentation:** Annotate your sketches with notes, labels, and annotations to provide context and clarity. Document design decisions, rationale, and considerations to ensure alignment with project requirements and objectives.
- **Collaboration and Feedback:** Involve stakeholders, clients, and team members in the wireframing and sketching process. Solicit feedback early and often, incorporating suggestions and insights into your design iterations.

Tips for Iterating and Refining UI Sketches

Iterating and refining UI sketches is a process that involves gathering feedback, making adjustments, and refining designs based on user needs and project requirements. Here are some tips for iterating and refining UI sketches effectively:

- **User Testing:** Conduct user testing sessions to gather feedback on your sketches from real users. Observe how users interact with your designs, identify pain points and usability issues, and use this feedback to refine your sketches.

- **Usability Heuristics:** Evaluate your sketches against established usability heuristics and design principles. Identify areas where your sketches may deviate from best practices and make adjustments to improve usability and user experience.
- **Prototype and Test:** Create interactive prototypes based on sketches and conduct usability testing sessions. Use prototyping tools to simulate user interactions and workflows, gather feedback on usability, and identify areas for improvement.
- **Iterative Design:** Embrace an iterative design approach, making incremental improvements to sketches based on user feedback and testing results. Iterate on your designs, refining and polishing them until they meet user needs and project objectives.
- **Feedback Loops:** Establish feedback loops with stakeholders, clients, and team members to gather ongoing feedback on your sketches. Schedule regular review sessions to share your progress, solicit feedback, and make adjustments based on input received.
- **Document Design Decisions:** Document design decisions, rationale, and considerations as you iterate. Maintain a record of changes and revisions, noting the reasons behind each decision to ensure alignment with project requirements.
- **Stay Flexible:** Remain open to feedback and be willing to make changes to your sketches based on user input and testing results. Stay flexible and adaptable throughout the design process, prioritizing user needs and usability above personal preferences or assumptions.

Crafting Navigation Components

Navigation components are the backbone of any UI, guiding users through digital experiences and helping them find the information they need efficiently. In this comprehensive section, we will delve into the examination of navigation bars, menus, tabs, and breadcrumbs in UI design. We will explore strategies for designing intuitive and user-friendly navigation systems and discuss considerations for responsive design and mobile navigation patterns.

Examination of Navigation Components

The following figure illustrates the examples of navigation components:

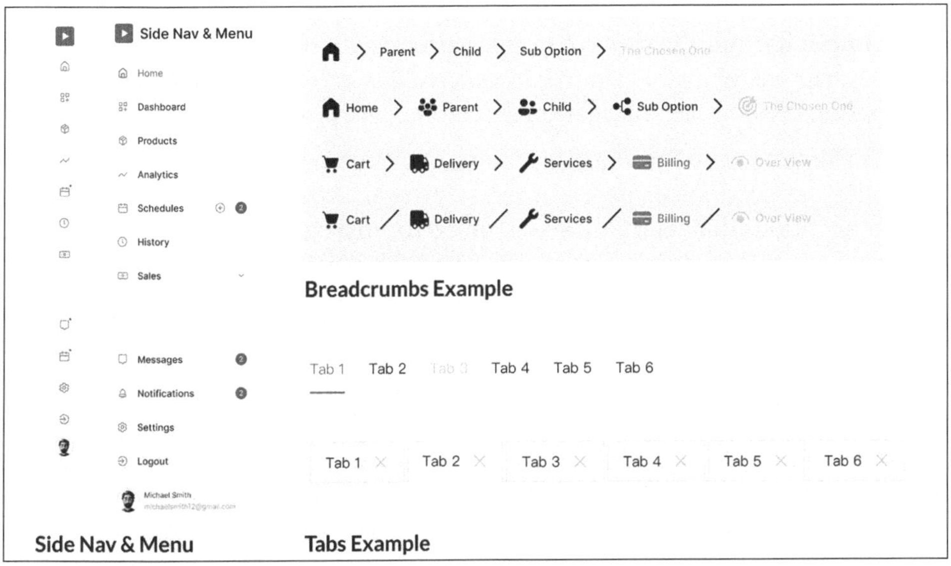

Figure 4.8: *Examples of navigation components*

- **Navigation bars**, also known as navbars or menus, are horizontal bars typically located at the top of a web page or application interface. They contain links or icons that allow users to navigate to different sections or pages of the interface. Navigation bars often include primary navigation options, such as home, about, products, and contact, providing users with quick access to essential content.
- **Menus** are hierarchical lists of options or commands that allow users to access additional functionality. They can be displayed as dropdown menus, flyout menus, or context menus, depending on the context and user interaction. Menus help organize and categorize content, making it easier for users to locate specific items or features within an interface.
- **Tabs** are visual indicators used to organize content into separate sections or categories. They are typically displayed as horizontal or vertical tabs, with each tab representing a distinct section of the interface. Tabs allow users to switch between different views or modes of content presentation, such as different pages, categories, or filters.
- **Breadcrumbs** are navigational aids that show users their current location within a website or application hierarchy. They display the path or trail of pages leading to the current page, allowing users to navigate backward or upward through the site structure. Breadcrumbs provide context and orientation, helping users understand their position within the overall navigation scheme.

Designing Intuitive Navigation Systems

Following are some key strategies to keep in mind when starting to design navigation systems to help you make them intuitive from the get-go:

- **Simplicity and Clarity:** Keep navigation systems simple, using clear labels, descriptive text, and intuitive icons. Avoid overwhelming users with too many options or complex navigation structures and prioritize clarity and usability.
- **Consistency and Familiarity:** Maintain consistency in navigation design across different sections or pages of the interface. Use familiar design patterns and conventions that users are accustomed to, ensuring a cohesive and predictable navigation experience.
- **Hierarchy and Organization:** Organize navigation elements hierarchically, grouping related items together and arranging them in a logical order. Use visual cues such as indentation, spacing, and typography to indicate hierarchy and relationships between navigation options.
- **Accessibility and Usability:** Design navigation systems with accessibility and usability in mind, ensuring that they are accessible to users of all abilities and devices. Use accessible design techniques such as proper contrast, keyboard navigation, and screen reader compatibility to accommodate diverse user needs.
- **Visual Feedback and Affordance:** Provide visual feedback and affordances to indicate interactive elements and states within the navigation system. Use hover effects, animations, and color changes to highlight active or selected items, giving users visual cues about their current navigation status.

Responsive Design for Mobile Navigation

Following are key considerations to keep in mind to create a user-friendly design for mobile navigation:

- **Adaptive Layouts:** Design navigation systems that adapt to different screen sizes and resolutions, ensuring a consistent and usable experience across devices. Use responsive design techniques such as fluid grids, flexible images, and media queries to create adaptive layouts that adjust to the user's device.
- **Mobile-Friendly Navigation:** Optimize navigation systems for mobile devices, where screen real estate is limited. Consider using mobile-specific navigation patterns such as hamburger menus, tab bars, or bottom navigation bars to maximize usability and efficiency on small screens.
- **Touch-Friendly Interactions:** Design navigation elements with touch-friendly interactions in mind, ensuring that they are easy to tap, swipe, or pinch on touchscreen devices. Use larger tap targets, generous spacing, and intuitive gestures to accommodate mobile users' interactions.

- **Progressive Disclosure**: Implement progressive disclosure techniques to prioritize essential navigation options and minimize clutter on mobile screens. Use collapsible menus, accordion panels, or hidden navigation elements to reveal additional options only when needed, keeping the interface clean and streamlined.

Creating Form Elements and Input Fields

In this section, we will explore the intricacies of designing form elements and input fields, crucial components of UI that facilitate data input and interaction. We will delve into form design principles, techniques for designing various form elements, and considerations for ensuring accessibility in form design.

Detailed Analysis of Form Design Principles

Effective form design is guided by a set of principles aimed at enhancing usability, clarity, and efficiency. Let us examine some key principles:

- **Alignment:** Consistent alignment of form elements creates visual harmony and makes it easier for users to scan and comprehend the form. Align labels and input fields uniformly to establish a clear visual hierarchy.
- **Spacing:** Proper spacing between form elements prevents visual clutter and enhances readability. Provide adequate spacing between labels, input fields, and groups of related elements to improve visual clarity and ease of use.
- **Labeling:** Clear and descriptive labels are essential for guiding users and indicating the purpose of each form element. Place labels adjacent to or above input fields, using concise and meaningful descriptions to facilitate accurate input.
- **Grouping:** Group related form elements together to convey logical relationships and streamline user interaction. Use visual cues such as borders, background colors, or whitespace to delineate distinct groups within the form.

Techniques for Designing Input Fields and Form Elements

Designing input fields and form elements requires careful consideration of usability, aesthetics, and functionality. Here are some techniques for creating effective forms:

- **Input Fields:** Design text input fields with sufficient width and height to accommodate anticipated input. Use appropriate placeholder text to provide context and instructions for users. Consider using input masks or validation patterns to guide input and prevent errors.
- **Text Areas:** Text areas are used for longer-form text input, such as comments

or messages. Provide ample space for users to input text comfortably and consider offering resizing handles to allow users to adjust the size of the text area.

- **Select Menus:** Dropdown select menus are used for selecting options from a predefined list. Design select menus with clear labels and consistent styling to ensure they are easily recognizable and accessible. Consider using hierarchical menus or multi-select options for complex selection scenarios.
- **Checkboxes and Radio Buttons:** Checkboxes and radio buttons are used for binary or mutually exclusive choices, respectively. Design checkboxes with clear labels and sufficient spacing to prevent selection errors. Use radio buttons for exclusive choices, arranging them in logical groups to facilitate selection.

Accessibility Considerations for Form Design

Accessible form design is essential for ensuring that all users, including those with special needs, can interact with forms effectively. Here are some accessibility considerations:

- **Input Validation:** Implement client-side and server-side input validation to ensure data integrity and prevent errors. Provide clear error messages and suggestions for correcting invalid input to assist users in completing the form accurately.
- **Error Handling:** Handle form errors gracefully, highlighting the fields with errors and providing descriptive error messages. Use aria-labels while coding to associate error messages with corresponding input fields, enhancing accessibility for screen reader users.
- **Keyboard Accessibility:** Ensure that all form elements are fully operable via keyboard navigation alone. Use tab index attributes to define the tab order of form elements and provide focus indicators to indicate the active element on keyboards.
- **Labeling and Descriptions:** Use descriptive labels and aria-label attributes to provide context and instructions for form elements. Ensure that labels are programmatically associated with their corresponding input fields to facilitate screen reader navigation.

Figure 4.9: *Best practices for form fields*

Designing Information Display Components

In this section, we will explore the art of designing information display components, elements essential to UI that convey data and content to users effectively. We will delve into various UI elements used to display information, guidelines for structuring and styling these components, and tips to incorporate visual hierarchy for enhancing readability and usability.

Exploration of UI Elements for Displaying Information

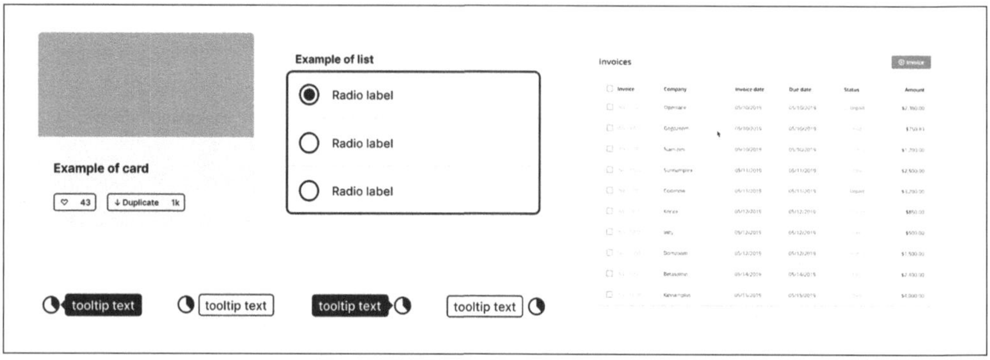

Figure 4.10: *Examples of information display components*

Information display components come in various forms, each serving a specific purpose in presenting data and content to users. Let us explore some commonly used UI elements:

- **Cards:** Cards are versatile UI components used to present bite-sized information or content snippets. They typically feature a title, image, description, and action buttons, making them ideal for displaying structured data or visual content in a compact format.
- **Tables**: Tables are used to organize and display tabular data in a structured grid format. They consist of rows and columns, with headers to label each column and rows to display data entries. Tables are effective for presenting data sets with multiple attributes.
- **Lists**: Lists are sequential arrangements of items or content elements, often displayed vertically or horizontally. They can be used for various purposes, such as navigation menus, item listings, or content sections. Lists provide a straightforward way to present information in a linear format.
- **Tooltips**: Tooltips are small, contextual pop-up boxes that appear when users hover over or interact with specific UI elements. They provide additional information, explanations, or instructions related to the element, enhancing clarity and usability.

Guidelines for Structuring and Styling Information Display

Structuring and styling information display components require careful consideration of readability, usability, and visual aesthetics. Here are some guidelines to follow:

- **Clarity and Readability:** Prioritize clarity and readability by using clear typography, appropriate font sizes, and sufficient contrast between text and background. Ensure that information is presented in a concise and scannable manner, avoiding clutter and unnecessary visual noise.
- **Consistency and Alignment:** Maintain consistency in the layout, alignment, and styling of information display components across the interface. Use a consistent grid system, spacing, and alignment to create visual harmony and cohesion.
- **Hierarchy and Organization:** Establish a clear visual hierarchy to guide users' attention and emphasize important information. Use visual cues such as typography, color, and size to differentiate between primary, secondary, and tertiary content elements.
    - **Contrast and Color:** Use contrast and color to differentiate between different levels of importance or significance within information display components. Use bold or vibrant colors to draw attention to key elements and actions.
    - **Typography and Formatting:** Experiment with typography and formatting to create visual hierarchy within text-based content. Use headings, subheadings, and bullet points to structure information and break up long blocks of text.
- **Iconography and Visual Cues:** Integrate iconography and visual cues to enhance visual hierarchy and aid in content navigation. Use icons to represent actions and concepts, and position them strategically to reinforce the content.
- **Whitespace and Breathing Room:** Use whitespace strategically to provide breathing room and separation between content. Adequate spacing improves readability and reduces cognitive load, allowing users to focus on the information presented.

Incorporating Icons and Illustrations in Design

Icons and illustrations play a crucial role in UI design, enhancing visual communication, aesthetics, and user engagement. In this section, we will explore the importance of icons and illustrations in UI design, strategies for selecting and designing icons that align with the overall visual language and brand identity, and best practices for integrating illustrations to provide context and enhance user engagement.

Importance of Icons and Illustrations in UI Design

Icons and illustrations serve as visual cues that help users navigate, understand, and interact with digital interfaces. They play a vital role in enhancing visual communication, conveying information quickly and effectively. Here is why icons and illustrations are essential in UI design:

- **Visual Communication:** Icons and illustrations facilitate visual communication by representing concepts, actions, and information in a concise and intuitive manner. They help users understand the functionality of interface elements and navigate through complex workflows with ease.
- **Aesthetics:** Icons and illustrations contribute to the overall aesthetics of UI design, adding visual interest, personality, and style to digital interfaces. They can enhance the visual appeal of interfaces and create a cohesive and engaging user experience.
- **User Engagement:** Well-designed icons and illustrations can captivate users' attention and evoke emotional responses, increasing user engagement and interaction with the interface. They can create memorable experiences and leave a lasting impression on users.

Strategies for Selecting and Designing Icons

Selecting and designing icons requires careful consideration of the overall visual language, brand identity, and usability. Here are some strategies for selecting and designing icons:

- **Consistency**: Maintain consistency in icon style, size, and color throughout the interface to create a cohesive visual language. Use a consistent grid system and design principles to ensure that icons align with the overall design aesthetic.
- **Clarity and Simplicity:** Design icons with clarity and simplicity to ensure that they are easily recognizable for users. Avoid unnecessary details and complexity, focusing on conveying the core concept or action represented by the icon.
- **Alignment with Brand Identity:** Select or design icons that align with the brand identity of the product or service. Consider the brand's visual style, color palette, and tone of voice when choosing or creating icons to maintain brand consistency.
- **Scalability:** Design icons in vector format to ensure scalability and adaptability to different screen sizes and resolutions. Vector icons remain crisp and clear at any size, allowing for seamless integration across various devices and platforms.

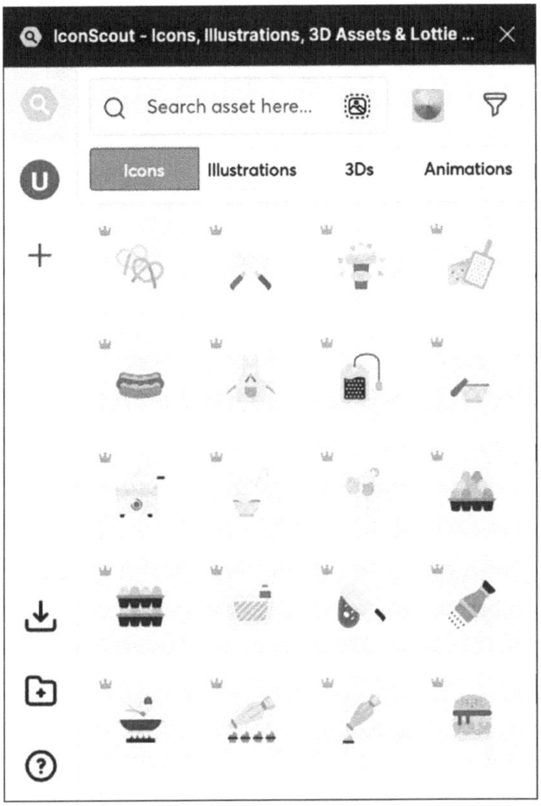

Figure 4.11: *Icons and illustrations can be sourced online from websites such as IconScout*

Best Practices for Integrating Illustrations

Integrating illustrations into UI design can provide context, tell stories, and enhance user engagement. Here are some best practices for integrating illustrations effectively:

- **Contextual Relevance:** Use illustrations that are relevant to the content, context, or message being conveyed. Ensure that illustrations provide meaningful context and enhance the user's understanding of the interface or content.
- **Consistency with Visual Language:** Maintain consistency between illustrations and other visual elements within the interface, such as icons, typography, and color palette. Use a consistent illustration style and visual language to create a cohesive and harmonious design.
- **Storytelling:** Use illustrations to tell stories, evoke emotions, and create memorable experiences for users. Consider incorporating narrative elements or characters into illustrations to engage users and guide them through the interface.

- **Accessibility:** Ensure that illustrations are accessible to all users, including those with visual impairments or disabilities. Provide alternative text descriptions or captions for illustrations to make them accessible to screen readers and other assistive technologies.

Prototyping and Iterating UI Elements

In this section, we will explore the prototyping and iteration process for UI elements, focusing on the importance of user testing and feedback, various prototyping tools and techniques, and case studies demonstrating the iterative design process.

Overview of Prototyping Tools and Techniques

Prototyping is a crucial stage in the UI design process, allowing designers to test and refine UI elements in context before final implementation. Here is an overview of prototyping tools and techniques:

- **Wireframing:** Wireframing is the initial stage of prototyping, where designers create low-fidelity sketches or mockups to outline the structure and layout of UI elements. Wireframes help visualize the overall design concept and identify potential usability issues early in the process.
- **Interactive Prototyping:** Interactive prototypes simulate the functionality and user interactions of the final product, allowing designers to test the usability and effectiveness of UI elements in a realistic context. Tools such as Figma, Adobe XD, and InVision enable designers to create interactive prototypes with clickable links, transitions, and animations.
- **User Flows:** User flows map out the sequence of actions and interactions that users take within the interface, from entry points to desired outcomes. Creating user flows helps designers understand the user journey and identify areas for improvement in UI element placement, navigation, and usability.
- **Usability Testing:** Usability testing involves gathering feedback from real users through observation, interviews, and surveys to evaluate the effectiveness and usability of UI elements. Usability testing provides valuable insights into user behavior, preferences, and pain points, informing the iteration process.

Importance of User Testing and Feedback

User testing and feedback are essential for iterating and refining UI designs based on real user interactions and preferences. Here is why user testing is crucial:

- **Identifying Pain Points:** User testing helps identify usability issues, navigation challenges, and other pain points that users encounter while interacting with UI elements. By observing user behavior and gathering feedback, designers can pinpoint areas for improvement and refinement.

- **Validating Design Decisions:** User testing validates design decisions and assumptions by providing real-world feedback from target users. It ensures that UI elements meet user needs, preferences, and expectations, leading to more user-centered and effective designs.
- **Iterative Improvement:** User testing facilitates an iterative design process, where designers can make incremental improvements to UI elements based on user feedback and testing results. Iterative refinement leads to better usability, engagement, and overall user experience.
- **Reducing Risks:** User testing reduces the risk of costly design errors and usability issues by identifying potential problems early in the design process. By addressing issues proactively through user testing, designers can avoid costly redesigns and rework later on.

Best Practices for Accessibility in UI Design

Accessibility in UI design ensures that digital products are usable by everyone, regardless of their abilities. Here are some best practices to follow:

- **Perceivable:** Use a sufficient color contrast ratio between text and background to improve readability. Provide alternative text for images to make them accessible to screen readers.
- **Clear and Concise Language:** Use simple language and avoid jargon to make content easier to understand. Use clear and consistent typography, spacing, and layout.
- **Operable:** Ensure all interactive elements are accessible via keyboard. Avoid imposing strict time limits that may disadvantage users with motor impairments. Design interfaces that minimize the risk of seizures by avoiding flashing animations or rapidly changing colors.
- **Understandable:** Maintain a consistent navigation structure throughout the website or app. Ensure elements behave as expected to avoid confusion.
- **Error Prevention:** Design inputs and forms in a way that minimize errors and provide clear error messages.
- **Robust:** Ensure compatibility with various assistive technologies, including screen readers and voice recognition software. Design with future technologies and standards in mind.

Case Studies Demonstrating the Iterative Design Process

Let us examine some case studies that illustrate the iterative design process for UI elements:

Figure 4.12: *E-Commerce checkout process*

E-Commerce Checkout Process: A team of designers is tasked with redesigning the checkout process for an e-commerce website to improve conversion rates and reduce cart abandonment. Through user testing and feedback, they identify usability issues such as confusing form fields, unclear error messages, and lengthy checkout steps. Design iterations address these issues by simplifying the form fields, providing clear error messaging, and streamlining the checkout flow. User testing validates the effectiveness of these changes, resulting in a significant increase in conversion rates and user satisfaction.

Figure 4.13: *Mobile app navigation*

Mobile App Navigation: A mobile app design team is challenged with improving the navigation experience for users by redesigning the app's navigation menu. Through prototyping and usability testing, they discover that users struggle to find specific features and navigate between sections efficiently. Iterative design involves restructuring the navigation menu, implementing intuitive icons, and adding contextual tooltips to guide users. User testing validates these changes, resulting in improved navigation efficiency and user satisfaction.

Figure 4.14: *Dashboard analytics*

Dashboard Analytics: A team of designers is redesigning a dashboard analytics interface to make data visualization and analysis more accessible and intuitive for users. Through prototyping and user testing, they uncover usability issues such as cluttered data displays, confusing chart labels, and hidden interaction options. Iterative design iterations focus on simplifying data visualization, improving chart readability, and enhancing interaction feedback. User testing validates these changes, leading to a more user-friendly and effective dashboard interface.

Future of UI Design

In the rapidly evolving landscape of UI design, emerging technologies and changing user behaviors are shaping the future of digital experiences. In this section, we will explore some of the most significant emerging trends and future directions in UI design, including voice interfaces, augmented reality (AR), and immersive experiences.

Voice Interfaces

Figure 4.15: *Voice interfaces*

Voice interfaces are revolutionizing the way users interact with digital devices and services, enabling hands-free and natural language interactions. With the rise of virtual assistants such as Amazon Alexa, Google Assistant, and Apple Siri, voice interfaces are becoming increasingly prevalent in various applications and devices. Here is how voice interfaces are shaping the future of UI design:

- **Conversational Interfaces:** Conversational UI design focuses on creating natural, human-like interactions between users and digital assistants through spoken language. Designers must consider factors such as speech recognition accuracy, natural language processing, and conversational flow when designing conversational interfaces.
- **Multimodal Experiences:** Multimodal interfaces combine voice, touch, and gestures to provide users with flexible and intuitive interaction options. Designing for multimodal experiences requires careful consideration of user context, device capabilities, and accessibility requirements to ensure a seamless and cohesive user experience.
- **Personalization and Context Awareness:** Voice interfaces enable personalized interactions based on user preferences, history, and context. Designers can leverage machine learning and AI algorithms to personalize responses and recommendations, enhancing user engagement and satisfaction.
- **Accessibility and Inclusivity:** Voice interfaces have the potential to improve accessibility and inclusivity by providing alternative interaction methods for users with disabilities or impairments. Designers must consider accessibility guidelines and best practices to ensure that voice interfaces are usable by all users, regardless of their abilities.

Augmented Reality (AR)

Figure 4.16: *Example of augmented reality [Pokémon Go]*

Augmented reality (AR) overlays digital content onto the physical world, blurring the line between the virtual and real environments. AR technology has the potential to transform various industries, from gaming and entertainment to education and retail. Here is how AR is influencing the future of UI design:

- **Spatial Interaction:** AR interfaces leverage spatial interaction techniques such as gesture recognition, gaze tracking, and object recognition to enable intuitive and immersive interactions. Designers must consider the physical environment, user context, and spatial constraints when designing AR experiences.
- **Contextual Information:** AR interfaces provide contextual information and visualizations overlaid onto real-world objects and environments, enhancing situational awareness and decision-making. Designers can use techniques such as spatial anchoring and contextual cues to guide user attention and interaction in AR experiences.
- **Virtual Product Experiences:** AR enables virtual product experiences, allowing users to visualize and interact with products in their real-world environment before making a purchase. Designers can create immersive product demonstrations, configurators, and virtual try-on experiences to enhance the shopping experience and drive conversions.
- **Collaborative Experiences:** AR enables collaborative experiences where multiple users can interact with shared virtual content in real time. Designers can design collaborative AR interfaces for remote collaboration, training simulations, and interactive storytelling, fostering social engagement and collaboration.

Immersive Experiences

Figure 4.17: *Example of immersive experiences*

Immersive experiences transport users into virtual environments, enabling rich and engaging interactions across various platforms and devices. From virtual reality (VR) and mixed reality (MR) to 360-degree video and interactive storytelling, immersive experiences are redefining the way users consume and interact with digital content. Here is how immersive experiences are shaping the future of UI design:

- **Presence and Immersion:** Immersive UI design focuses on creating a sense of presence and immersion, where users feel fully immersed in virtual environments and experiences. Designers must prioritize factors such as spatial audio, haptic feedback, and realistic graphics to enhance immersion and presence.
- **Interactive Storytelling:** Immersive experiences enable interactive storytelling, where users can actively participate and influence the narrative outcome. Designers can use branching narratives, interactive elements, and gamification techniques to engage users and create compelling storytelling experiences.
- **Virtual Collaboration:** Immersive interfaces facilitate virtual collaboration and communication, allowing users to interact with remote clients and partners in virtual environments. Designers can create virtual meeting spaces, collaborative workspaces, and virtual events to facilitate remote collaboration and engagement.
- **Training and Simulation:** Immersive experiences are increasingly used for training simulations and educational purposes, allowing users to practice skills, procedures, and scenarios in a safe and controlled environment. Designers can create immersive training simulations, virtual labs, and interactive tutorials to enhance learning outcomes and retention.

Conclusion

In this chapter, we engaged with the intricacies of creating UI elements, while exploring the importance of consistency, usability, and accessibility in UI design. We discussed various strategies for designing and incorporating UI elements effectively, from buttons and forms to navigation bars and cards. Throughout the chapter, we emphasized the significance of clarity, simplicity, and user-centered design principles in crafting intuitive and engaging UIs.

By understanding the principles of UI design and mastering the techniques for creating UI elements, designers can elevate the overall user experience and create interfaces that are both functional and aesthetically pleasing. Whether designing for web, mobile, or other digital platforms, the principles and best practices covered in this chapter serve as valuable guidelines for designers seeking to create impactful and user-friendly interfaces.

As we conclude this chapter, it is essential to recognize that UI design is a dynamic and evolving field. New technologies, trends, and user expectations continually shape the landscape of UI design, challenging designers to adapt and innovate. By staying informed about emerging trends, experimenting with new tools and techniques, and embracing a user-centered mindset, designers can continue to push the boundaries of UI design and create experiences that delight and engage users in the digital age.

Transition to the next chapter

As we conclude our exploration of creating UI elements in *Chapter 4, Designing UI in Figma*, we now shift our focus to the next phase of UI design in *Chapter 5, Prototyping and Iterating User Interface Design*. In the upcoming chapter, we will dive into the process of prototyping and iterating UI elements, exploring how designers can test, refine, and improve their designs based on user feedback and real-world interactions. We will further explore the iterative design process and the importance of user testing in creating user interfaces that truly resonate with audiences.

Recap of Key Points

- **Importance of Consistency:** We highlighted the significance of maintaining consistency in UI design, including visual elements such as buttons, forms, navigation bars, and cards. Consistency fosters familiarity, usability, and brand identity across different interfaces and platforms.
- **Usability and Accessibility:** We discussed the importance of designing UI elements with usability and accessibility in mind. By prioritizing clarity, simplicity, and intuitive design principles, designers can create interfaces that are easy to navigate and inclusive for all users.
- **Clarity and Simplicity:** We emphasized the value of clarity and simplicity in UI

design, advocating for clear labeling, logical layout, and intuitive interactions. Simple and straightforward UI elements enhance user comprehension and reduce cognitive load, leading to a more enjoyable user experience.

- **User-Centered Design Principles:** Throughout the chapter, we underscored the importance of adopting a user-centered approach to UI design. By understanding user needs, preferences, and behaviors, designers can create interfaces that meet user expectations and facilitate seamless interactions.
- **Crafting Engaging UI Elements:** We explored techniques for crafting engaging UI elements, such as buttons with clear call-to-action (CTA) labels, forms with intuitive input fields, and navigation bars that provide easy access to key features.

CHAPTER 5
Prototyping and Iterating User Interface Design

Introduction

Welcome to *Chapter* 5 of our journey through the intricacies of UI design. In this chapter, we will learn further about the dynamic world of prototyping and iterating UI elements. We will uncover the importance of user testing and feedback, explore various prototyping tools and techniques, and delve into real-world case studies that showcase the power of iteration in creating exceptional user experiences.

Prototyping and iteration are not just stages in the UI design process; they are fundamental pillars that drive innovation, refine ideas, and ultimately shape the success of digital products and experiences. By embracing an iterative mindset and incorporating user feedback at every stage, designers can create UI elements that resonate with users, enhance usability, and deliver delightful interactions.

Join us as we unravel the iterative design process, discover the significance of user-centric design principles, and dive into the realm of prototyping tools and techniques. Through practical insights, actionable strategies, and inspiring case studies, we will equip you with the knowledge and tools to prototype, test, and iterate UI elements effectively, ensuring your designs meet the needs and expectations of users in an ever-evolving digital landscape.

Structure

In this chapter, we will cover the following topics:

- Understanding the Iterative Design Process
- Techniques of User Testing and Feedback

- Wireframing and Sketching User Interface
- Learning How to Prototype in Figma
- Advanced Prototyping in Figma
- Testing User Flows with Figma
- Case Study Demonstrating the Iterative Design Process
- Hands-On Exercises

Understanding the Iterative Design Process

The iterative design approach is a cyclical and user-centric methodology that lies at the heart of UI design. User-centered design (UCD) is a design approach that prioritizes the needs and experiences of users throughout the entire design process. It involves understanding user goals, behaviors, and pain points, and then designing products and services that meet their needs. Key principles of UCD include early and continuous user involvement, empathy, iterative design, and user testing. By understanding user needs, conducting thorough research, and continuously refining designs based on feedback, UCD ensures that products and services are not only functional but also delightful to use.

The UCD approach emphasizes user research, prototyping, and testing to ensure that the final product is usable, efficient, and satisfying.

The Cyclical Nature of Iteration in UI Design

Iteration in UI design follows a cyclical process, where designers create, test, gather feedback, and refine their designs in multiple iterations. Each iteration builds upon the insights gained from previous iterations, leading to incremental improvements and enhancements in the UI elements.

The cyclical nature of iteration ensures that the design evolves iteratively, with each cycle bringing the interface closer to its optimal state. By embracing iteration as an ongoing process rather than a one-time activity, designers can continuously refine and optimize UI elements to deliver a seamless and intuitive user experience.

Benefits of Iterative Design for Improving User Experience

Iterative design offers several benefits for improving the user experience:

- **User-Centered Design:** Iterative design puts users at the center of the design process, allowing designers to gather feedback and insights directly from real users. By incorporating user feedback into the design process, designers can create interfaces that are tailored to user needs, preferences, and behaviors.

- **Incremental Improvement**: Through iterative design, UI elements undergo multiple rounds of refinement and enhancement, leading to incremental improvements in usability, functionality, and aesthetics. Each iteration builds upon the success and learning from previous iterations, resulting in a more polished final product.
- **Faster Iteration Cycles**: Iterative design enables designers to work in shorter and more frequent iteration cycles, allowing them to test ideas, gather feedback, and make improvements rapidly. This iterative approach fosters agility and flexibility, allowing designers to respond quickly to changing requirements and user feedback.
- **Reduced Risk**: By testing and validating UI elements iteratively, designers can identify and address potential issues and usability problems early in the design process. This proactive approach helps mitigate risks and ensures that the final product meets user expectations and business objectives.
- **Continuous Learning**: Iterative design promotes a culture of continuous learning and improvement, where designers constantly seek to understand user needs, preferences, and behaviors. By learning from each iteration and applying insights to future designs, designers can evolve and grow as practitioners, ultimately delivering better user experiences.

Overview of the Iterative Design Phases

An iterative design process is a dynamic approach to creating and refining designs, characterized by continuous cycles of feedback, prototyping, testing, and refinement. Unlike linear design processes, iteration allows for flexibility and adaptability, enabling designers to respond to changing requirements and user needs. Central to iterative design is the continuous solicitation of feedback from users, stakeholders, and other relevant parties, which informs revisions and improvements to the design. Designs are developed incrementally through multiple rounds of prototyping and testing, with each iteration building upon the insights gained from previous iterations. The ultimate goal of iterative design is to deliver a final product that meets user expectations and addresses their pain points through ongoing refinement and iteration.

- **Discover Phase:**

  Embark on a journey of exploration and insight as you delve into the Discover phase of the Double Diamond process. Here, curiosity reigns supreme as you immerse yourself in research, observation, and empathetic understanding. Uncover hidden truths and unearth user needs through rigorous analysis and exploration, laying the foundation for inspired design solutions.

- **Define Phase:**
  In the Define phase, clarity emerges from the chaos as you distill your findings into actionable insights and tangible design challenges. Define your direction with precision and purpose, articulating clear objectives and setting the stage for focused ideation and innovation. Here, ideas take shape and visions coalesce into tangible goals, guiding your design journey forward.

- **Develop Phase:**
  Enter the Develop phase, where creativity flourishes and concepts come to life through iterative prototyping and experimentation. Here, the boundaries of possibility are stretched as you refine and iterate upon your ideas, pushing the boundaries of innovation to create solutions that resonate deeply with user needs and aspirations.

- **Deliver Phase:**
  In the Deliver phase, witness the culmination of your efforts as your designs are brought to fruition and shared with the world. Here, meticulous attention to detail ensures that your creations are polished to perfection, ready to make a meaningful impact and inspire lasting change in the lives of users. Embrace the thrill of seeing your designs come to life as you deliver solutions that transcend expectations and elevate the human experience.

- **Post-Delivery: Refine Phase:**
  The Refine phase focuses on incorporating user feedback and iterating on the design to improve its usability, functionality, and overall user experience. Designers analyze the feedback collected during the Test phase, prioritize design changes, and make iterative improvements to the UI elements. This iterative process of refinement continues until the design meets the desired level of usability and user satisfaction.

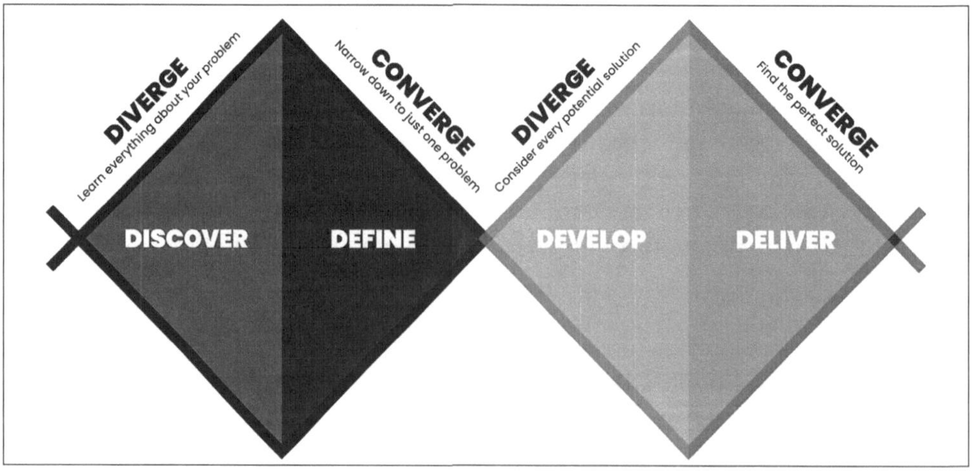

Figure 5.1: *An example of an iterative design process – 'Double Diamond'*

Techniques of User Testing and Feedback

User-centered design principles form the foundation of the iterative design process, guiding designers to create interfaces that prioritize usability, satisfaction, and effectiveness. These principles emphasize the importance of understanding users' needs, preferences, and behaviors, and iterating designs based on user feedback. In the iterative design process, user-centered design principles serve as a compass, ensuring that every design decision is driven by empathy and a deep understanding of the target audience. By aligning with these principles, designers can create interfaces that resonate with users, enhance usability, and ultimately lead to better outcomes.

Putting Users at the Center of the Design Process

Putting users at the center of the design process is paramount to ensuring usability and satisfaction. By empathizing with users, designers can gain valuable insights into their needs, motivations, and pain points, informing design decisions at every stage of the iterative process. User-centered design involves users actively in the design process through techniques such as user research, persona development, and usability testing. By soliciting feedback from users early and often, designers can identify usability issues, validate design assumptions, and iterate on their designs to better meet user needs. By prioritizing usability and satisfaction, designers can create interfaces that are intuitive, user-friendly, and enjoyable to use. Thus, a user-centric design process not only improves the quality of the final product but also fosters a sense of ownership and investment among users, leading to increased adoption and engagement.

Importance of Empathy and Understanding User Behaviors

Empathy is a fundamental aspect of user-centered design, allowing designers to put themselves in the shoes of their users and understand their needs and behaviors. By developing a deep understanding of users' motivations, challenges, and goals, designers can create interfaces that address their needs effectively. Understanding user needs and behaviors requires empathy and active listening. Designers must immerse themselves in the users' world, observing their interactions, listening to their feedback, and empathizing with their experiences. By doing so, designers can uncover insights that inform the design decisions and drive innovation. Empathy also plays a crucial role in fostering collaboration and empathy among team members. By empathizing with users, designers can bridge the gap between stakeholders, developers, and other team members, ensuring that everyone is aligned with the user's needs and goals.

Gathering User Feedback:

- **Usability Testing**: Usability testing involves observing users as they interact with a prototype or product to identify usability issues and gather feedback on their experience. Through tasks and scenarios, designers can observe user behaviors, reactions, and difficulties, providing valuable insights for iteration.
- **Surveys**: Surveys are useful for collecting quantitative data and understanding user opinions, preferences, and demographics at scale. Designers can create surveys to gather feedback on specific aspects of the design or overall user satisfaction, helping to identify trends and patterns among users.
- **Interviews**: Interviews allow designers to have in-depth conversations with users to gain qualitative insights into their needs, motivations, and pain points. By asking open-ended questions and probing for details, designers can uncover deeper insights and understand the context behind user behaviors and preferences.
- **Observation**: Observation involves directly observing users in their natural environment to understand how they interact with products or systems in real-life situations. By observing user behaviors, routines, and environments, designers can gain insights that may not be captured through other methods.

Establishing Clear Objectives and Hypotheses for User Testing:

- **Recruitment**: When recruiting participants for user testing, designers should strive to recruit a diverse range of users who represent the target audience. This may involve reaching out to existing customers, leveraging user research panels, or using recruitment agencies to find participants with specific demographics or characteristics.
- **Incentives:** Offering incentives can encourage participation and improve the quality of user testing sessions. Designers can offer incentives such as gift cards, discounts, or product samples to compensate participants for their time and effort.
- **Moderation:** During user testing sessions, it is crucial to have a skilled moderator who can guide participants through tasks, ask probing questions, and facilitate discussions. The moderator should create a comfortable and non-judgmental environment where participants feel free to share their thoughts and feedback openly.
- **Data Collection:** Designers should use a variety of methods to collect data during user testing, including video recordings, screen captures, notes, and surveys. This multi-method approach ensures that designers capture a comprehensive picture of user behaviors, preferences, and feedback.
- **Analysis:** After user testing sessions, designers should analyze the data collected to identify trends, patterns, and insights. This analysis helps designers distill the findings into actionable recommendations for iteration and improvement.

Methods for Analyzing and Interpreting User Feedback:

- **Thematic Analysis:** Thematic analysis involves identifying recurring themes and patterns in qualitative data, such as interview transcripts or open-ended survey responses. By categorizing responses into themes, designers can uncover insights about user needs, preferences, and pain points.
- **Quantitative Analysis:** Quantitative analysis involves analyzing numerical data collected through surveys, usability tests, or analytics tools. This may include calculating averages, percentages, or correlations to identify trends and patterns in user behavior and preferences.
- **Affinity Diagramming:** Affinity diagramming is a collaborative method for organizing and synthesizing qualitative data. Designers and stakeholders can group related insights and observations into categories or themes, helping to identify common patterns and prioritize design improvements.

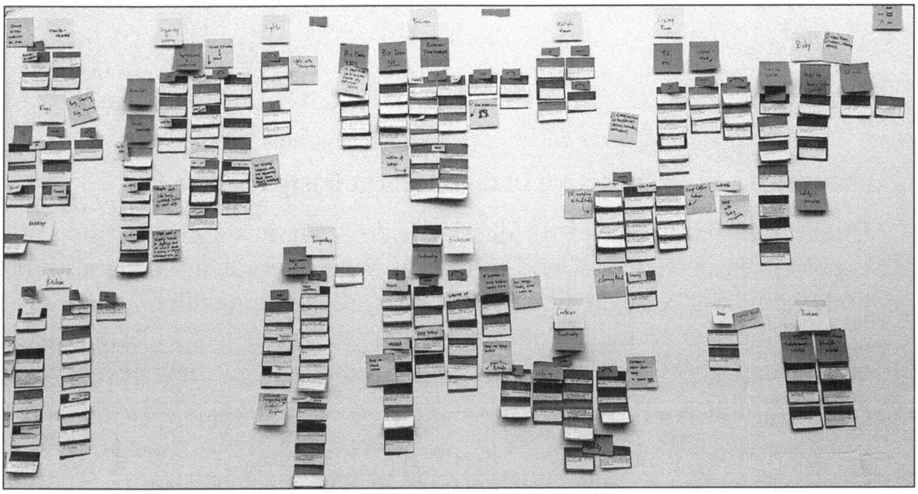

***Figure* 5.2**: *An example of affinity diagramming*

- **Heatmaps and Clickmaps:** Heatmaps and clickmaps provide visual representations of user interactions with a digital interface. By analyzing where users click, scroll, or hover, designers can identify areas of interest, engagement, and friction, informing design decisions and optimizations.

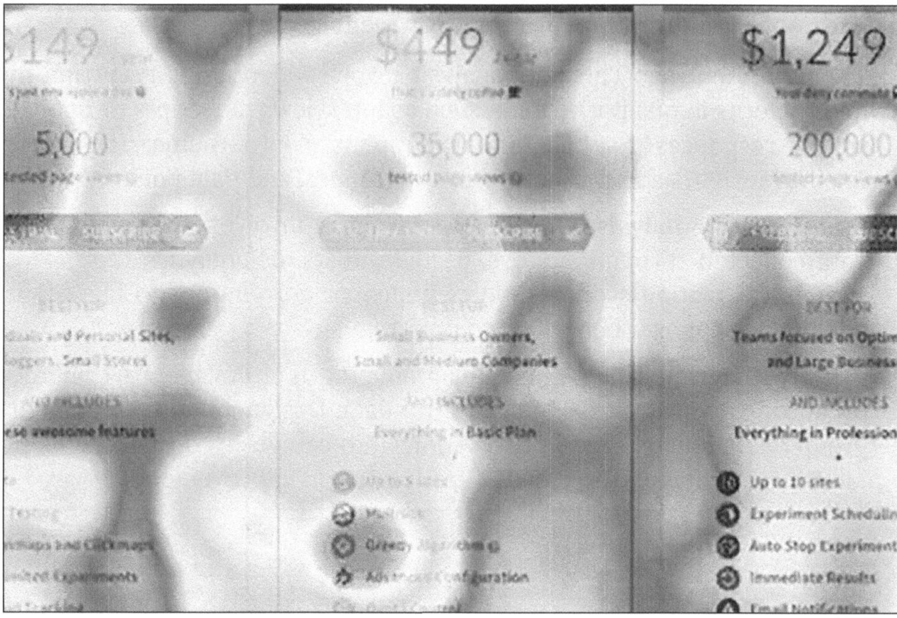

Figure 5.3: *An example of a heatmap*

Using Qualitative and Quantitative Data to Inform Design Decisions:

- **Qualitative Data**: Qualitative data provides rich, in-depth insights into user experiences, preferences, and behaviors. Designers can use qualitative data to understand the "why" behind user actions, uncovering underlying motivations and emotions that drive behavior. Qualitative data is particularly valuable for generating hypotheses, identifying user needs, and informing design direction.
- **Quantitative Data:** Quantitative data provides numerical insights into user behavior, preferences, and performance metrics. Designers can use quantitative data to measure the frequency and severity of usability issues, track key performance indicators (KPIs), and assess the impact of design changes over time. Quantitative data is valuable for identifying trends, benchmarking performance, and making data-driven decisions.

Incorporating Feedback into the Iterative Design Process:

- **Prioritize Actionable Insights:** Designers should prioritize actionable insights that have the potential to drive meaningful improvements in the user experience. By focusing on insights that align with project goals and user needs, designers can maximize the impact of their iterative design efforts.
- **Iterative Testing and Validation:** Designers should iteratively test and validate design changes with real users to ensure their effectiveness. By incorporating user feedback into each iteration of the design process, designers can identify and address usability issues, refine design solutions, and ultimately create a more user-centered product.

- **Continuous Improvement:** The iterative design process is inherently iterative, with each cycle of iteration leading to incremental improvements in the user experience. By embracing a mindset of continuous improvement, designers can constantly refine and optimize their designs based on user feedback, evolving the product to better meet user needs and preferences over time.

Wireframing and Sketching User Interface

Effective wireframing and sketching require careful consideration of user needs, project requirements, and design objectives. Here are some techniques to help you plan and sketch UI elements effectively:

- **Define User Needs:** Start by understanding the needs, goals, and preferences of your target users. Conduct user research, gather feedback, and create user personas to gain insights into user behaviors, preferences, and pain points.

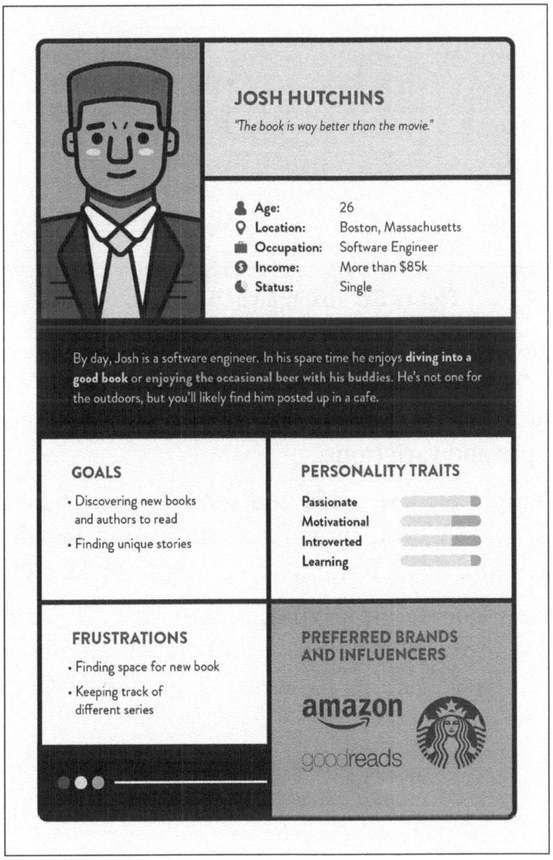

Figure 5.4: *Example of a user persona*

- **Establish Design Objectives:** Define clear design objectives and goals for your UI project. Determine what you want to achieve with your design, whether it is improving usability, increasing engagement, or driving conversions.
- **Storyboarding:** Use storyboarding techniques to visualize user interactions and workflows. Create sequential sketches or storyboards to illustrate how users will navigate through the interface and accomplish tasks.

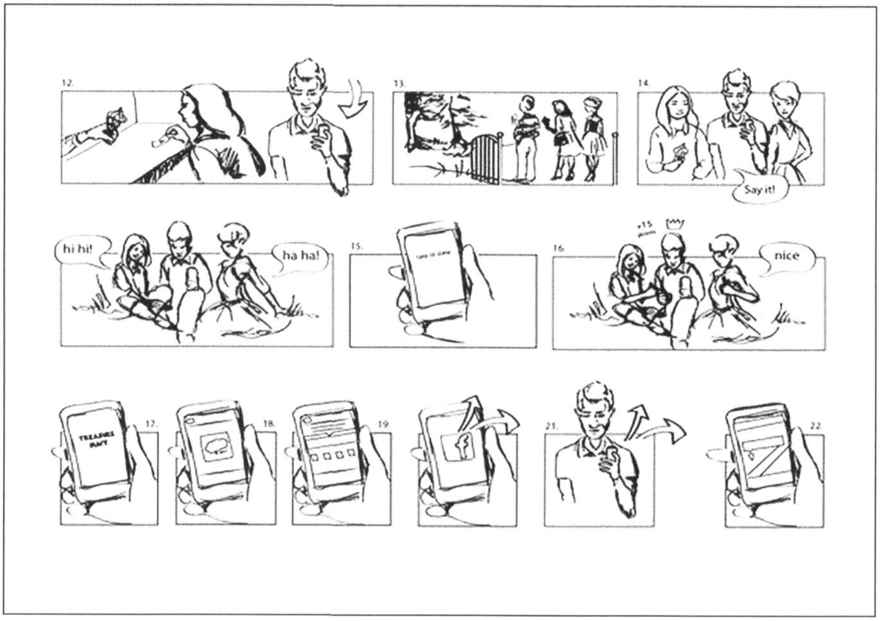

***Figure 5.5**: Example of a storyboard*

- **Iterative Sketching:** Adopt an iterative approach to sketching, starting with rough, low-fidelity sketches and gradually refining them over time. Experiment with different layout, structure, and functionality options, exploring multiple design concepts and variations.
- **Grids and Templates:** Use grids and templates to maintain consistency and alignment. Grids help you organize content and establish visual hierarchy, while templates provide a framework for common UI elements and layouts.
- **Annotation and Documentation:** Annotate your sketches with notes, labels, and annotations to provide context and clarity. Document design decisions, rationale, and considerations to ensure alignment with project requirements and objectives.

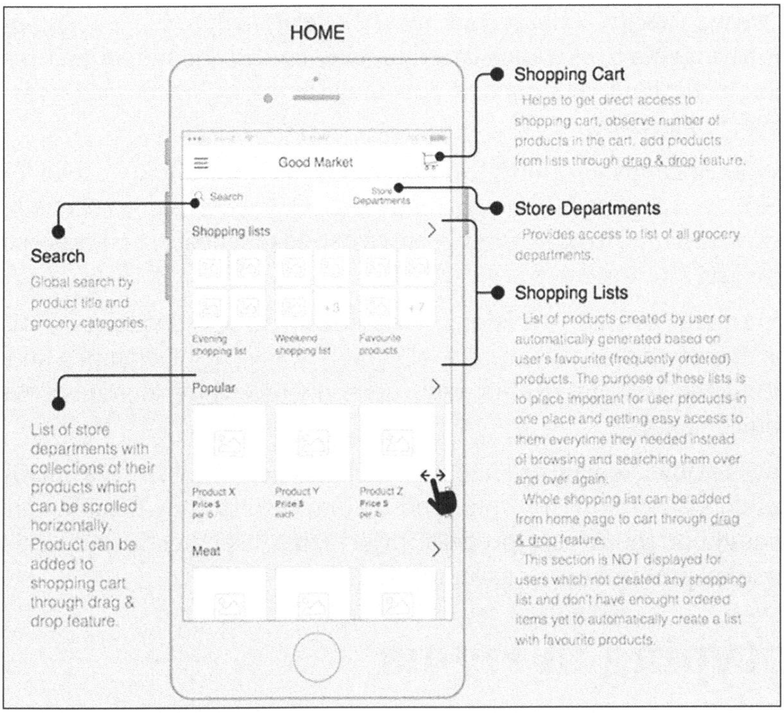

***Figure 5.6**: Example of an annotated wireframe*

- **Collaboration and Feedback:** Involve stakeholders, clients, and team members in the wireframing and sketching process. Solicit feedback early and often, incorporating suggestions and insights into your design iterations.

Tips for Refining UI Wireframes

Refining UI wireframes is an iterative process that involves gathering feedback, making adjustments, and refining designs based on user needs and project requirements. Here are some tips for iterating and refining UI sketches effectively:

- **User Testing:** Conduct user testing sessions to gather feedback on your sketches from real users. Observe how users interact with your designs, identify pain points and usability issues, and use this feedback to refine your sketches.
- **Usability Heuristics:** Evaluate your sketches against established usability heuristics and design principles. Identify areas where your sketches may deviate from best practices and make adjustments to improve usability and user experience.
- **Prototype and Test:** Create interactive prototypes based on sketches and conduct usability testing sessions. Use prototyping tools to simulate user interactions and workflows, gather feedback on usability, and identify areas for improvement.

- **Iterative Design:** Embrace an iterative design approach, making incremental improvements to sketches based on user feedback and testing results. Iterate on your designs, refining and polishing them until they meet user needs and project objectives.
- **Feedback Loops:** Establish feedback loops with stakeholders, clients, and team members to gather ongoing feedback on your sketches. Schedule regular review sessions to share your progress, solicit feedback, and make adjustments based on input received.
- **Document Design Decisions:** Document design decisions, rationale, and considerations as you iterate. Maintain a record of changes and revisions, noting the reasons behind each decision to ensure alignment with project requirements.
- **Stay Flexible:** Remain open to feedback and be willing to make changes to your sketches based on user input and testing results. Stay flexible and adaptable throughout the design process, prioritizing user needs and usability above personal preferences or assumptions.

Prototyping in Figma

Prototyping is a crucial phase in the design process that bridges the gap between static designs and fully developed products. In Figma, prototyping is made accessible and efficient through its robust set of tools that allow designers to create interactive and animated prototypes directly within the design interface. This chapter will explore the fundamentals of prototyping in Figma, offering detailed guidance on how to create interactive prototypes and touch upon advanced techniques.

Creating Prototypes to Simulate User Interactions

Before starting with the prototype, ensure all your frames (screens) are designed and laid out in Figma. In Figma, switch from the '`Design`' tab to the '`Prototype`' tab to link elements between frames and define interactions. Click an element you want to make interactive and drag the blue node to the target frame. Once this connection is established, a properties panel will appear where you can define the type of interaction (for example, `On Click`, `On Hover`) and the resulting action (for example, `Navigate to`, `Open Overlay`).

- **Click Interactions:**
    - **Setting Up Click Interactions:** To create a clickable interaction, select an element such as a button, and drag the blue arrow to the frame that represents the next step or screen. This action sets up a click interaction.

- **Defining Click Actions:** In the properties panel, you can define what happens when the element is clicked. Options include navigating to another frame, opening an overlay, or triggering a different action such as a scroll or a pop-up.

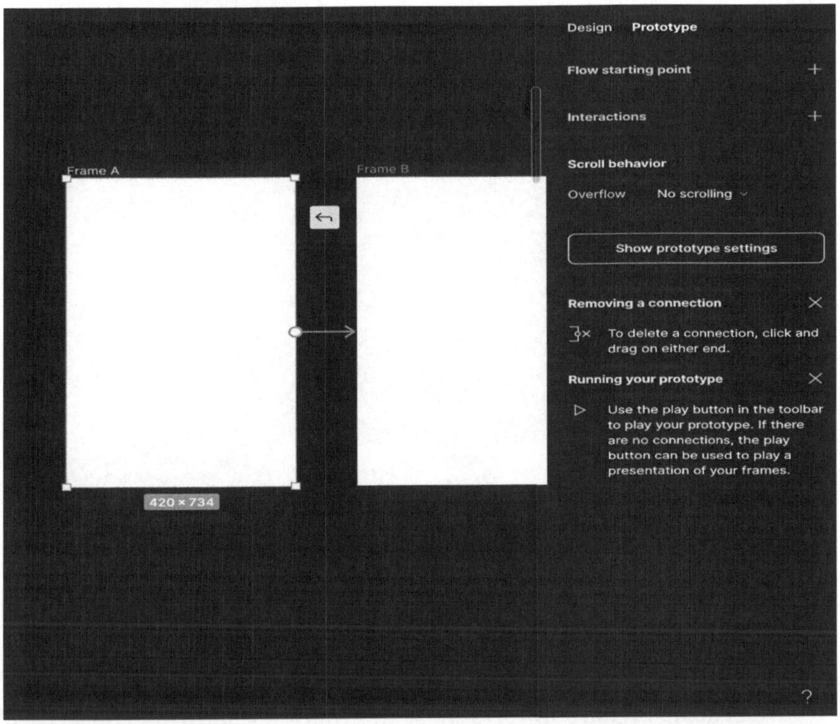

***Figure 5.7:** Setting up click interactions in the prototype tab of Figma*

- **Hover Interactions:**
  - **Hover States:** Figma allows you to define hover states for elements. This is particularly useful for web designs where hover interactions are common. By creating component variants, you can easily switch between states.
  - **Implementing Hover Effects:** To implement hover interactions, select the element, define its default state, and create a variant for the hover state. Link these variants in the prototype settings to simulate the hover effect.

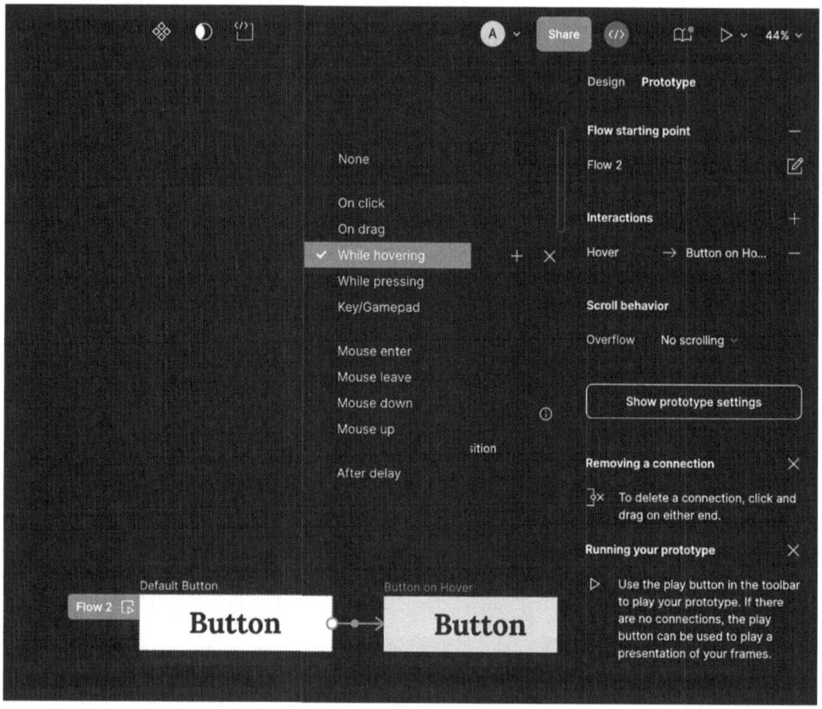

***Figure 5.8**: Setting up a hover state in Figma under prototype settings*

- **Swipe and Drag Interactions:**
    - **Mobile Gestures:** For mobile app prototypes, swipe and drag interactions are crucial. Figma supports these interactions, allowing you to create more realistic mobile experiences.
    - **Setting Up Swipe Gestures:** To set up a swipe interaction, link the element to the frame that represents the next state in the swipe sequence. Define the interaction as a swipe left, right, up, or down in the same properties panel as shown in *Figure 5.8*.

Animate Transitions

You can choose how the transition between frames should occur (for example, **`Instant`**, **`Dissolve`**, **`Slide`**). Adjust the easing and duration settings to fine-tune the animation, options include linear, ease-in, ease-out, and custom bezier curves.

Add animations between different states or screens:

- **Transition Types:**
    - **Instant:** This transition type changes screens immediately without any animation. It is useful for quick and direct navigation.
    - **Dissolve:** Creates a fade effect between screens, making the transition smoother and more visually appealing.

- **Move In/Move Out:** Slides the new screen in from a direction (left, right, up, down) and moves the old screen out. This is ideal for creating a sense of continuity in the user flow.
- **Push:** Similar to move in/out, but both the new and old screens move simultaneously, giving a more dynamic effect.
- **Smart Animate:** This advanced feature animates changes between frames by automatically animating properties such as position, scale, and opacity of layers that exist in both frames. It is ideal for creating smooth and sophisticated animations.

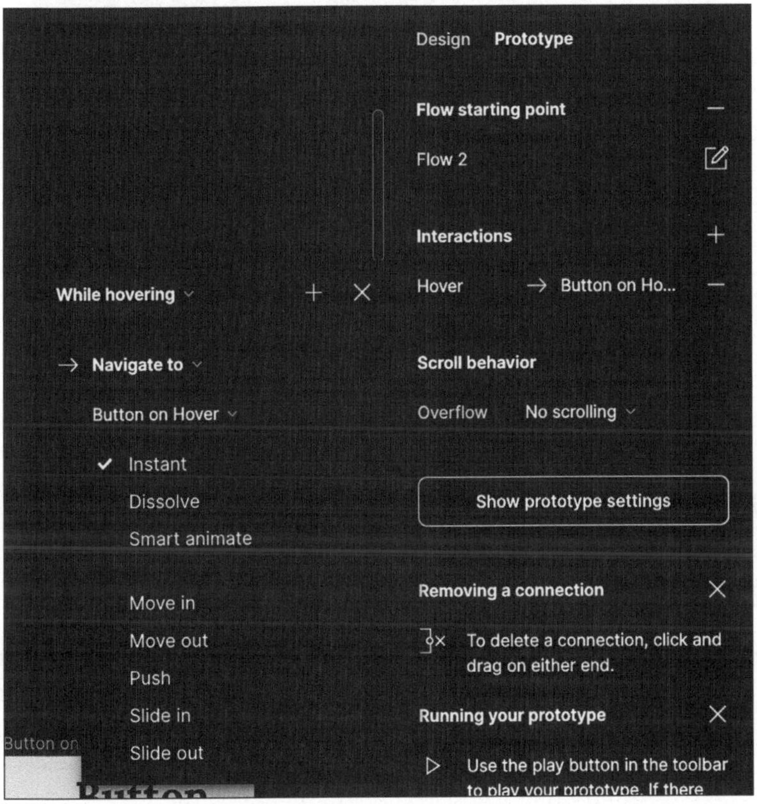

Figure 5.9: *Animation types in the prototyping settings of Figma*

- **Customizing Animations:**
  - **Easing Functions:** Easing functions control the acceleration and deceleration of animations. Options include linear, ease-in, ease-out, and ease-in-out. Custom easing curves can be created to fine-tune the animation.
  - **Duration:** The duration setting controls how long the transition takes. Adjusting the duration can make animations feel faster or slower, depending on the desired effect.

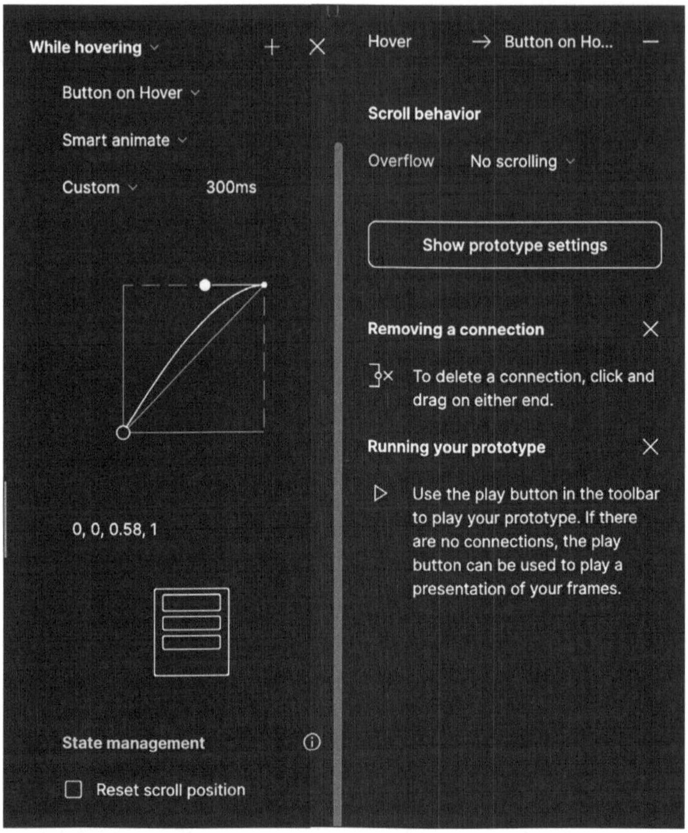

***Figure 5.10**: Custom animation in Figma prototyping under 'Smart Animate'*

Advanced Prototyping in Figma

Figma offers a range of advanced prototyping techniques that allow designers to create sophisticated, interactive prototypes. These features go beyond basic linking and transitions, enabling the creation of more realistic and dynamic user experiences. This section delves into three key advanced prototyping techniques: overlays and modals, interactive components, and scroll and fixed positioning.

Overlays and Modals

Use overlays to create modal dialogs, tooltips, and dropdown menus. Overlays can be positioned relative to the trigger element and have their own interactions.

- **Creating Overlays:**
  - **Setting Up Overlays:** To create an overlay, first design the element that will serve as the overlay (for example, a modal dialog, tooltip, or dropdown menu). Ensure it is placed on its own frame.

   - **Linking Overlays:** Select the trigger element (for example, a button or icon) and drag the blue node to the overlay frame. In the interaction details, choose "Open overlay" as the action.

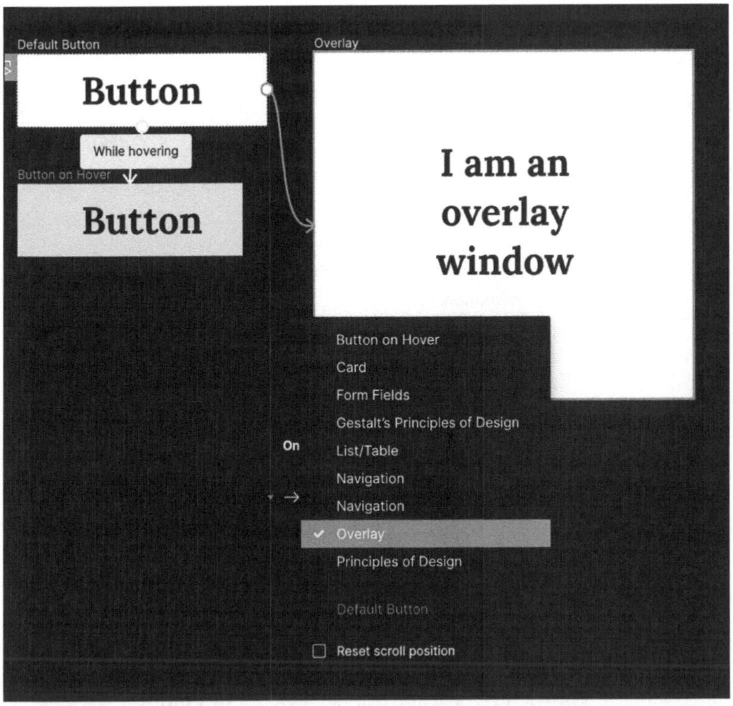

Figure 5.11: *Setting an overlay in Figma*

- **Positioning Overlays:**
   - **Relative Positioning:** Figma allows you to position overlays relative to the trigger element. Options include centering the overlay on the screen, aligning it to the top, bottom, left, or right of the trigger, or customizing the offset.
   - **Fixed Position:** Ensure the overlay remains fixed in place while the background can be interacted with. This is particularly useful for modal dialogs that need to remain prominent on the screen.

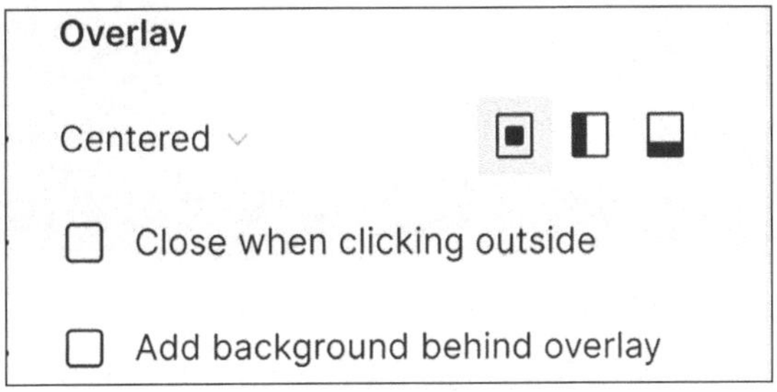

Figure 5.12: *Positioning an overlay in Figma*

- **Overlay Interactions:**
  - **Interactive Overlays:** Overlays themselves can contain interactive elements, such as buttons or links, which can trigger additional actions. For example, a dropdown menu overlay might have clickable items that navigate to frames.
  - **Closing Overlays:** Define how overlays should be dismissed. This can be done by clicking outside the overlay, clicking a close button within the overlay, or setting a timer for automatic dismissal.

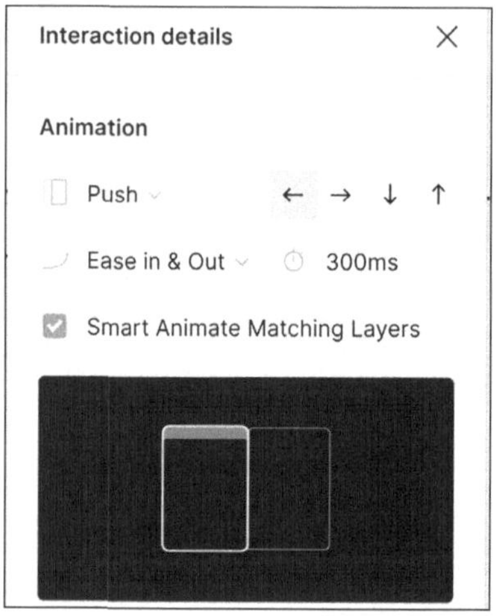

Figure 5.13: *Animating an overlay in Figma*

- **Use Cases:**
  - **Modal Dialogs:** Useful for alerts, confirmations, or forms that require user input without navigating away from the current screen.

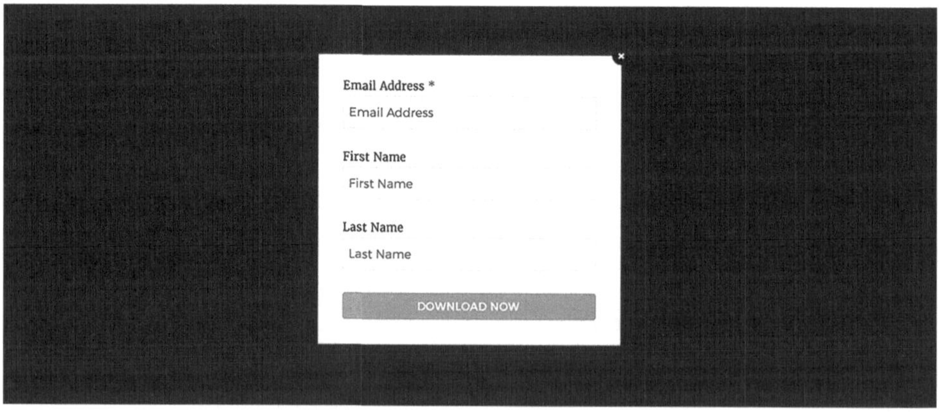

Figure 5.14: *Example of a modal dialog*

  - **Tooltips:** Provide additional information or guidance when users hover over or click specific elements.

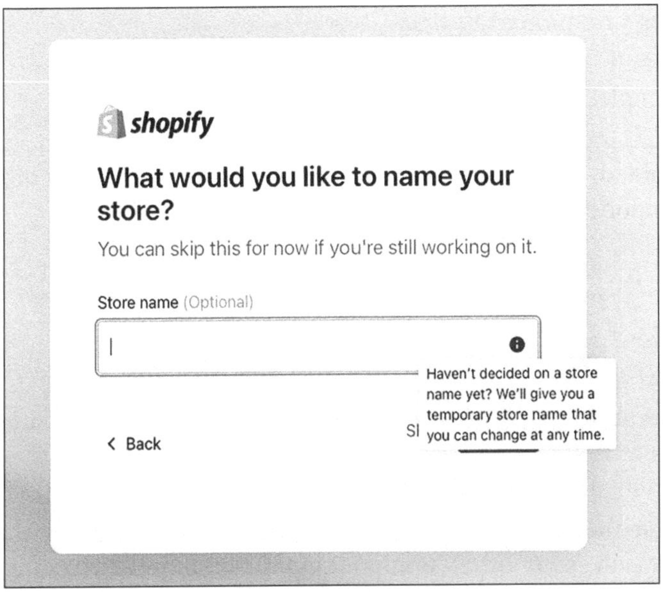

***Figure 5.15**: Example of a tooltip, courtesy Shopify*

- **Dropdown Menus:** Create interactive navigation elements that expand to show additional options.

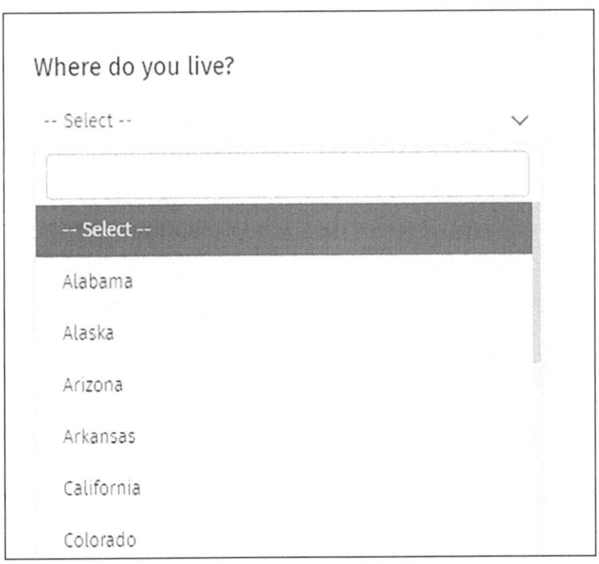

***Figure 5.16**: Example of a dropdown*

Interactive Components

Figma allows for interactive components, where different states (for example, default, hover, pressed) can be defined within a single component. This helps in creating more realistic prototypes with dynamic interactions.

- **Creating Component States:**
  - **Default State:** Design the default appearance of the component (for example, a button in its normal state).
  - **Additional States:** Add variants for different states such as hover, pressed, disabled, and active. Each variant represents a unique visual state of the component.

Figure 5.17: *Example of button states*

- **Linking States:**
  - **Interaction Definitions:** Define interactions that transition between the different states. For example, set a hover interaction to switch from the default state to the hover state.
  - **Component Interactions:** Components can trigger interactions within themselves or other components. This allows for complex, multi-step interactions within a single component setup.
- **Using Interactive Components:**
  - **Realistic Prototypes:** Interactive components make prototypes feel more realistic by accurately simulating user interactions. For example, a button that changes appearance when hovered over or clicked.
  - **Consistency:** By defining states within a single component, you can ensure consistency across your design. Any changes to the component will automatically apply to all instances.
- **Use Cases:**
  - **Buttons:** Define hover, pressed, and disabled states to simulate real-world button interactions.
  - **Form Fields:** Show different states for focus, input, error, and success.
  - **Navigation Elements:** Create interactive menus and tabs with active and inactive states.

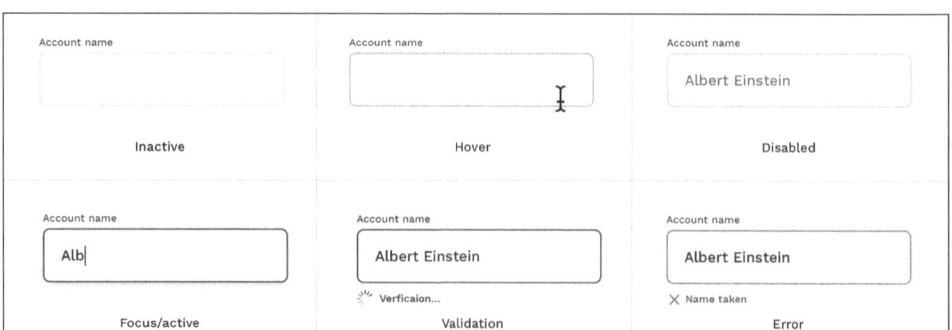

Figure 5.18: *Example of form field states*

Scroll and Fixed Positioning

Define scrollable regions within your frames to simulate content scrolling. Keep certain elements fixed (for example, headers, footers) while the rest of the content scrolls. This is useful for maintaining navigational consistency.

- **Scrollable Areas:**
    - **Creating Scrollable Regions:** To make an area scrollable, place the content within a frame that is smaller than the content itself. In the properties panel, enable the "`Clip content`" option and set the overflow behavior to "`Scroll`".
    - **Vertical and Horizontal Scrolling:** Define whether the scrolling should be vertical, horizontal, or both. This is useful for creating scrollable lists, carousels, and larger content areas.

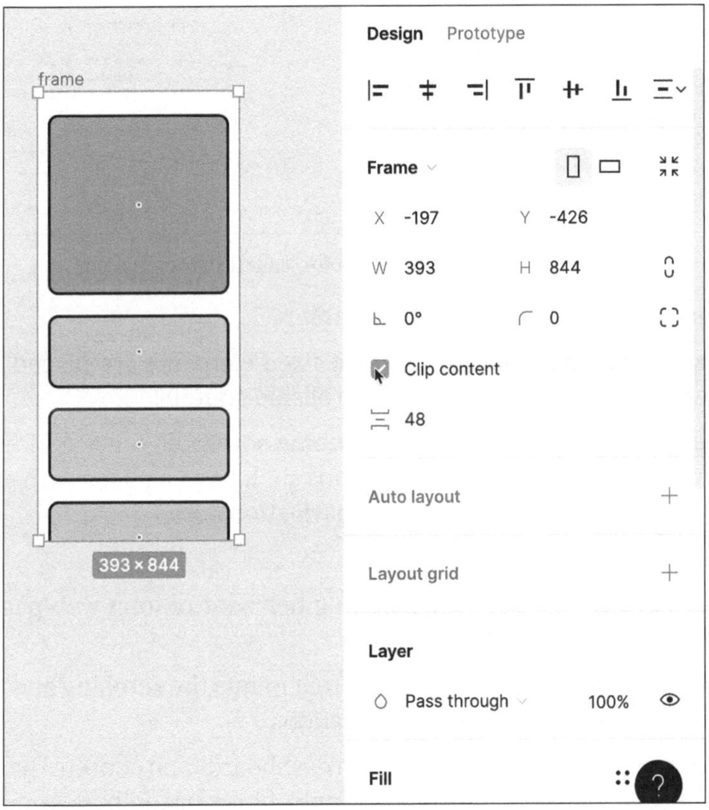

***Figure 5.19**: Scrolling by clipping content in Figma, courtesy Figma.com*

- **Fixed Elements:**
    - **Pinning Elements:** Keep certain elements fixed in place while the rest of the content scrolls. This can be achieved by placing the fixed element in a separate frame layer above the scrollable content.

   - **Common Use Cases:** Fixed headers, footers, and side navigation bars that stay visible as users scroll through the content.

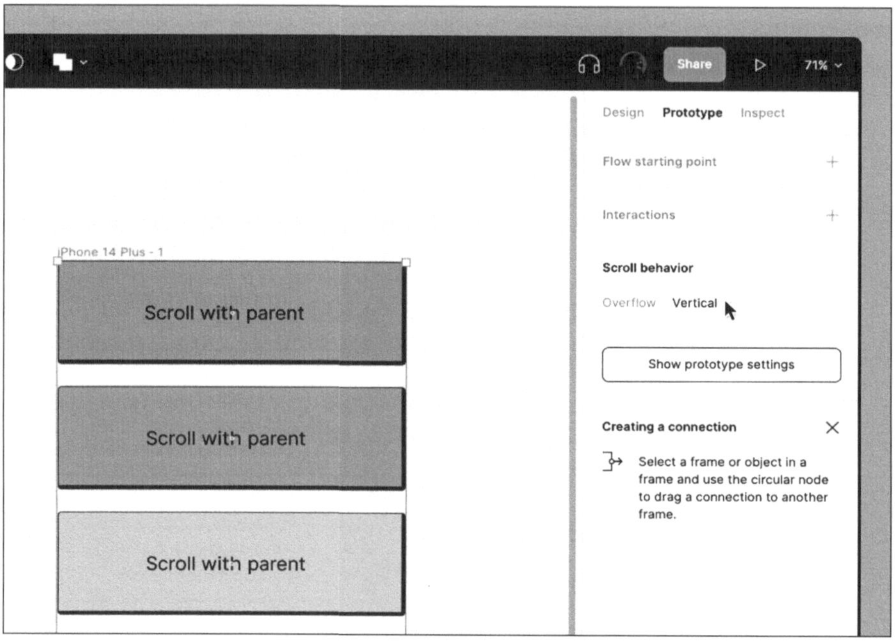

***Figure* 5.20**: *Scrolling behavior, courtesy Figma.com*

- **Combining Scroll and Fixed Elements:**
   - **Layer Management:** Ensure that fixed elements are placed on top layers and do not interfere with the scrollable content.
   - **Simulating Real Scenarios:** Combine scrollable areas and fixed elements to simulate real-world applications such as web pages with sticky headers or mobile apps with persistent navigation bars.
- **Use Cases:**
   - **Web Pages:** Simulate the scrolling behavior of long web pages with fixed headers and navigation.
   - **Mobile Apps:** Create prototypes that mimic the scrolling and fixed element behavior of native mobile applications.
   - **Content-Rich Interfaces:** Design dashboards and content-heavy interfaces where certain elements (for example, filters or toolbars) remain accessible while the user scrolls through the data.

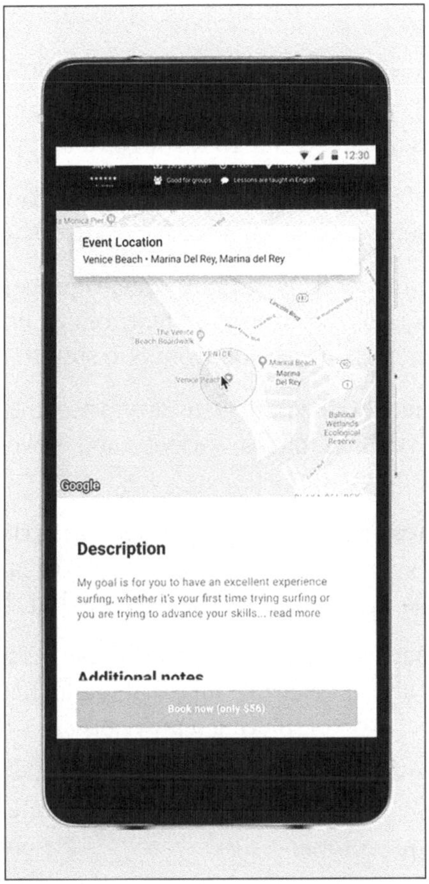

Figure 5.21: *A mobile app is a good example of a mix of fixed, and scrollable content. In the maps section of the Figma prototype, you can set scrolling to both vertical or horizontal, simulating a real user behavior*

Testing User Flows with Figma

Testing user flows is a crucial step in validating design assumptions and ensuring that your prototype meets user needs and expectations. This section will guide you through the process of creating, testing, and refining user journeys within your Figma prototypes.

Validating Design Assumptions by Testing the Entire User Journey

Validating your design assumptions involves testing the entire user journey from start to finish. This comprehensive approach ensures that your design is intuitive and functional.

Creating User Journeys:

1. **Mapping Out Flows:** Begin by mapping out the different user journeys within your prototype. This involves linking multiple frames together to represent the entire process a user would go through to complete a task.
    a. Start by identifying the key user paths within your application. These paths should represent the main tasks or goals users will want to accomplish.
    b. In Figma, create multiple frames that represent each step in the user journey. Use Figma's prototyping features to link these frames together, ensuring a seamless transition from one step to the next.
    c. For each frame, detail what the user will see and do. Include all necessary interactions, such as clicks, swipes, and hovers, to simulate the user experience.
2. **Scenario-Based Testing:** Create specific scenarios that users might encounter, for example, an e-commerce checkout flow or a mobile app onboarding process. This helps in testing specific paths within the prototype.
    a. Develop scenarios based on real-life use cases. For example, for an e-commerce site, scenarios might include browsing products, adding items to a cart, and completing a purchase.
    b. Consider different types of users and their potential interactions with your design. This helps in understanding how various user groups will navigate through your prototype.
    c. Focus on specific paths within the prototype to identify any issues or areas that may require improvement. This targeted testing helps in refining particular aspects of the user journey.

Identifying Pain Points:

1. **Usability Testing:** Conduct usability testing sessions where real users interact with the prototype. Observe how users navigate through the prototype and identify any pain points or areas of confusion.
    a. Conduct Sessions with Real Users: Organize usability testing sessions with actual users. This provides valuable insights into how users interact with your design and where they encounter difficulties.
    b. Pay close attention to how users navigate through the prototype. Note any areas where they hesitate, get confused, or make errors.
    c. Ask users for their feedback on the design. Inquire about their overall experience, what they found intuitive, and what they found challenging.

2. **Task Completion Rates:** Measure how easily and quickly users can complete tasks within the prototype. High task completion rates indicate a more intuitive design, while low rates suggest areas needing improvement.

    a. Identify the main tasks users need to complete within the prototype. These tasks should align with the core functionalities of your design.

    b. Track how easily and quickly users can complete these tasks. High task completion rates indicate that the design is user-friendly, while low rates highlight areas that need improvement.

    c. Measure the time it takes for users to complete each task. Long completion times may suggest that certain elements of the design are not intuitive.

Iterative Testing and Refinement:

1. **Continuous Feedback Loop:** Use feedback from usability testing to refine the prototype. Make necessary adjustments and continue testing until the design meets user expectations and requirements.

    a. Continuously collect feedback from users throughout the testing process. This feedback is essential for understanding how the design performs and where it can be improved.

    b. Use the feedback to make necessary adjustments to the prototype. This could involve tweaking interactions, rearranging elements, or enhancing visual cues.

    c. After making changes, test the prototype again to see if the adjustments have resolved the issues. This iterative process ensures that the design evolves based on user input and becomes more refined over time.

2. **A/B Testing:** Conduct A/B testing by creating multiple versions of a user flow or interface element. Compare performance and user preference to determine the most effective design.

    a. Develop multiple versions of a user flow or interface element. These variants should differ in specific ways that you want to test (for example, different button placements, color schemes, or interaction styles).

    b. Test each variant with a group of users and compare their performance. Look for differences in task completion rates, user satisfaction, and overall efficiency.

    c. Analyze user feedback to determine which variant is preferred and why. This helps in choosing the most effective design that resonates with users and enhances their experience.

Case Study Illustrating the Design Process

Following is an example case study for an e-commerce website redesign to help readers understand how the design process works end-to-end.

- **Define Phase**: In the Define phase of the e-commerce website redesign project, the design team conducted extensive research to understand the goals, needs, and pain points of the target users. They analyzed user feedback, conducted surveys, and reviewed analytics data to identify key areas for improvement. The team defined clear objectives for the redesign, focusing on enhancing user engagement, streamlining the checkout process, and improving conversion rates. They created user personas to represent the different segments of their target audience, helping to prioritize design decisions and ensure alignment with user needs. Through stakeholder interviews and brainstorming sessions, the team established design principles and success criteria for the project. These guiding principles served as a framework for the subsequent design phases, ensuring that the redesign remained user-centered and aligned with the business goals.
- **Design Phase**: Armed with insights from the Define phase, the design team entered the Design phase, where they began exploring design solutions and concepts. They created wireframes and mockups to visualize the layout, structure, and functionality of the redesigned e-commerce website. Using tools like Figma, the team iteratively refined the designs based on feedback from stakeholders and user testing sessions. They focused on improving the user interface, navigation flow, and product presentation to enhance the overall user experience. The design team also paid special attention to the checkout process, aiming to simplify and streamline the steps involved in completing a purchase. They experimented with different layouts, form designs, and payment options to optimize the checkout flow and reduce cart abandonment rates. Throughout the Design phase, the team collaborated closely with developers and other stakeholders to ensure that the design concepts were technically feasible and aligned with the project timeline and budget.
- **Prototype Phase**: With the design concepts finalized, the team moved into the Prototype phase, where they created interactive prototypes to simulate the functionality and user interactions of the redesigned e-commerce website. Using prototyping tools like Figma's prototyping feature, they added interactive elements such as buttons, dropdown menus, and form fields to the designs. The interactive prototypes allowed the team to test the user experience in a realistic environment, gathering feedback on usability, navigation flow, and overall functionality. They conducted usability testing sessions with

real users, observing how they interacted with the prototype and identifying areas for improvement. Based on the feedback from user testing sessions, the team iteratively refined the prototypes, making adjustments to the layout, navigation, and interaction design to address usability issues and enhance the overall user experience.

- **Test Phase**: In the Test phase, the design team conducted comprehensive usability testing sessions with real users to validate the effectiveness of the redesigned e-commerce website. They recruited participants representing the target audience demographics and observed their interactions with the prototype. During the usability testing sessions, participants were asked to complete specific tasks, such as browsing products, adding items to the cart, and completing the checkout process. The team observed how users navigated the website, identified usability issues and pain points, and gathered feedback on their overall experience. Based on the insights from the usability testing sessions, the team identified several areas for improvement, including clarifying navigation labels, optimizing page load times, and enhancing mobile responsiveness. They documented these findings and prioritized design changes for the Refine phase.
- **Refine Phase**: In the Refine phase, the design team iteratively refined the designs based on the insights gathered from usability testing sessions. They prioritized design changes and implemented improvements to address usability issues, enhance user experience, and align with the project goals and objectives. Using feedback from stakeholders and users, the team made adjustments to the layout, navigation flow, and visual design elements of the e-commerce website. They conducted additional rounds of usability testing to validate the effectiveness of the refinements and gather further feedback for iteration.

Through continuous refinement and iteration, the design team achieved significant improvements in the user experience of the redesigned e-commerce website. They reduced cart abandonment rates, increased conversion rates, and enhanced user engagement, ultimately delivering a more intuitive, user-friendly, and successful e-commerce platform.

Hands-On Practice

To solidify your understanding of prototyping in Figma, the following hands-on exercises will guide you through creating various interactive elements and user flows. These exercises range from basic to advanced, allowing you to progressively build your skills.

Exercise 1: Creating a Simple Interactive Prototype

Objective: Link frames and elements to simulate basic user interactions such as clicks and page navigation.

Steps:

1. **Create Frames:**
    a. Create two frames (for example, Home and Details) with distinct content.
    b. On the Home frame, add a button labeled "`Go to Details`".
2. **Link Frames:**
    a. Select the button on the Home frame.
    b. Click the blue node and drag it to the Details frame.
    c. In the interaction details, set the action to "`On click`" and the transition to "`Navigate to`" Details frame.
3. **Preview:**
    a. Click the `Present` button to view the prototype.
    b. Click the button to navigate from the Home frame to the Details frame.

Expected Outcome: When you click the button on the Home frame, it navigates to the Details frame.

Exercise 2: Adding Overlays and Modals

Objective: Use overlays to create a modal dialog that appears upon clicking a button.

Steps:

1. **Design Modal:**
    a. Create a new frame for the modal (for example, modal).
    b. Design the modal content, including a close button.
2. **Link Modal as Overlay:**
    a. On your main frame (for example, Home), add a button labeled "`Show Modal`".
    b. Select the button and link it to the Modal frame.

    c. Set the interaction to "`On click`" and action to "`Open overlay`".
    d. Position the overlay to the center of the screen.

3. **Close Overlay:**
    a. On the Modal frame, select the close button.
    b. Link the close button back to the Home frame or set the action to "`Close overlay`".

4. **Preview:**
    a. Click the **`Present`** button.
    b. Click the "`Show Modal`" button to display the modal overlay.
    c. Use the close button to dismiss the overlay.

Expected Outcome: Clicking the "`Show Modal`" button opens the modal overlay, and clicking the close button dismisses it.

Exercise 3: Interactive Components with States

Objective: Create a button with hover and pressed states for dynamic interactions.

Steps:

1. **Create Button Component:**
    a. Design a button with default styling.
    b. Convert the button to a component (*Ctrl/Cmd* + Alt + K).

2. **Add Variants:**
    a. In the component properties, add two variants: Hover and Pressed.
    b. Modify the styling for each state (for example, change color on hover, apply shadow on pressed).

3. **Define Interactions:**
    a. Select the default variant.
    b. Set an interaction to change to the Hover variant on hover.
    c. Set another interaction to change to the Pressed variant on click.

4. **Preview:**
    a. Click the `Present` button.
    b. Hover over and click the button to see the state changes.

Expected Outcome: The button changes appearance when hovered over and clicked, simulating real-world interactions.

Exercise 4: Creating a Scrollable Area

Objective: Design a scrollable content area within a frame.

Steps:

1. **Design Content:**
    a. Create a frame with a height smaller than the content inside it (for example, a long list of items).
    b. Ensure the content extends beyond the frame boundaries.
2. **Enable Scrolling:**
    a. Select the frame.
    b. In the properties panel, enable the "`Clip content`" option.
    c. Set the overflow behavior to "`Vertical scroll`".
3. **Preview:**
    a. Click the `Present` button.
    b. Scroll through the content within the frame.

Expected Outcome: The frame allows vertical scrolling, displaying content that extends beyond its initial boundaries.

Exercise 5: Fixed Position Elements

Objective: Keep certain elements (for example, headers or footers) fixed while the rest of the content scrolls.

Steps:

1. **Design Layout:**
    a. Create a frame with content that requires scrolling.
    b. Add a header or footer element at the top or bottom of the frame.

2. **Fix Position:**
    a. Select the header or footer element.
    b. In the properties panel, enable the "`Fix position when scrolling`" option.
3. **Preview:**
    a. Click the `Present` button.
    b. Scroll through the content and observe the fixed position of the header or footer.

Expected Outcome: The header or footer remains fixed in place while the rest of the content scrolls.

Exercise 6: Testing User Flows

Objective: Validate design assumptions by testing a complete user journey, from onboarding to task completion.

Steps:

1. **Create Multiple Frames:**
    a. Design frames representing different steps in the user journey (for example, Login, Dashboard, Profile).
2. **Link Frames to Create Flow:**
    a. Set up interactions to navigate between these frames (for example, login button navigates to Dashboard, profile icon navigates to Profile).
3. **Simulate User Journey:**
    a. Click the `Present` button.
    b. Navigate through the frames to simulate the user journey.
4. **Collect Feedback:**
    a. Share the prototype with team members or stakeholders.
    b. Gather feedback on the flow and usability.

Expected Outcome: A complete, navigable user journey that can be tested for usability and design effectiveness.

Exercise 7: Animating Transitions

Objective: Add animations between different states or screens to create a more engaging user experience.

Steps:

1. **Design States:**
    a. Create frames representing different states or screens (for example, Home and Details).
2. **Link Frames with Animation:**
    a. Select the trigger element on the Home frame.
    b. Link it to the Details frame.
    c. Set the interaction to "`On click`" and choose an animation (for example, "`Smart Animate`").
3. **Customize Animation:**
    a. Adjust the animation duration and easing for a smooth transition.
4. **Preview:**
    a. Click the `Present` button.
    b. Click the trigger element to see the animated transition.

Expected Outcome: A smooth, animated transition between states or screens, enhancing the user experience.

Conclusion

This chapter has provided an in-depth look at the iterative design process, emphasizing its crucial role in creating user-centered UI designs. We began by understanding the iterative methodology, highlighting how continuous refinement based on user feedback ensures the development of highly functional and user-friendly interfaces. The importance of user testing and gathering feedback was underscored, with various techniques such as usability testing, surveys, and interviews discussed to gain valuable insights into user behavior and preferences.

We then explored the foundational stages of UI design, focusing on wireframing and sketching as essential tools for planning and visualizing the interface. Prototyping in Figma was introduced, showcasing how interactive prototypes can simulate user interactions and validate design assumptions. Advanced prototyping techniques, including overlays, interactive components, and scrollable areas, were covered to enhance the realism and dynamism of prototypes. Testing user flows with Figma was emphasized as a method to validate the entire user journey, identify pain points, and measure task completion rates, all of which contribute to refining the design.

A practical case study demonstrated the iterative design process in action, providing a real-world example of how an e-commerce website redesign was approached and refined. Hands-on exercises were included to solidify the concepts covered, allowing readers to practice creating wireframes, prototyping, and testing user flows in Figma.

Transition to the next chapter

Having explored the iterative design process and advanced prototyping techniques in Figma, we have established a strong foundation for creating user-friendly interfaces through continuous feedback and refinement. We turn further to the critical aspect of collaboration in modern UI design. *Chapter 6, Advanced Design Techniques in Figma,* will delve into Figma's collaborative features and best practices for effective teamwork, enhancing communication and feedback among designers, developers, and stakeholders. This chapter will empower you to leverage Figma's real-time collaboration tools to create cohesive and integrated designs.

Recap of Key Points

- **Continuous Improvement:** In this chapter, we emphasized the cyclical nature of iterative design, which involves continuous refinement based on user feedback to improve user experience.
- **Gathering user feedback:** Covered various methods for gathering user feedback, including usability testing, surveys, interviews, and observations, and stressed the importance of clear testing objectives.
- **Defining a design vision:** Discussed the foundational stages of UI design, highlighting the importance of wireframing and sketching to plan and visualize interface structure and layout.
- **Prototyping in Figma:** Introduced basic prototyping in Figma, including creating interactive prototypes that simulate user interactions such as clicks, hovers, and swipes. Explored advanced techniques such as overlays, interactive components, scrollable areas, and fixed positioning to create more dynamic and realistic prototypes.
- **Testing user flows in Figma:** Emphasized the importance of validating entire user journeys by mapping out user flows, conducting usability testing, and measuring task completion rates to identify and resolve pain points.

CHAPTER 6
Advanced Design Techniques in Figma

Introduction

In this chapter, we will embark on an exploration of advanced design techniques that will empower you to take your creations to new heights. Figma is not just a tool for basic design tasks; it is a powerhouse of features that allow for intricate and visually stunning designs.

This chapter takes you into the realm of blending modes, effects, and advanced typography, unlocking the full potential of Figma's capabilities. These techniques will enable you to create designs that are not only visually captivating but also strategically crafted to convey your message effectively.

Through practical examples, step-by-step tutorials, and hands-on exercises, you will gain a deeper understanding of how to apply techniques to leverage these advanced features that elevate your designs. Whether you are a seasoned designer looking to expand your skillset or a newcomer eager to push the boundaries of your creativity, this chapter will equip you with the knowledge and tools needed to create impactful and memorable designs in Figma. So, let us dive in and explore the endless possibilities that await us in the world of advanced design techniques!

Structure

In this chapter, we will cover the following topics:

- Exploring Advanced Design Features in Figma
- Blending Modes
- Effects
- Advanced Typography
- Guidance to Apply Advanced Design Techniques in Real-World Projects

Exploring Advanced Design Features in Figma

In today's competitive design landscape, where innovation and creativity are paramount, mastering advanced features in Figma is not just advantageous–it is essential. Figma's advanced features offer a plethora of tools and capabilities that enable designers to push the boundaries of their creativity and craft truly exceptional designs. By delving into these advanced features, designers can create designs that not only meet but exceed user expectations, resulting in more engaging and memorable experiences for users. Mastering advanced features in Figma empowers designers to streamline their workflow and increase their productivity. With advanced techniques at their disposal, designers can work more efficiently, iterate on designs more quickly, and ultimately deliver projects on time and within budget. This efficiency not only benefits designers but also enhances collaboration within teams, as it allows for smoother communication and faster decision-making processes.

As the design industry continues to evolve and new trends and technologies emerge, staying ahead of the curve becomes increasingly important. By mastering advanced features in Figma, designers can future-proof their skillset and remain competitive in the ever-changing design landscape. Whether it is creating cutting-edge visual effects, implementing the latest typography trends, or experimenting with new design paradigms, having a deep understanding of advanced features in Figma enables designers to stay relevant and adaptable in a rapidly evolving industry.

Creating Complex Illustrations and Graphics: Blending Modes, Effects, and Typography

Blending modes in Figma are a powerful tool for controlling how layers interact with each other, allowing designers to achieve a wide range of visual effects. From simple overlays to complex blending operations, blending modes offer endless possibilities for creative expression. Effects such as shadows, gradients, and blurs add depth and dimensionality to designs, enhancing their visual appeal and realism. By mastering these effects, designers can create designs that not only look great but also feel immersive and engaging to users. Advanced typography techniques in Figma enable designers to manipulate text in sophisticated ways, allowing for greater control over typography and layout. By adjusting kerning, leading, and applying text effects, designers can create typography treatments that are both visually striking and highly readable. This level of control over typography is essential for creating designs that effectively communicate the intended message and evoke the desired emotional response from users. By the end of this chapter, readers will gain a deeper understanding of these advanced design techniques and learn how to apply them effectively in their own projects in Figma.

Blending Modes

Blending modes in Figma are a set of mathematical algorithms that determine how layers interact with each other when they overlap. Each blending mode produces a different result, allowing designers to create various visual effects and compositions. For example, blending modes can be used to blend colors together, create transparency effects, or enhance contrast and brightness. Understanding blending modes and their applications enables designers to make informed decisions about how to achieve specific visual effects in their designs and experiment with different blending modes.

There are several types of blending modes available, each producing different visuals.

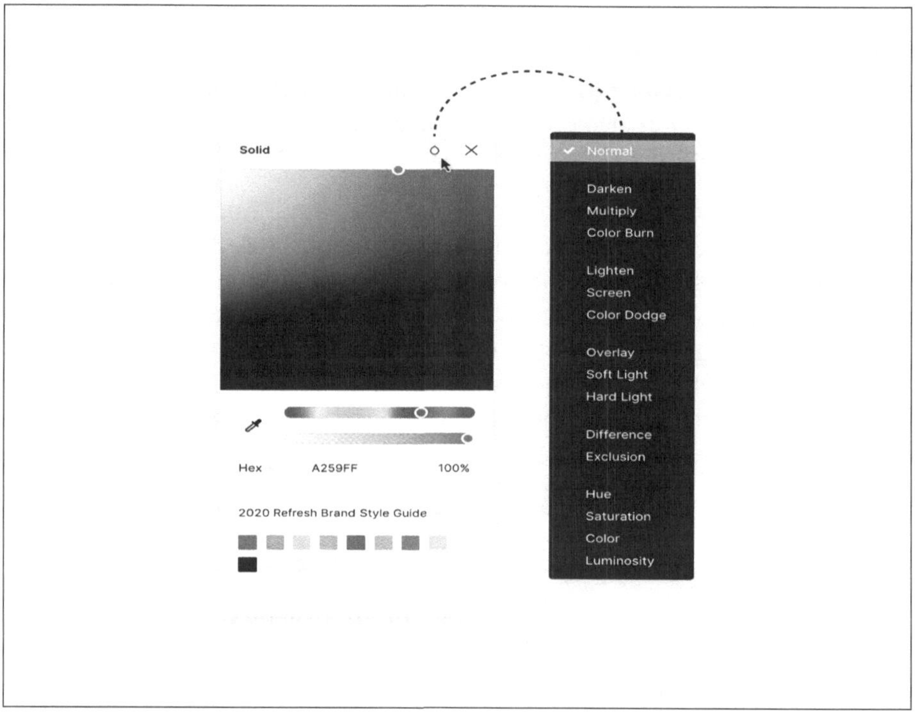

***Figure 6.1**: How to apply blending modes in Figma*

Here are some common blending modes found in Figma:

- **Normal:** This is the default blending mode where layers are simply stacked on top of each other without any blending or transparency effects.
- **Multiply:** This blending mode multiplies the colors of the layers together, resulting in darker colors. It is commonly used for creating shadows and adding depth to designs.
- **Screen:** The Screen blending mode lightens the colors of the layers, resulting in brighter colors. It is often used for creating highlights and glowing effects.

- **Overlay:** Overlay combines the Multiply and Screen blending modes, resulting in enhanced contrast and saturation. It is useful for adding dramatic effects to designs.
- **Darken:** This blending mode compares the colors of the layers and selects the darker color for each pixel. It is useful for removing white backgrounds or creating silhouette effects.
- **Lighten:** Lighten does the opposite of Darken, selecting the lighter color for each pixel. It is useful for creating transparent effects or blending layers with white backgrounds.
- **Difference:** Difference subtracts the colors of the layers from each other, resulting in inverted colors. It is often used for special effects and color corrections.
- **Color Burn:** Color Burn darkens the base color to reflect the blend color. It is useful for creating intense color effects and deepening shadows.
- **Color Dodge:** Color Dodge lightens the base color to reflect the blend color. It is useful for creating bright highlights and glowing effects.
- **Hue:** This blending mode preserves the luminance and saturation of the base color while adopting the hue of the blend color. It is useful for applying color adjustments without affecting brightness or saturation.

Hands-On Exercises for Experimenting with Blending Modes

Designers can start by creating simple shapes or text layers and applying different blending modes to see how they affect the appearance of the layers. For example, they can experiment with blending modes such as "**`Overlay`**," "**`Soft Light`**," and "**`Hard Light`**" to see how they change the colors and contrast of the layers. Designers can also try combining multiple layers with different blending modes to create more complex effects. By engaging in hands-on exercises, designers can develop a practical understanding of blending modes and how to use them creatively in their designs. Following are some exercises to help you gain a better understanding of how blending modes work in Figma and how they can be used creatively to enhance your designs.

***Figure 6.2**: Different types of blending modes and their effects*

Creating a Shadow Effect

1. Start by creating a simple shape, such as a square or circle, on the canvas.
2. Duplicate the shape layer to create a copy.
3. Apply a dark color to the duplicate shape layer.
4. Experiment with different blending modes, such as Multiply or Overlay, to see how they affect the appearance of the duplicate shape layer.
5. Adjust the opacity of the duplicate shape layer to fine-tune the shadow effect.
6. Once satisfied with the result, group the original shape layer and the shadow layer together to create a cohesive design.

Adding Texture to a Background:

1. Create a new rectangle shape that covers the entire canvas to serve as the background.
2. Import an image or texture file into Figma and place it on top of the background rectangle.

3. Experiment with different blending modes, such as Overlay or Soft Light, to blend the texture with the background.
4. Adjust the opacity of the texture layer to control the intensity of the texture effect.
5. Use masking techniques, such as applying a shape mask to the texture layer, to create custom texture effects.
6. Once satisfied with the result, group the background rectangle and the texture layer together to keep the design organized.

Creating a Double Exposure Effect:

1. Import two different images into Figma and place them on the canvas.
2. Resize and position the images so that they overlap each other partially.
3. Experiment with different blending modes, such as Screen or Multiply, to blend the images together and create a double exposure effect.
4. Adjust the opacity of the images to control the intensity of the effect.
5. Use masking techniques, such as applying a shape mask to one of the images, to create custom blending effects.
6. Once satisfied with the result, group the images together to keep the design organized.

Effects in Figma

Effects in Figma are powerful tools that allow designers to add depth, dimensionality, and visual interest to their designs. They include a variety of options such as shadows, gradients, blurs, and more. Effects can be applied to individual layers or groups of layers, allowing for precise control over the appearance of design elements. By using different types of effects listed below, designers can create designs that are visually compelling:

Shadows: Shadows add depth and realism to design elements by simulating the appearance of light casting shadows. They can be adjusted in terms of color, opacity, blur radius, and angle to achieve different effects.

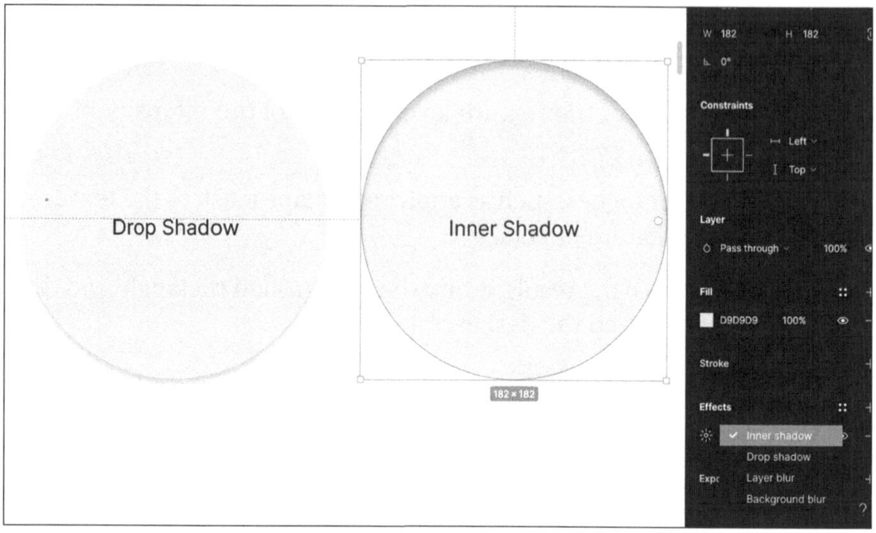

Figure 6.3: *Shadow effects in Figma*

Some examples include:

- **Drop Shadow:** Adds a shadow behind the layer to simulate depth and elevation. It can be customized in terms of color, opacity, blur radius, and angle.
- **Inner Shadow**: This effect adds a shadow inside the layer, giving the appearance of depth and dimension. Designers can adjust parameters such as color, blur radius, and angle to control the intensity and direction of the shadow.

Gradients: Gradients allow designers to create smooth transitions between colors, adding visual interest and dimension to design elements. They can be linear or radial, and their colors, opacity, and angle can be customized.

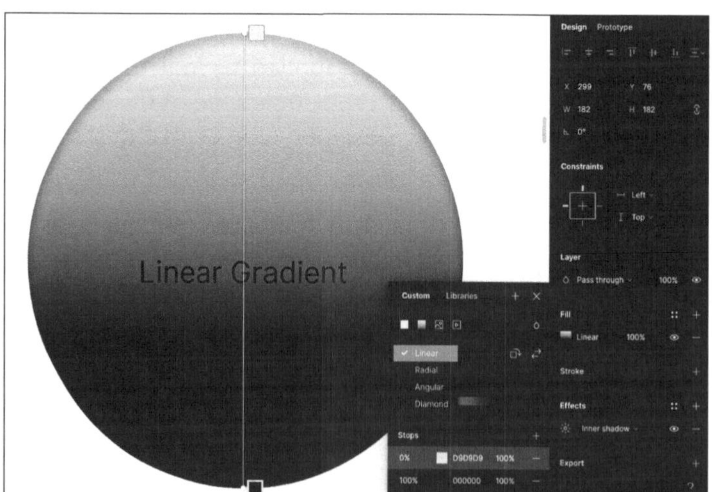

Figure 6.4: *Types of gradients in Figma under fill*

Some examples include:

- **Linear Gradient:** Creates a smooth transition between two or more colors in a straight line. The angle and position of the gradient can be adjusted.
- **Radial Gradient:** Creates a smooth transition between two or more colors in a circular pattern. The center and size of the gradient can be adjusted.
- **Angular Gradient:** This gradient type creates a smooth transition between colors radiating from a center point, following a circular pattern. It is useful for creating radial designs or circular elements with dynamic color shifts.
- **Diamond Gradient:** With this gradient style, colors transition from the center of the layer outward, forming a diamond-shaped pattern. It offers a unique aesthetic for backgrounds, logos, or decorative elements.

Blurs: Blurs soften the edges of design elements, creating a sense of depth and focus. They can be applied to individual layers or entire groups of layers, and their intensity can be adjusted to achieve different effects.

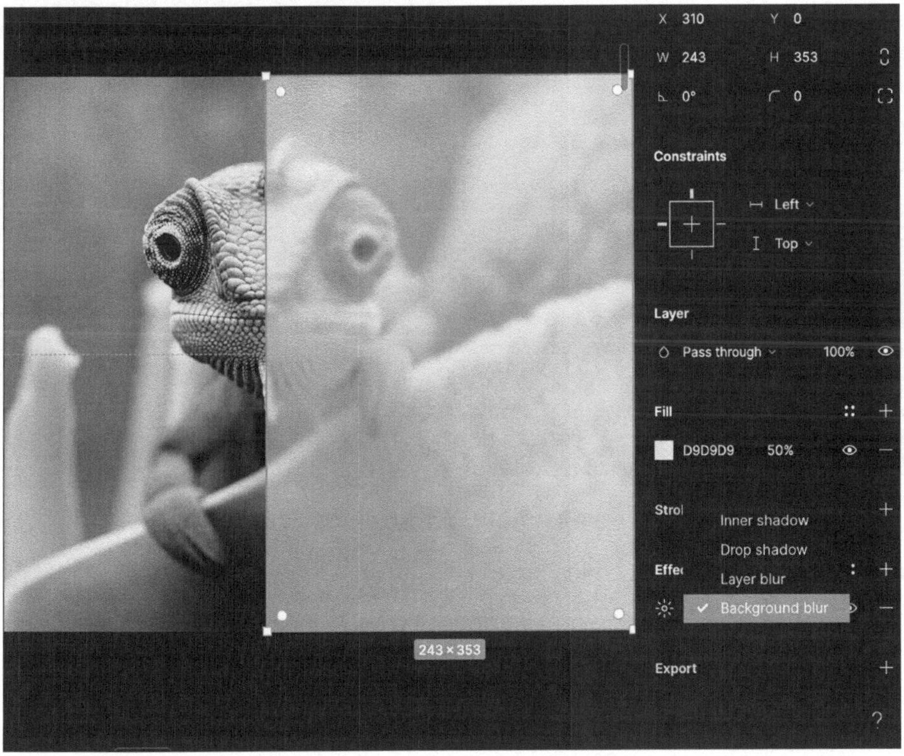

Figure 6.5: *Types of blurs in Figma*

Some examples include:

- **Background Blur:** Applies a blur effect to the background behind the layer, simulating depth of field. It is useful for creating UI overlays or pop-up dialogs.

- **Layer Blur:** Applies a blur effect to the entire layer, including its contents. This can be useful for creating frosted glass or frosted acrylic effects. You can get this effect by superimposing two images but remember that you should have an opacity applied to the layer to apply a layer blur effect.

Other Layer Effects and Styles: From adding subtle shadows and glows to creating intricate patterns and textures, designers can customize every aspect of their layers to achieve the desired look and feel. There are multiple tutorials available in the Figma community with options for embossing, pattern fills, and customizable borders. Figma empowers designers to create polished and professional designs with ease.

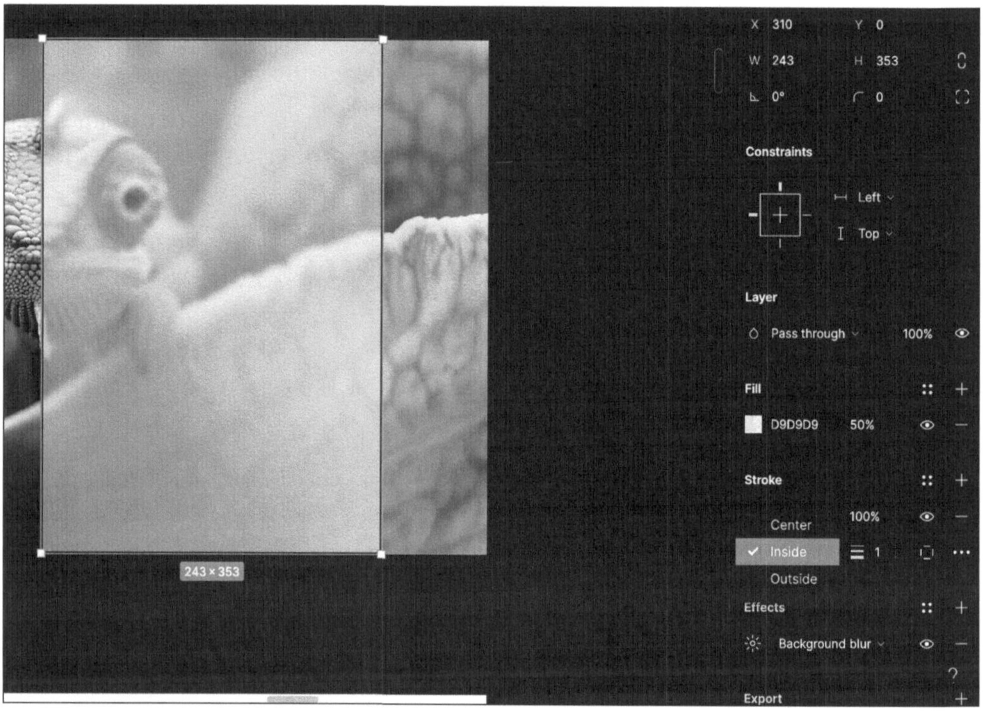

Figure 6.6: *Stroke styles in Figma*

Some additional effects and styles include:

- **Border Styles:** Allows you to apply various border styles to layers, including solid, dashed, and dotted lines. You can customize the color, width, and corner radius of the border.
- **Fill Styles:** Allows you to apply solid colors, gradients, or images as fills to layers. You can also adjust the opacity and blending mode of the fill.

Tips for Applying Effects to Enhance Designs

To apply effects in Figma, select the desired layer or group of layers, then access the "`Effects`" panel located within the properties panel. Here, designers can choose from a variety of effects such as shadows, gradients, and blurs, and fine-tune their parameters to achieve the desired visual effect. Experimenting with different settings and combinations of effects is key to finding the perfect look for your design, allowing for creative exploration and customization.

Here are some tips for using effects effectively in Figma:

- **Use shadows sparingly**: Shadows can add depth and dimension to key design elements, but overuse can lead to cluttered or distracting visuals. Apply shadows selectively to important elements to create emphasis and hierarchy within design.
- **Experiment with gradients**: Gradients offer a versatile tool for creating smooth color transitions and visual effects. Experiment with different gradient types, angles, and color combinations to achieve interesting color effects and dynamic visual transitions in your designs.
- **Utilize blurs for focus and depth**: Blurs can be used to soften the edges of design elements, creating a sense of focus or depth of field. Use blurs strategically to draw attention to focal points, simulate motion, or create a sense of depth in your designs. Experiment with different blur intensities and types to achieve the desired visual effect.

Hands-On Exercises with Effects Using a Real-World Project

In real-world projects, designers often use effects to enhance the visual appeal and usability of their designs. For example, a designer might use shadows to make buttons appear raised or interactive, gradients to create depth in a background, or blurs to soften the edges of a photograph. By studying real-world examples, designers can gain inspiration and insight into how effects can be used creatively to achieve specific design goals.

Elevating Brand Identity with Visual Effects in Mobile Banking App

Let us consider a hypothetical scenario given under to help you communicate your Figma designs as a case study. A prominent mobile banking app sought to differentiate itself from competitors and reinforce its brand identity through design. The existing app interface lacked visual appeal and failed to convey the brand's modern and innovative image, leading to stagnant user engagement and limited market penetration.

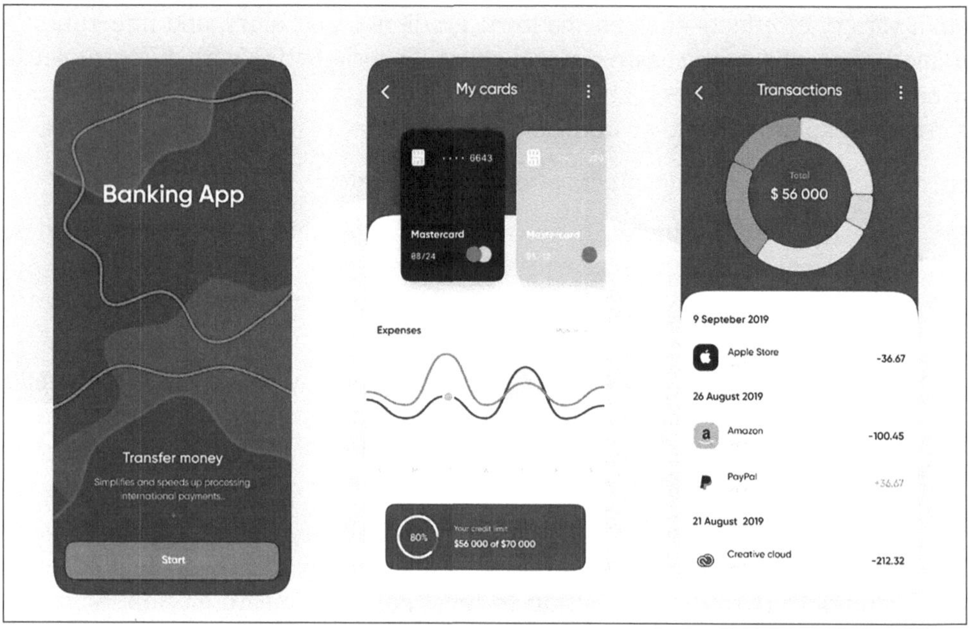

***Figure 6.7:** An example of a mobile banking app*

Objective: The primary objective was to redesign the mobile banking app interface to reflect the brand's identity and values while enhancing the overall user experience. The focus was on integrating visual effects strategically to create a visually stunning and user-friendly interface that resonated with the target audience.

Implementation:

- **Dynamic Gradients for Brand Consistency:** Vibrant and dynamic gradients were incorporated into various elements of the app interface, including headers, buttons, and backgrounds. These gradients reflected the brand's color palette and added a modern and dynamic touch to the design, reinforcing brand identity and consistency.
- **Subtle Animations for Delightful Interaction:** Subtle animations and transitions were introduced throughout the app interface to provide feedback and enhance user interaction. Smooth transitions between screens, subtle button animations, and micro-interactions added a layer of delight to the user experience, making interactions more engaging and intuitive.
- **Soft Shadows for Depth and Hierarchy:** Soft drop shadows were applied to key elements such as cards, buttons, and icons to create a sense of depth and hierarchy. These shadows helped differentiate elements from the background and provided visual cues for interaction, thus enhancing usability and clarity.
- **Blur Effects for Focus and Emphasis:** Gaussian blur effects were strategically applied to background elements behind important content sections, such as

transaction details and account summaries. These blur effects helped draw attention to the foreground content and provided a visual hierarchy, thus improving readability and focus.

Results: The redesigned mobile banking app interface received overwhelmingly positive feedback from users and stakeholders, leading to a significant improvement in key performance metrics. User engagement increased by 30%, with users spending more time navigating the app and exploring its features. App retention rates saw a notable improvement of 25%, indicating higher user satisfaction and loyalty. The visually stunning design and enhanced user experience contributed to 35% increase in app downloads and installations, expanding the app's user base and market reach.

Conclusion: By strategically integrating visual effects such as gradients, animations, shadows, and blur effects, the mobile banking app was able to elevate its brand identity and create a visually stunning and user-friendly interface. The successful implementation of these effects not only reinforced the brand's image but also improved user engagement, retention, and app performance.

Advanced Typography in Figma

Advanced typography techniques encompass a range of practices aimed at enhancing the visual appeal and readability of text in design projects. This includes techniques such as kerning, leading, tracking, and text effects, all of which play a crucial role in creating compelling typography compositions. By mastering these techniques, designers can effectively convey hierarchy, emphasis, and mood through typography, elevating the overall design aesthetic.

Typography Features

Figma offers a range of features and tools to support advanced typography techniques, empowering designers to create sophisticated and visually engaging text compositions.

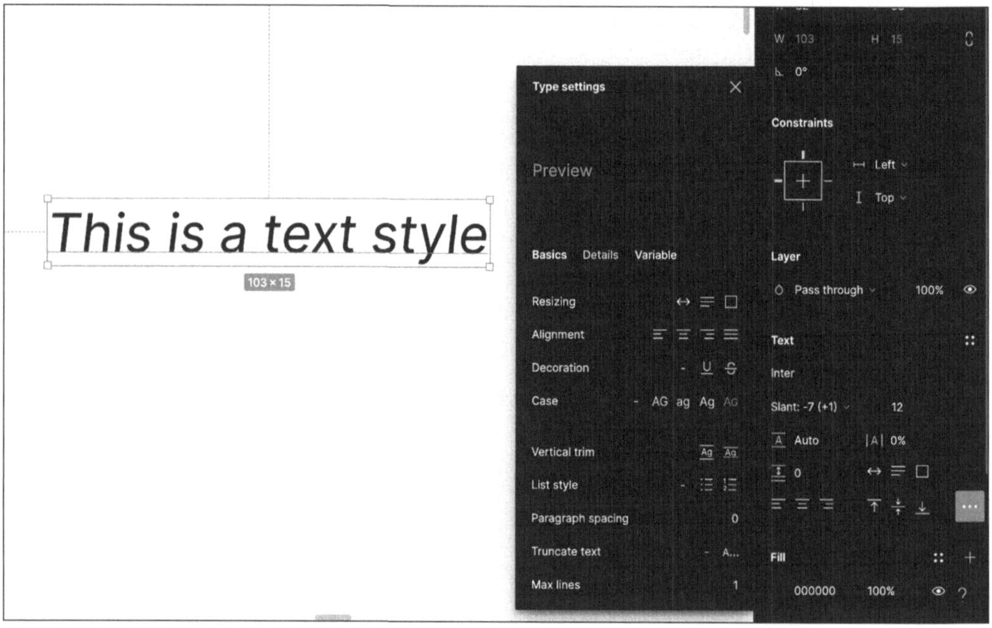

Figure 6.8: *An example of a variable font setting where users can access multiple options to manipulate typography and text styles in user interface. It can be accessed from the text panel*

Some of the key features include:

- **Typography Panel:** Figma's typography panel provides comprehensive controls for adjusting text properties such as font family, font size, weight, alignment, and line spacing (leading). Designers can easily customize text styles to achieve the desired typographic effect.
- **Character Spacing:** Figma allows designers to adjust the spacing between individual characters (kerning) and groups of characters (tracking) to fine-tune the visual appearance of text. Precise control over character spacing helps improve readability and visual consistency.
- **Line Height Adjustment:** Designers can adjust the spacing between lines of text (leading) to improve readability and visual harmony in typography compositions. Figma offers both automatic and manual line height adjustment options, giving designers flexibility in controlling text density and spacing.
- **Font Styles and Variants:** Figma supports a wide range of font styles and variants, including regular, bold, italic, and variable fonts. Designers can easily switch between font styles and variants to create typographic hierarchy and emphasis within their designs.
- **Text Effects:** Figma enables designers to apply various text effects such as shadows, outlines, and gradients to add visual interest and emphasis to typography. These effects can be customized and adjusted to create unique and impactful treatments.

- **Web Fonts and Variable Fonts:** Figma supports the use of web fonts and variable fonts, allowing designers to access a vast library of fonts and styles for their typography needs. Variable fonts offer additional flexibility by allowing designers to adjust font properties such as weight, width, and optical size dynamically.
- **Typography Styles and Libraries:** Designers can create and organize typography styles and libraries within Figma, making it easy to maintain consistency and efficiency in typography across multiple design projects. Typography styles can be saved and reused, streamlining the design process and ensuring brand consistency.

Tips for Manipulating Text Effectively Using Figma's Typography Tools

In Figma, designers have access to a comprehensive set of typography tools that enable precise control over text properties. Utilizing features such as character spacing, line height adjustment, and font styles, designers can manipulate text effectively to achieve desired typographic effects. Additionally, leveraging Figma's support for web fonts and variable fonts allows for greater flexibility and creativity in typography design. Here are some tips for getting the most out of Figma's typography features:

- **Use Consistent Typography Styles:** Establishing consistent typography styles across your designs helps maintain visual coherence and reinforces brand identity. Create predefined text styles for headings, body text, and other elements to ensure consistency throughout your project.
- **Pay Attention to Hierarchy:** Establish a clear hierarchy within your typography by varying font sizes, weights, and styles to indicate different levels of importance. Use larger font sizes and bolder weights for headings and titles, while reserving lighter weights and smaller sizes for body text and secondary content.
- **Optimize Line Spacing:** Adjusting line spacing (leading) can significantly impact the readability and visual appearance of text. Experiment with different line height values to find the optimal spacing for your typography compositions. Aim for a balance between readability and visual harmony, avoiding excessively tight or loose line spacing.
- **Fine-Tune Character Spacing:** Pay attention to the spacing between individual characters (kerning) and groups of characters (tracking) to ensure optimal readability and visual consistency. Use Figma's typography panel to adjust kerning and tracking values as needed, especially for display text and logo designs.
- **Consider Typography Accessibility:** When designing text elements, consider accessibility guidelines to ensure that your typography is legible for all users,

including those with visual impairments. Choose fonts with good readability and sufficient contrast against the background and avoid using text sizes that are too small or too light.

- **Experiment with Text Effects:** Explore Figma's text effects, such as shadows, outlines, and gradients, to add visual interest and emphasis to your typography. However, use these effects judiciously and avoid overdoing it, as excessive effects can distract from the content and detract from readability.
- **Test Across Devices and Platforms:** Test your typography designs across different devices and platforms to ensure that they display correctly and maintain visual consistency. Consider how typography renders on various screen sizes and resolutions and make adjustments as needed to optimize legibility and appearance.

Hands-On Exercises for Practicing Advanced Typography

By engaging in these hands-on exercises, designers can gain practical experience in applying advanced typography techniques within Figma, ultimately enhancing their ability to create visually compelling and effective typography compositions. Let us cover three main areas to master typography:

- **Kerning and Tracking Practice:** Experiment with adjusting the spacing between individual characters (kerning) and groups of characters (tracking) to achieve optimal spacing and readability. Use Figma's typography panel to adjust kerning and tracking values and observe the impact on text appearance.
- **Leading Adjustment Exercise:** Practice adjusting line spacing (leading) to improve readability and visual harmony in typography compositions. Experiment with different leading values to find the optimal balance between line spacing and text density.
- **Text Effects Exploration:** Explore various text effects such as text shadows, outlines, and gradients to add visual interest and emphasis to typography. Experiment with different effect settings and combinations to create unique and impactful text treatments.

Here are three exercises to help you sharpen your typography techniques:

1. **Character Spacing Exploration:**
    a. Start by creating a simple text box in Figma and entering a phrase of your choice.

    b. Experiment with adjusting the character spacing (kerning) to see how it affects the spacing between individual letters.

c. Try increasing and decreasing the character spacing to observe the visual impact on the text. Pay attention to how adjusting the kerning affects the overall readability and appearance of the text.

d. Practice fine-tuning the character spacing until you achieve an optimal balance between readability and visual aesthetics.

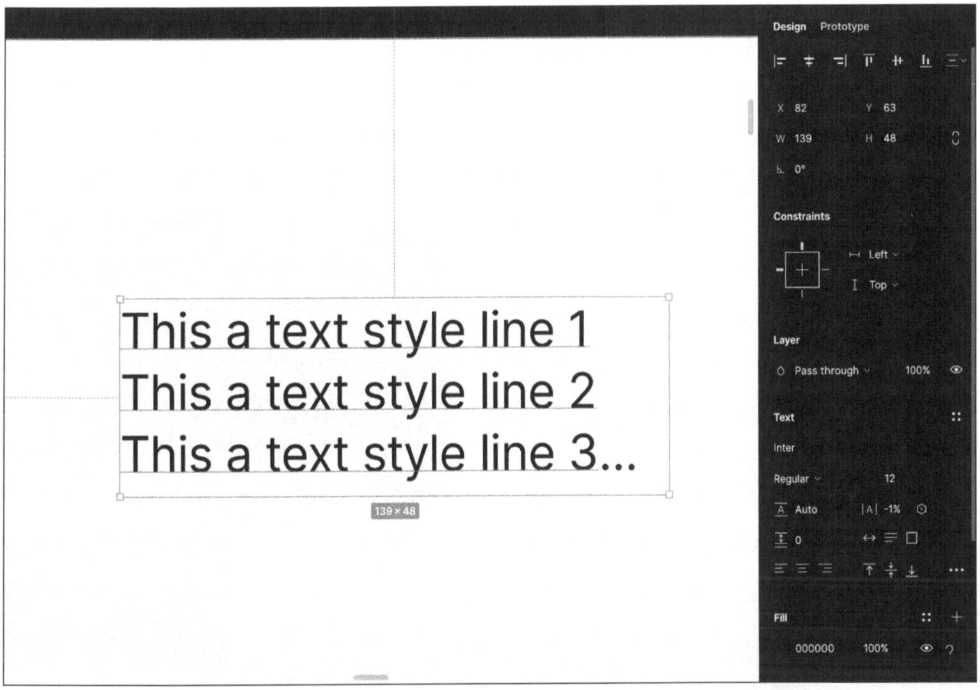

***Figure 6.9**: An example of character spacing and line height controls*

2. **Line Height Adjustment Exercise:**

    a. Create another text box in Figma and type out a paragraph of lorem ipsum text or any other content.

    b. Experiment with adjusting the line height (leading) to see how it affects the spacing between lines of text.

    c. Try increasing and decreasing the line height to observe the visual impact on the text layout. Pay attention to how adjusting the leading affects the overall readability and visual flow of the text.

    d. Practice finding the ideal line height that provides sufficient spacing between lines without causing the text to look too cramped or too spread out.

3. **Typography Effects Application:**
   a. Create a new text box in Figma and enter a word or short phrase.
   b. Experiment with applying various text effects such as shadows, outlines, or gradients to the text.
   c. Explore different effect settings and combinations to see how they enhance the visual appearance of the typography.
   d. Practice applying text effects creatively to achieve unique and visually compelling typography designs. Experiment with layering multiple effects or using effects selectively to emphasize specific parts of the text.

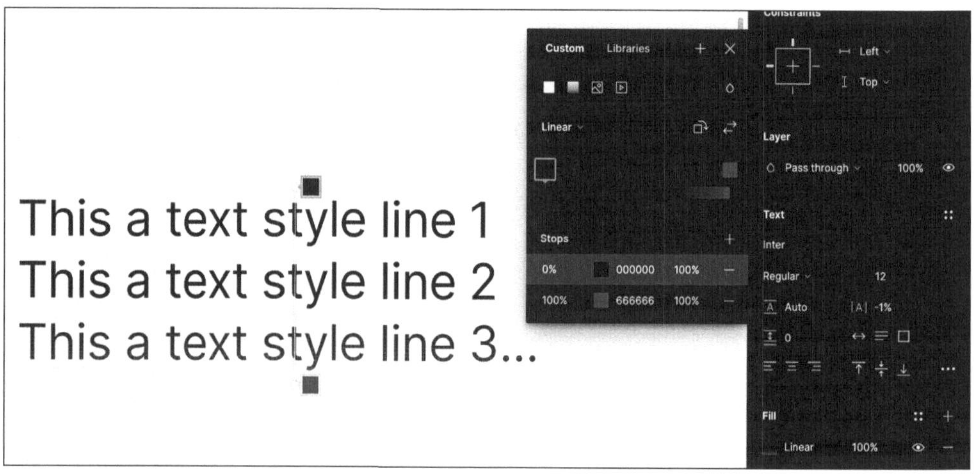

Figure 6.10: *An example of typography effects in Figma, such as gradient fill*

Accessibility Considerations

When using advanced design techniques such as blending modes and effects, accessibility should be a primary consideration to ensure that your designs remain usable for all users, including those with visual impairments. Here are key points to keep in mind:

- **High Contrast for Visual Clarity:** Blending modes and effects can create complex visual interactions between layers, but these interactions can reduce contrast, making text and important elements harder to read. Always check that there is sufficient contrast between text, backgrounds, and graphical elements to ensure readability, especially for users with low vision or color blindness.
- **Avoiding Overuse of Visual Effects:** While blending modes and effects such as drop shadows, glows, or gradients can add visual appeal, overusing them can create visual clutter, making it harder for users to focus on key information.

Simplicity is often more accessible, so use effects sparingly and ensure they do not interfere with the clarity of important content.

- **Testing with Color Blindness Simulators:** Some blending modes and color effects can be difficult for users with color blindness to perceive correctly. Use color blindness simulators to ensure that color combinations and effects are legible for all users or offer alternative text or symbols that convey the same information.
- **Providing Clear Focus Indicators:** Effects such as blurred backgrounds or complex patterns can obscure focus areas, which are crucial for keyboard and screen reader users. Make sure that interactive elements such as buttons and links have clear visual focus indicators (such as borders or highlights) and that they stand out from the background, regardless of blending effects.
- **Ensure Proper Layer Hierarchy:** Complex visual effects and blending modes can sometimes create confusion about the hierarchy of elements. Ensure that the most important content, such as buttons or headings, remains prominent and does not get lost in visually complex layers. This can be achieved by controlling opacity, ensuring contrast, or using subtle effects that do not overpower the content.

Accessibility of Animations: If you are using animation or transitions in combination with effects, ensure that these are not distracting or disorienting. Provide users with the option to disable animations if they have conditions like motion sensitivity, as recommended by WCAG (Web Content Accessibility Guidelines).

Guidance to Apply Advanced Design Techniques in Real-World Projects

Guidance on incorporating advanced typography techniques into real-world projects can elevate the visual appeal and effectiveness of your designs. Here are some tips to help you integrate these techniques seamlessly:

- **Start with a Clear Vision:** Before diving into your project, take some time to define your goals and vision. Consider the overall tone, style, and message you want to convey through your typography. Having a clear vision will guide your decision-making process as you incorporate advanced techniques.
- **Choose the Right Typeface:** Selecting the appropriate typeface is crucial for achieving your desired aesthetic and conveying your message effectively. Experiment with different fonts to find one that aligns with the mood and personality of your project. Consider factors such as readability, style, and compatibility with other design elements.
- **Establish a Visual Hierarchy:** Establishing a clear visual hierarchy is essential for guiding the viewer's attention and organizing information effectively.

Use a combination of font sizes, weights, and styles to differentiate between headings, subheadings, body text, and other elements. Ensure that important information stands out while maintaining overall coherence and readability.

- **Experiment with Typography Effects:** Incorporate advanced typography effects such as shadows, gradients, and textures to add depth and visual interest to your designs. Experiment with different effect settings and combinations to create unique and dynamic typography compositions. However, be mindful of not overdoing it – use effects judiciously to enhance rather than detract from your message.
- **Consider Context and Audience:** When applying advanced typography techniques, consider the context in which your design will be viewed and the preferences of your target audience. Tailor your typography choices and effects to suit the specific needs and expectations of your audience. Keep accessibility in mind to ensure that your typography is legible and inclusive for all users.
- **Iterate and Refine:** Design is an iterative process, so do not be afraid to experiment, iterate, and refine your typography designs. Solicit feedback from peers, mentors, or online communities to gain valuable insights and perspectives. Use this feedback to iterate on your designs, making adjustments as needed to achieve the desired outcome.
- **Document Your Process:** Throughout your project, document your process, including design decisions, challenges faced, and lessons learned. Keeping a design journal or project log can help you track your progress and reflect on your growth as a designer. Additionally, documenting your process can serve as a valuable resource for future projects and portfolio presentations.

Conclusion

In this chapter, we delved into advanced design techniques within Figma, aiming to empower readers with the tools and knowledge needed to create visually stunning designs. Beginning with an overview of the chapter, we emphasized the importance of mastering advanced features in Figma, setting the stage for a deeper exploration of blending modes, effects, and advanced typography.

The exploration of blending modes provided readers with insights into their applications and practical examples in design. Through hands-on exercises, readers were encouraged to experiment with blending modes, thus fostering creativity and sparking innovative design solutions. Additionally, the examination of effects such as shadows, gradients, and blurs offered insights into enhancing designs with depth and dimensionality, with real-world case studies providing concrete examples of their application.

In the section on advanced typography, readers learned valuable tips for manipulating text effectively using Figma's typography tools. Hands-on exercises provided opportunities to practice advanced typography skills and apply them in practical design scenarios, empowering readers to craft typography-driven designs with confidence. As we conclude this chapter, readers are encouraged to leverage the knowledge and skills acquired here in their design practice, unlocking new possibilities for creative expression and contributing to the creation of impactful designs in Figma and beyond.

Transition to the next chapter

Having explored the intricacies of advanced design techniques in Figma, we now turn our attention to the collaborative capabilities of this versatile platform. In *Chapter 7, Collaboration and Team Workflows*, we will delve into how Figma revolutionizes the way design teams collaborate, share feedback, and iterate on designs in real-time. From sharing prototypes to conducting design reviews, we will explore the myriad features that make Figma a powerhouse for collaborative design work. Join us as we discover how Figma streamlines teamwork and enhances productivity in the design process.

Recap of Key Points

- **Introduction to Advanced Design Techniques:** We emphasized the importance of mastering advanced features in Figma and provided a brief overview of blending modes, effects, and advanced typography.
- **Blending Modes:** Readers gained insights into blending modes and their applications, experimented with practical examples in design, and engaged in hands-on exercises to explore blending modes creatively.
- **Effects:** The exploration of effects such as shadows, gradients, and blurs offered insights into enhancing designs with depth and dimensionality. Real-world case studies demonstrated the application of effects in design projects.
- **Advanced Typography:** Readers learned valuable tips for manipulating text effectively using Figma's typography tools. Hands-on exercises enabled them to practice advanced typography skills and apply them in practical design scenarios.

CHAPTER 7
Collaboration and Team Workflows

Introduction

This chapter delves into the collaborative features of Figma and explores best practices for effective teamwork within the platform. It begins by highlighting the importance of collaboration in design projects and how Figma facilitates real-time collaboration among team members, regardless of their location. Readers learn how to leverage Figma's collaborative features, such as commenting, sharing, and version control, thereby improving communication and workflow management. Practical examples demonstrate how team members can collaborate on design projects simultaneously, providing feedback, making revisions, and tracking changes in real time.

The chapter also covers strategies for managing design iterations and version control within Figma. Readers gain insights into how to organize files, create design systems, and maintain consistency across projects, ensuring efficient collaboration and smooth project delivery. Through case studies and examples, readers learn how teams can effectively collaborate on complex design projects using Figma, from initial concept development to final execution. By mastering collaboration and team workflows in Figma, readers are empowered to work more efficiently and effectively with colleagues, ultimately leading to better outcomes.

Structure

In this chapter, we will cover the following topics:

- Sharing Prototypes (*Interactive Designs*)
- Gathering Feedback
- Real-Time Collaboration
- Version Control
- Best Practices for Collaborating in Figma

Sharing Prototypes

Sharing prototypes, that is, clickable interactive user interface designs, is a crucial aspect of the process, enabling designers to effectively communicate their vision and gather valuable feedback from stakeholders and team members. Figma's powerful sharing capabilities allow you to generate shareable links, customize permissions, and embed prototypes into various platforms. This ensures that everyone involved in the project can easily access, review, and interact with the user interface designs, fostering collaboration and accelerating the design iteration process. With Figma, sharing prototypes becomes efficient, enhancing transparency and engagement throughout the project lifecycle.

Generating Prototypes

Generating Shareable Links: Figma allows you to generate shareable links for your prototypes, making it easy to distribute your work to team members and stakeholders.

Generating shareable links is straightforward:

1. Click the "`Share`" button in the top-right corner.

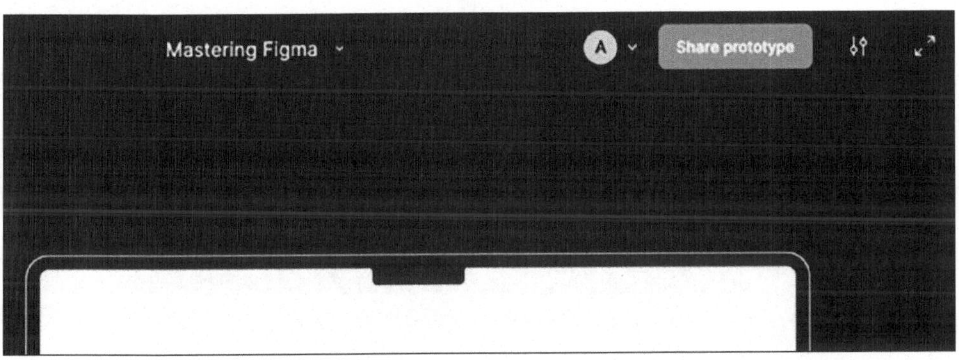

Figure 7.1: *Share Prototype button in Figma*

2. Set the appropriate permissions.

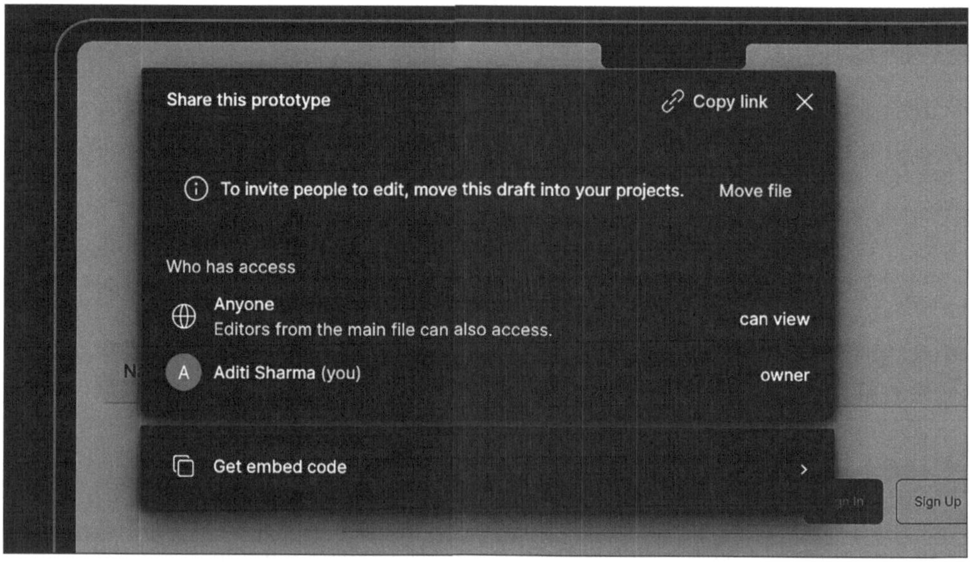

Figure 7.2: *Setting constraints for sharing in Figma*

3. Copy the generated link and share it with your team.

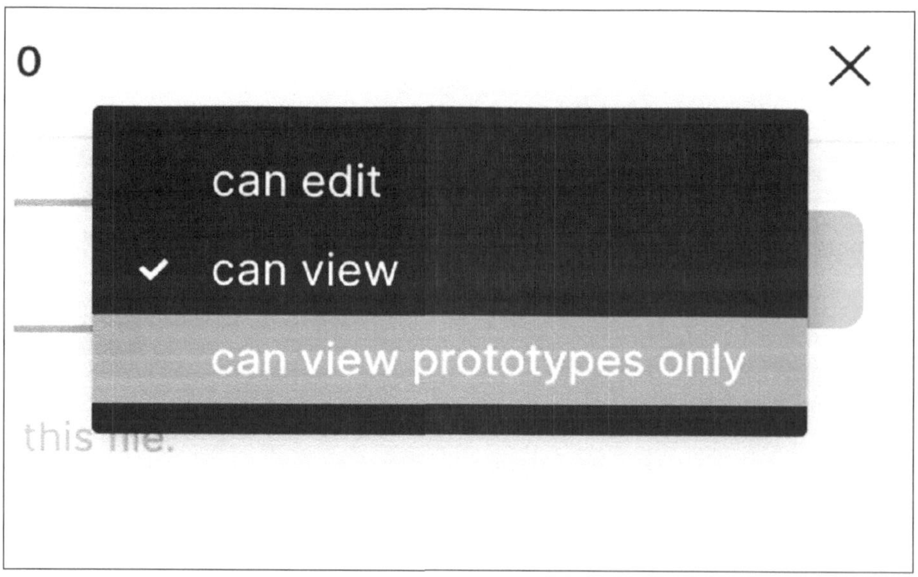

Figure 7.3: *Permission types for prototypes in Figma*

These links can be customized with different levels of access:

- **View-Only:** Allows recipients to view the prototype without making any changes.
- **Comment**: Enables recipients to leave comments and suggestions without editing the design.

- **Edit**: Grants full access to make changes to the prototype.

Embed Options

Figma also provides options to embed prototypes into web pages or presentations. This feature is particularly useful for showcasing user interface designs in various contexts, such as client presentations or internal documentation.

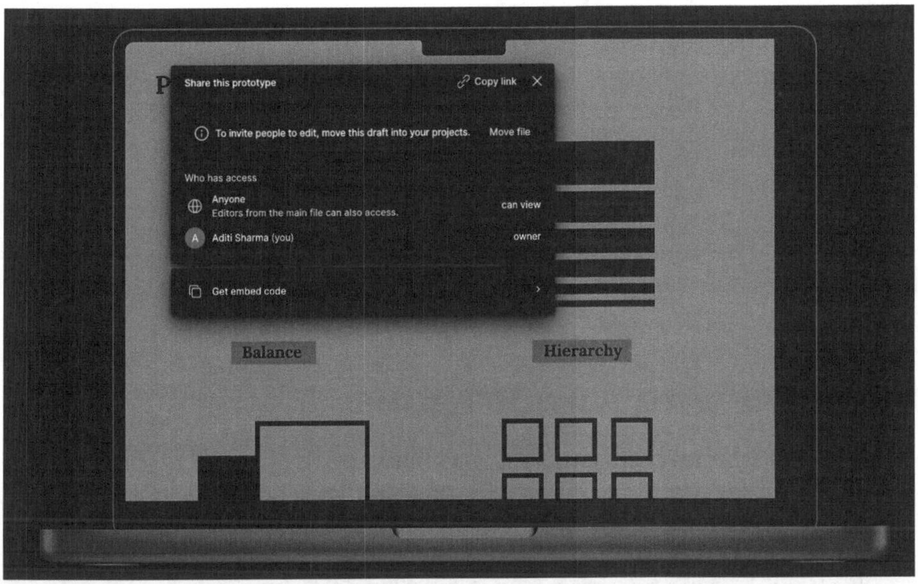

Figure 7.4: *Embedding Prototype Options in Figma*

You can get code which can be copied and inserted into any website using Figma.

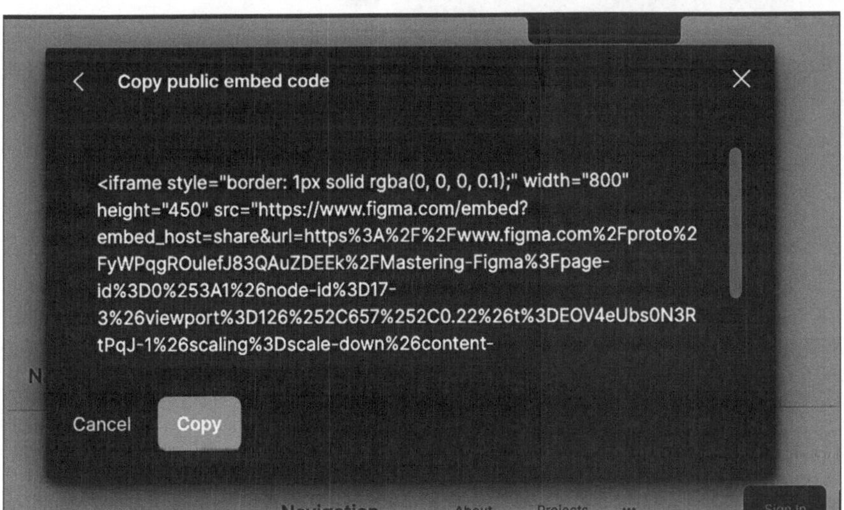

Figure 7.5: *Copying code from Figma to embed when building websites/apps*

To embed a prototype:

1. Click the "**Share**" button and select the "**Embed**" tab.
2. Customize the embed settings (size, permissions).
3. Copy the embed code and paste it into your web page or presentation.

Gathering Feedback

Gathering feedback is an essential part of the design process, ensuring that your work aligns with user needs and stakeholder expectations. Figma makes this process effective by enabling real-time comments and annotations directly on your user interface designs. Stakeholders and team members can leave precise and actionable feedback, fostering a collaborative environment and streamlining the review process. By addressing and resolving comments within Figma, designers can efficiently iterate on their work, leading to better-informed design decisions and improved final products.

Comments and Annotations

One of Figma's most powerful features is the ability to leave comments and annotations directly on the prototype. This fosters real-time feedback and discussion, streamlining the review process.

Figure 7.6: *Step-by-step guide to adding a new comment in Figma*

To leave a comment:

1. Select the "**`Comment`**" tool from the toolbar.
2. Click on the area of the prototype where you want to leave a comment.
3. Type your feedback and click "**`Post`**."
4. Team members and stakeholders can reply to comments, creating a threaded discussion that is easy to follow. This feature ensures that all feedback is documented and easily accessible within the design file.

Resolving Comments

Once feedback has been addressed, comments can be resolved to keep the discussion organized.

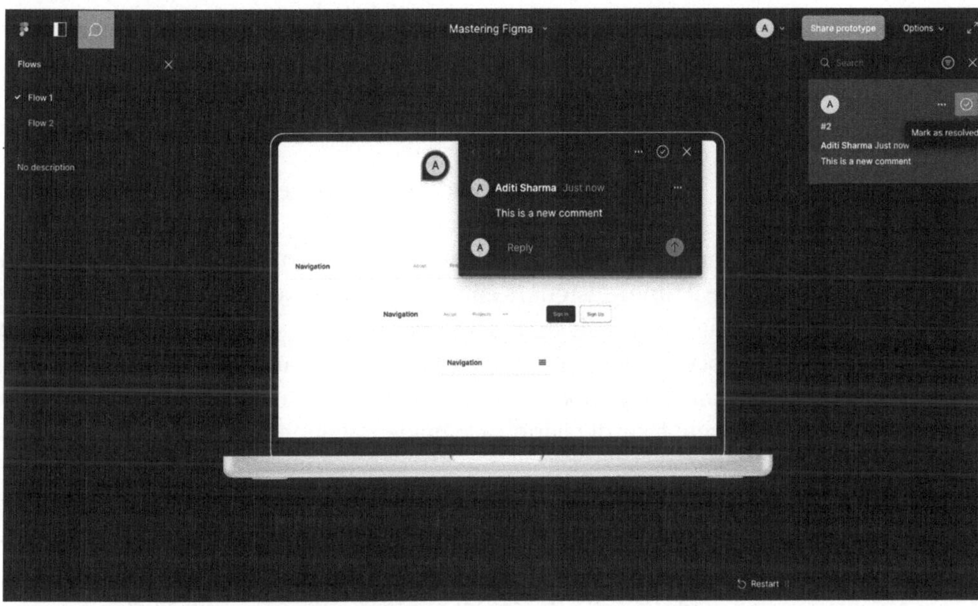

Figure 7.7: *Resolving a comment in Figma*

To resolve a comment:

1. Click on the comment.
2. Select "**`Resolve`**."
3. The comment will be marked as resolved, and the discussion thread will be collapsed.
4. This feature helps in keeping track of changes and ensuring that all feedback has been addressed.

Real-Time Collaboration

Figma's real-time collaboration features revolutionize the way design teams work together, facilitating collaboration regardless of geographical location.

Here is how Figma empowers teams to collaborate in real time:

Co-Editing

Figma allows multiple team members to work on the same prototype simultaneously, enabling true collaboration in real time. Whether designers are working from the same office or across different time zones, co-editing ensures that everyone can contribute to the project efficiently. As team members make edits, their cursors and changes are visible to others, fostering a collaborative environment and reducing the need for constant back-and-forth communication. This feature is particularly advantageous for remote teams, where face-to-face collaboration may not be possible, allowing for accelerated design processes and improved productivity.

Design Reviews

Conducting live design reviews with stakeholders is effortless with Figma's intuitive platform. During a design review session, team members can share the prototype link with stakeholders and use video conferencing tools to facilitate discussion. As feedback is provided in real time, designers can make changes on-the-fly, incorporating suggestions and iterating on the design. This immediate feedback loop streamlines the decision-making process, allowing teams to quickly advance the design and move towards completion. By involving stakeholders in live design reviews, everyone remains on the same page, ensuring that decisions are made collaboratively, and project goals are met effectively.

Tips for Successful Design Reviews

To ensure successful design reviews in Figma, consider the following tips:

- **Prepare Ahead of Time**: Have the prototype ready and any specific areas of focus identified before the review session.
- **Set Clear Objectives**: Define the purpose and goals of the design review to guide discussions and keep the team focused.
- **Encourage Participation**: Encourage all stakeholders to actively participate and provide feedback during the review session.
- **Document Decisions**: Record decisions and action items during the review session to ensure accountability and follow-up.
- **Follow Up**: After the design review, follow up with stakeholders to address any outstanding feedback and confirm next steps.

Accessibility when Collaborating

Accessibility starts with inclusivity, even when sharing Figma links. Ensure your links are set to the appropriate permission level: *view-only* for broader audiences or *edit access* for collaborators. Include descriptive link text instead of generic phrases like «click here» to provide context for screen readers. When collaborating in Figma, organize layers and frames with clear labels to improve navigation for those using assistive technologies. Lastly, when presenting designs, export assets with alt text to describe visuals meaningfully. Accessibility is not just a checklist–it is a mindset for creating equal opportunities for collaboration and understanding.

Version Control and Managing Iterations

Keeping track of changes and different versions of your design are critical aspects of the design process, also known as Version Control. Figma provides robust tools to help manage your design iterations effectively.

Version Control

Figma automatically saves version history, allowing you to access and restore previous versions of your design. This feature ensures that no work is lost and that you can easily revert to an earlier state if needed.

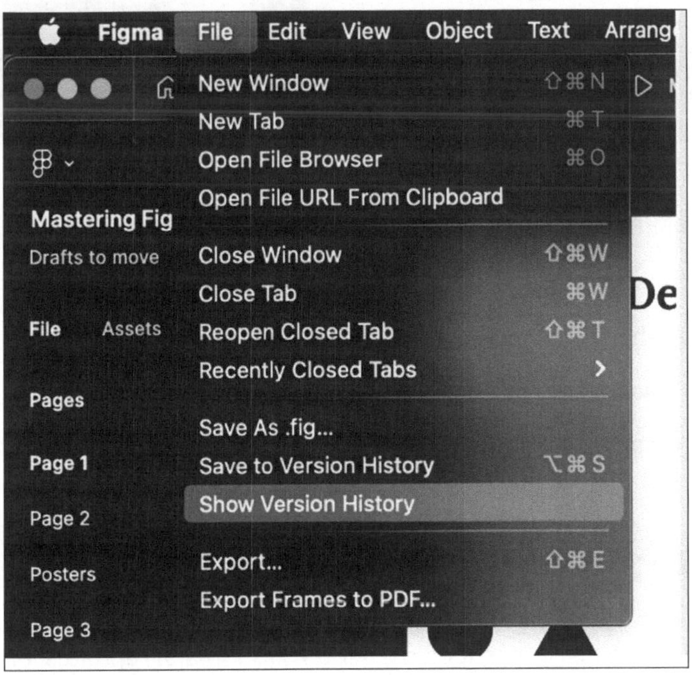

Figure 7.8: *Viewing version history in Figma*

A side panel will open up that shows all actions that have been taken within a specific Figma project.

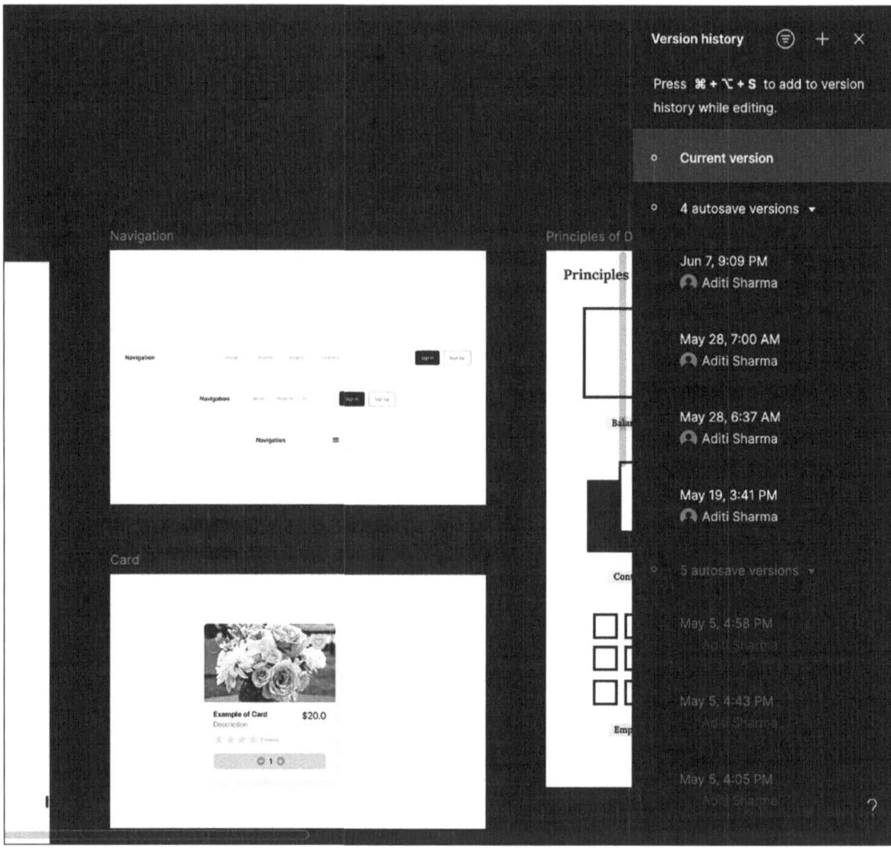

***Figure 7.9**: A side panel opens up to view the version history in Figma*

To view version history:

1. Open the design file.
2. Click on the "**`File`**" menu.
3. Select "**`Show Version History`**."
4. In the version history panel, you can see a timeline of all changes, who made them, and restore any previous version as needed.

Managing Design Iterations

To manage design iterations effectively, Figma allows you to create and name specific versions manually. This is particularly useful after major updates or before client presentations.

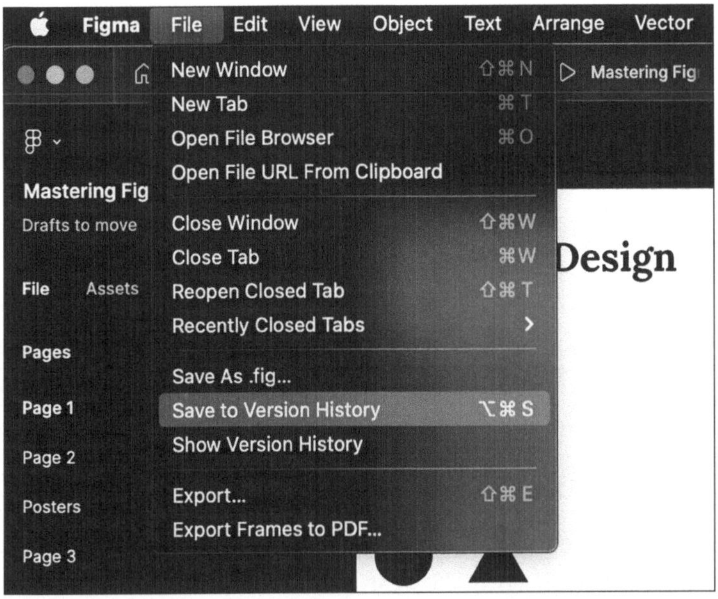

Figure 7.10: *Under the file menu, Figma provides an option to save a version*

You can provide a specific name for the version specific to the context of the project.

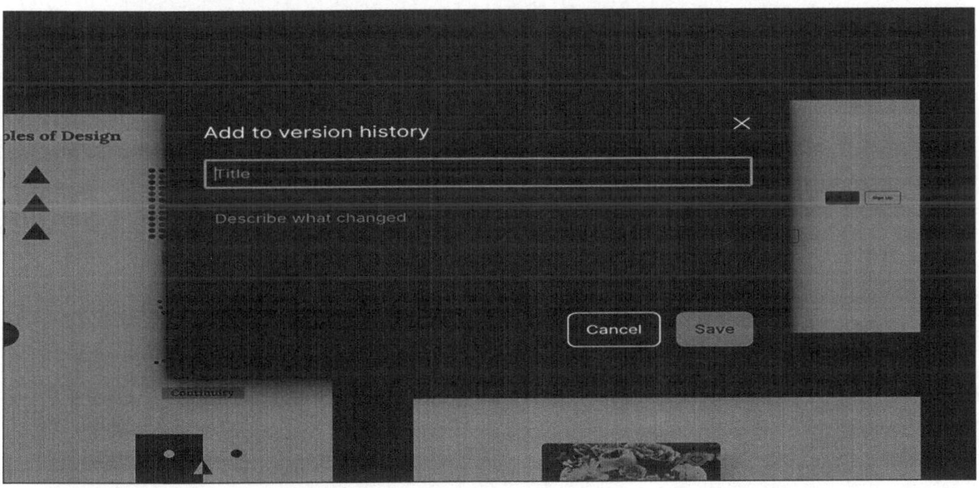

Figure 7.11: *Naming a version in Figma*

To create a named version:

1. Open the design file.
2. Click on the "**`File`**" menu.
3. Select "**`Save to Version History`**".
4. Name the version and add a description if needed.

This practice helps in keeping track of major milestones and ensuring that you can always refer back to important iterations.

Additional Collaborative Features of Figma

Figma's collaborative capabilities extend far beyond basic real-time editing and commenting. It offers a comprehensive suite of tools designed to streamline communication, improve project management, and enhance the overall collaborative experience. This section explores these advanced collaborative features and provides insights on how to utilize them effectively within your design teams.

Team Libraries

Figma's Team Libraries feature allows design teams to create and share a consistent set of components, styles, and assets across multiple projects. This ensures that everyone on the team is using the same design elements, thereby promoting consistency and reducing duplication of effort.

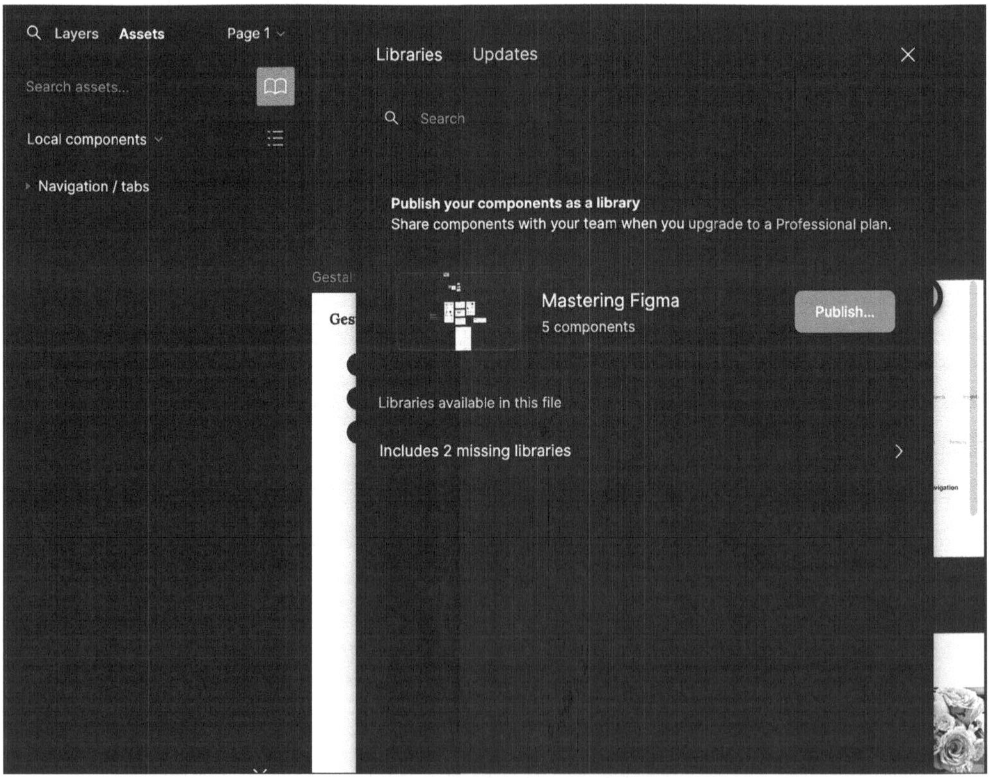

Figure 7.12: *Image showing the assets and libraries tab selected in Figma*

Creating a Team Library

1. Create a new Figma file or open an existing one.
2. Design the components and styles you want to share.
3. Click on the "`Assets`" tab in the left sidebar.
4. Click on the "`Library`" icon and select "`Publish`".
5. Name your library and click "`Publish`" to make it available to your team.

Using Shared Components and Styles

- Open the design file where you want to use the shared components.
- Click on the "`Assets`" tab in the left sidebar.
- Enable the desired team library from the list of available libraries.
- Drag and drop the shared components and styles into your design.
- By leveraging Team Libraries, design teams can maintain a unified design language and streamline the handoff process to developers.

Design Systems

A design system is a collection of reusable components, guided by clear standards, that can be assembled together to build any number of applications. Figma's design system capabilities allow teams to build, document, and maintain comprehensive design systems directly within the platform.

Building a Design System

- Start by defining the foundational elements such as color palettes, typography, and spacing guidelines.
- Create reusable components such as buttons, input fields, and navigation bars.
- Document the usage guidelines for each component to ensure consistent application across projects.

Maintaining a Design System

- Regularly update the components and styles based on feedback and new requirements.
- Use Figma's version control to track changes and updates to the design system.
- Communicate changes to the team and ensure everyone is using the latest version of the design system.

- A well-maintained design system enhances efficiency, reduces redundancy, and ensures a consistent user experience across all products.

Design Tokens

Design tokens are a way to store design decisions in a central place and apply them consistently across different platforms. In Figma, you can create and manage design tokens to ensure a consistent look and feel. Design tokens bridge the gap between design and development, ensuring that design decisions are applied consistently in code.

Creating Design Tokens

- Define your design tokens for colors, typography, spacing, and other properties.
- Use Figma's styles and components to implement these tokens in your user interface designs.

Managing and Updating Tokens

- Store design tokens in a central library.
- Update tokens as needed and ensure changes propagate across all designs using the tokens.

Project Management and Organization

Effective project management is crucial for successful collaboration. Figma provides tools to organize and manage design projects efficiently. Proper organization and management of design projects help keep everyone aligned and ensure smooth collaboration.

Using Folders and Projects

- Create folders to group related design files together.
- Organize projects by teams, clients, or specific initiatives.

Managing Permissions

- Set permissions at the project or file level to control access.
- Use Figma's team and project settings to manage who can view, comment, and edit.

Activity Log

- Use the activity log to track changes and updates made to design files.
- Monitor who made changes and when, ensuring accountability and transparency.

Best Practices for Collaborating in Figma

Sharing and collaborating effectively in Figma is essential for efficient workflows and successful project outcomes. As referenced in leading articles on designproject.io, sassdesign.io, and toxigon.com, here are some best practices to ensure smooth sharing and effective collaboration:

1. Establishing Clear Roles and Permissions

Define Team Roles: Clearly define the roles of team members such as designers, developers, project managers, and stakeholders. Assign appropriate permissions (view, comment, or edit) based on each team member's role to ensure that everyone has the access they need without compromising the integrity of the design.

Use Team Projects: Organize files into team projects to keep related user interface designs and assets in one place. Manage project-level permissions to streamline access control and ensure consistency across projects.

2. Maintaining a Consistent Naming Convention

File and Component Naming: Use clear and consistent naming conventions for files, pages, frames, and components to make it easy for team members to find and understand the structure of the design. Include version numbers or dates in file names if necessary to keep track of iterations.

Layer Naming: Name layers descriptively to make the design more readable and easier to navigate, especially for new team members or developers.

3. Utilizing Comments and Annotations Effectively

Provide Clear Feedback: Use Figma's commenting feature to provide clear and specific feedback on user interface designs. Comments should be concise, actionable, and directed at specific elements or sections of the design. Utilize annotations to explain design decisions or provide additional context that may not be immediately obvious.

Resolve Comments Promptly: Address comments and feedback as soon as possible to keep the project moving forward. Mark comments as resolved once they have been addressed to maintain a clear and organized feedback loop.

4. Fostering Collaboration and Seeking Feedback

Co-Editing: Take advantage of Figma's real-time collaboration capabilities by having multiple team members work on the same design simultaneously. This is particularly useful for design sprints and collaborative brainstorming sessions. Use Figma's multiplayer cursors to see where team members are working and avoid conflicts.

Generate Shareable Links: Create shareable links for your prototypes and customize permissions based on the level of access needed (view, comment, or edit). Embed prototypes in web pages or presentations for broader visibility and easier sharing with stakeholders.

Feedback Mechanisms: Conduct live design reviews where stakeholders can provide instant feedback and see changes being made in real time. This fosters a more dynamic and interactive review process. Use Figma's presentation mode to walk through designs and prototypes during review meetings. Collect feedback from stakeholders and team members through comments directly on the prototype. Encourage detailed and constructive feedback to inform design decisions. Use surveys or usability testing sessions to gather more in-depth feedback from users.

5. Implementing Version Control and Iterations

Version History: Use Figma's version history to track changes over time and revert to previous versions if necessary. This helps maintain a record of design decisions and iterations. Save key milestones as named versions to provide clear reference points throughout the project.

Design Iterations: Encourage iterative design by regularly reviewing and updating prototypes based on feedback. This continuous improvement cycle helps refine designs and meet user needs better.

6. Organizing Design Assets and Libraries

Component Libraries: Create and maintain component libraries to ensure consistency across designs and Figma projects. Shared libraries allow team members to use standardized components, reducing redundancy and errors. Regularly update and review component libraries to incorporate improvements and new design standards.

Asset Management: Organize design assets, such as images, icons, and styles, within Figma to make them easily accessible to all team members. Proper asset management helps streamline the design process and ensures consistency.

Conclusion

This chapter demonstrated the transformative impact of Figma's collaborative features on design teamwork. By learning about prototype sharing, feedback gathering, real-time collaboration, and version control, teams can achieve heightened efficiency and creativity. The chapter began by emphasizing the significance of sharing prototypes, showcasing Figma's ability to generate shareable links and embed options for effective presentations and stakeholder engagement, thereby ensuring efficient feedback collection.

Furthermore, the methods for gathering feedback within Figma were discussed, highlighting how comments and annotations enable precise and actionable feedback directly on designs, thereby streamlining the review process. The importance of promptly resolving comments to maintain an organized feedback loop and continuous progress was also emphasized. Real-time collaboration emerged as another critical aspect, with Figma's co-editing feature empowering multiple team members to work simultaneously on designs, enhancing productivity and fostering collaboration. Live design reviews benefit from this feature, facilitating instant feedback and dynamic adjustments.

Additionally, the chapter underscored the importance of version control in managing design iterations, with Figma's version history enabling teams to track changes over time and revert to previous versions as needed, thus ensuring well-documented design decisions. Saving key milestones as named versions provides clear reference points throughout the project lifecycle. Lastly, best practices for sharing and collaborating in Figma were outlined, emphasizing the need for clear roles and permissions, consistent naming conventions, effective use of comments, and leveraging real-time collaboration features to create a smooth and productive environment for design projects.

Transition to the next chapter

Having explored Figma's collaborative features in this chapter, we have established a solid foundation for efficient teamwork and streamlined design processes. Transitioning to the next chapter, we will explore the integration of plugins and external tools within Figma's versatile ecosystem. These integrations expand the functionality of Figma, allowing designers to access additional features, streamline workflows, and enhance productivity. From design asset management to prototyping and beyond, *Chapter 8, Integrating Plugins and External Tools*, will demonstrate how plugins and external tools can augment your design process within Figma, empowering you to create even more efficiently and effectively. Let us delve into the world of plugin integration and external tool collaboration to unlock new possibilities in your design journey.

Recap of Key Points

- **Sharing Prototypes:** Figma allows designers to create links that can be shared with team members and stakeholders, with customizable view, comment, or edit permissions. Prototypes can be embedded into web pages or presentations, facilitating easy showcase of designs in various contexts.
- **Commenting and Annotations:** Stakeholders and team members can leave comments directly on the prototype, fostering real-time feedback and discussion. Feedback can be addressed and resolved directly in Figma, ensuring all input is accounted for and tracked.
- **Real-Time Collaboration:** Multiple team members can work on the same prototype simultaneously, accelerating the design process and enhancing collaboration, especially for remote teams. Live design reviews allow for immediate feedback and on-the-fly adjustments, facilitating quick decision-making.
- **Managing Design Iterations:** Figma's version history helps track changes, allowing teams to revert to previous versions if needed and ensuring well-documented design decisions. Key project milestones can be saved as named versions, providing clear reference points throughout the design process.
- **Best Practices for Collaborating:** Define roles and permissions to manage access and contributions effectively. Use consistent naming for files and components to maintain organization. Utilize comments for clear and actionable feedback. Make full use of co-editing and live review features to enhance team productivity.

CHAPTER 8
Integrating Plugins and External Tools

Introduction

In the rapidly evolving field of UI/UX design, efficiency and innovation are paramount. Figma, a leading design tool, has revolutionized the way designers create and collaborate. One of the key strengths of Figma lies in its robust ecosystem of Figma plugins and the ability to integrate with various external tools outside of Figma. These integrations not only extend the functionality of Figma but also streamline workflows, making it an indispensable tool for designers.

This chapter delves into the world of plugins and external tools in Figma. We will explore the extensive plugin ecosystem that Figma offers, discuss how to integrate third-party tools to enhance your design process, and provide tips for optimizing your workflow with these powerful additions. Whether you are a seasoned designer or new to Figma, understanding and leveraging these tools can significantly boost your productivity.

Structure

In this chapter, we will cover the following topics:

- Introduction to Integrating Plugins and External Tools
- Overview of Figma's Plugin Ecosystem
- Integrating Third-Party Tools for Enhanced Functionality
- Tips for Optimizing Workflow with Plugins
- Case Studies
- Hands-On Exercises

Overview of Figma's Plugin Ecosystem

Figma's plugin ecosystem is a vibrant and dynamic collection of tools that extend the core capabilities of the Figma design platform. These plugins are created by both Figma and third-party developers, providing users with a wide range of functionalities that can be seamlessly integrated into their design workflows. From automating repetitive tasks to introducing new design capabilities, plugins can transform the way you work in Figma.

To use a plugin:

- Open the Figma file.
- Go to the "**`Resources`**" panel or search for plugins in the community.
- Install and run the desired plugin directly from your project.

Explore more via Figma's Community Resources [https://www.figma.com/community].

Key Features and Benefits of Using Plugins

Users can access and search for specific plugins from the main menu.

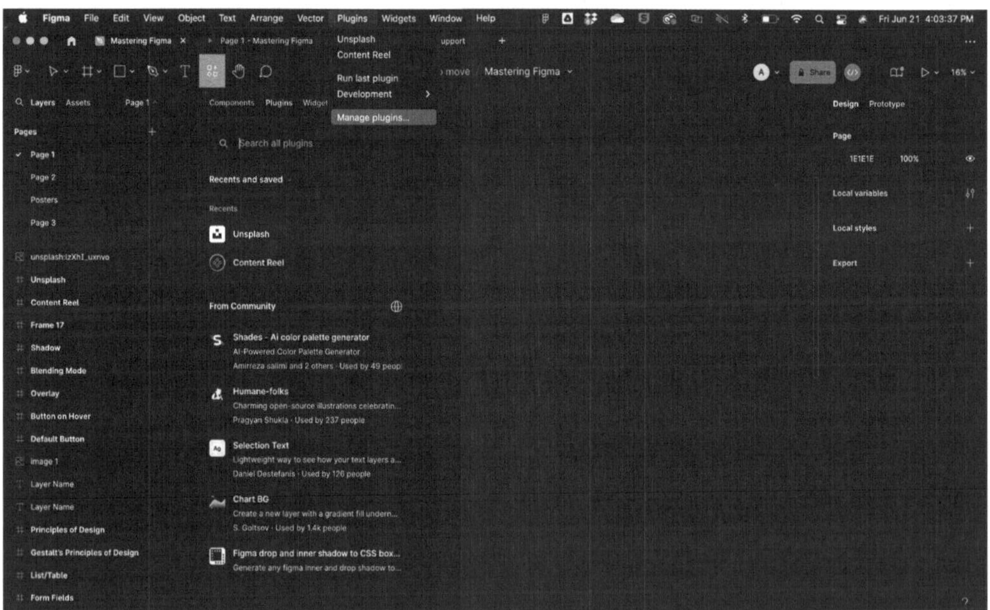

Figure 8.1: *Plugins in Figma*

- **Enhanced Functionality:** Plugins add new features and capabilities to Figma that are not available in the base application. This can include everything from advanced typography tools to specialized design elements.

- **Efficiency and Productivity:** By automating routine tasks, plugins save time and reduce the potential for errors. This allows designers to focus on more creative aspects of their projects.
- **Collaboration:** Some plugins are designed to enhance team collaboration by integrating with project management tools, enabling better communication and project tracking.
- **Customization:** Plugins allow designers to tailor Figma.

Popular Plugins in Figma

- **Unsplash**: Provides access to a vast library of free stock photos that can be easily inserted into designs.

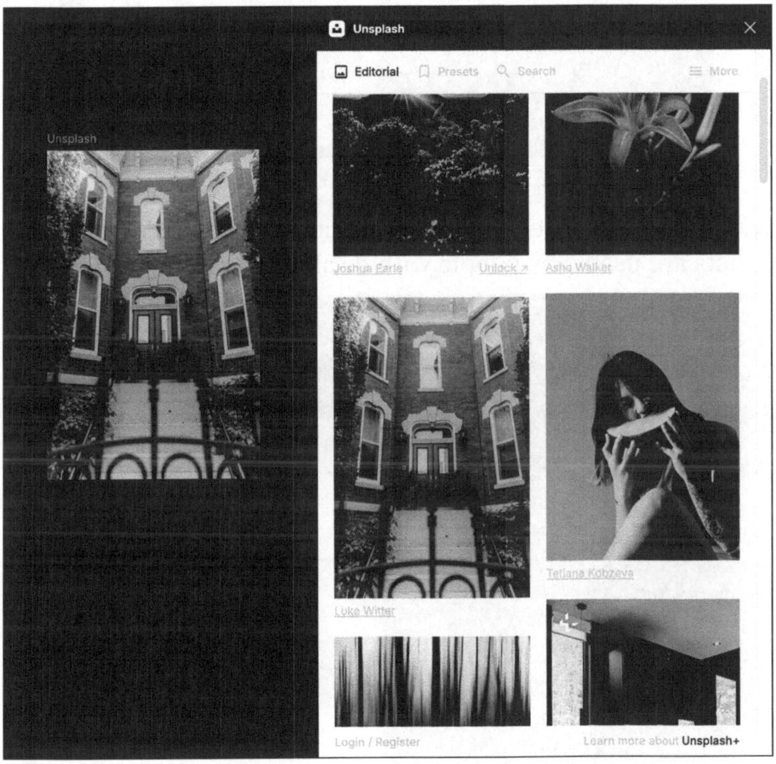

Figure 8.2: *Unsplash plugin in Figma*

- **Content Reel:** Allows designers to generate placeholder text, avatars, and other content elements, streamlining the prototyping process.

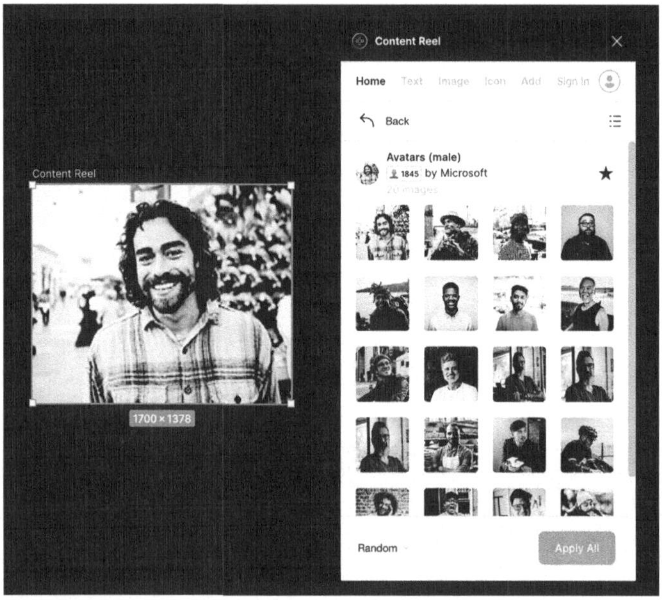

Figure 8.3: *Content Reel plugin in Figma*

- **Stark**: A tool for checking accessibility issues in designs, ensuring that products are usable by people with disabilities.

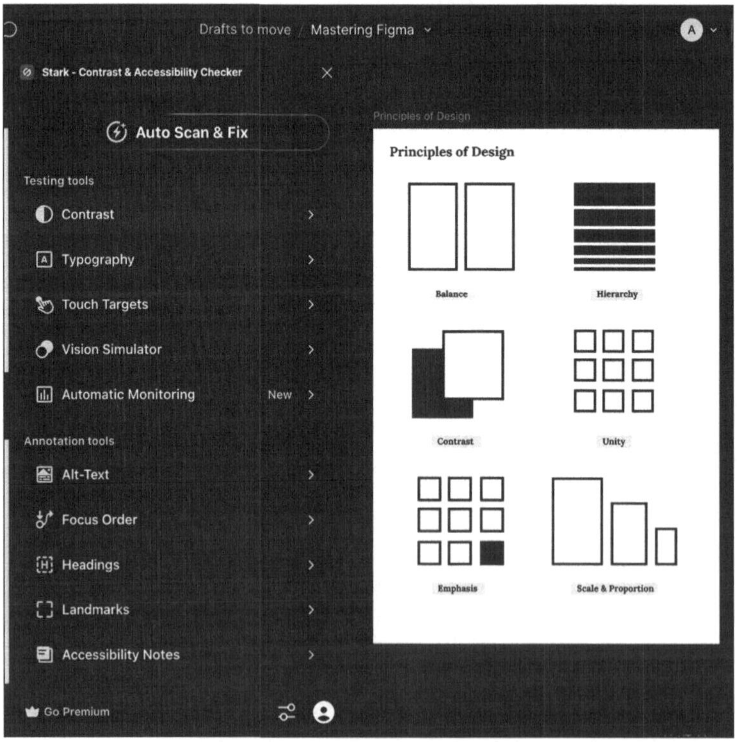

Figure 8.4: *Stark plugin in Figma*

- **Figmotion**: Adds animation capabilities to Figma, enabling designers to create interactive and animated prototypes directly within the platform.

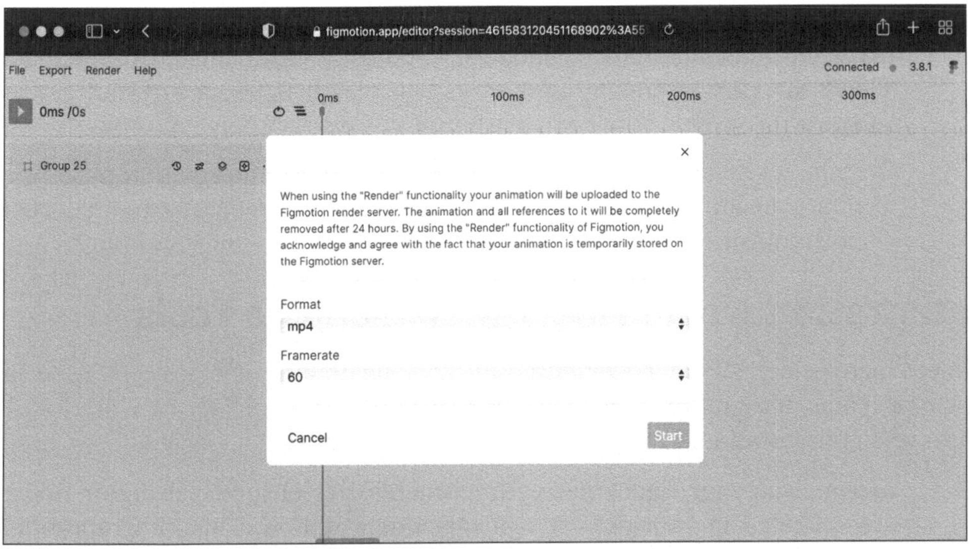

Figure 8.5: *Figmotion plugin in Figma*

Integrating Third-Party Tools for Functionality

Integrating third-party tools into Figma can significantly enhance your design workflow by adding powerful capabilities and streamlining processes with preconfigured content . Whether it is for advanced prototyping, animation, asset management, or user testing, these integrations allow designers to extend Figma's native features and tailor their workspace to meet their project needs better. Tools such as Principle, Zeplin, and Figmotion, among others, seamlessly connect with Figma, enabling smoother transitions between design and development, more robust animations, and more efficient feedback cycles. By leveraging these integrations, teams can collaborate more effectively, iterate faster, and ultimately deliver higher-quality designs with greater ease.

Connecting Figma with Third-Party Design Tools

Figma's open architecture allows for seamless integration with various third-party design tools, enhancing its functionality and making it a central hub for all design activities. These integrations enable designers to incorporate features and tools from other design software, providing a more comprehensive design environment.

- **Adobe Creative Cloud:** Integrate Figma with Adobe's suite of tools such as Photoshop and Illustrator to enhance your design capabilities. This integration allows for easy importing and exporting of assets, ensuring that you can leverage the strengths of both platforms.
- **Sketch**: For teams that use both Sketch and Figma, integration plugins can facilitate the import and export of design files between the two tools, ensuring smooth transitions and collaborative work.

Integration with Project Management Tools

Project management tools are essential for coordinating design projects, especially in larger teams. Integrating Figma with these tools can streamline the workflow and improve communication.

- **Asana**: Sync your Figma files with Asana tasks to ensure that design updates are reflected in your project management workflow. This integration helps keep all team members on the same page and ensures that deadlines are met.
- **Trello**: Use Figma's Trello integration to attach design files to Trello cards. This makes it easy to track design progress and provides context for tasks and project updates.

Using Development and Code Tools with Figma

Figma also integrates well with development tools, facilitating a smoother handoff between design and development.

- **Zeplin:** Zeplin bridges the gap between designers and developers by providing detailed specs, assets, and code snippets for Figma designs. This ensures that the design vision is accurately implemented in the final product.
- **Avocode:** Avocode provides tools for generating code from Figma designs, making it easier for developers to understand and implement design elements.

Integrating Your Figma file with These Tools

Taking an example of Zeplin, let us review, step-by-step, images of how to integrate Figma files with any third-party tool. You can use a similar process to add any other listed plugins.

1. Under the **`Plugins`** navigation menu of Figma, select **`Manage plugins`**.

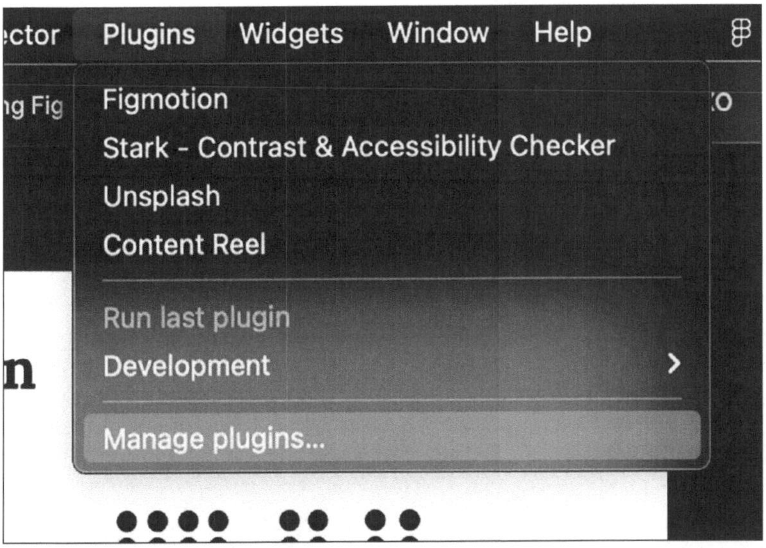

Figure 8.6: *Step 1, go to manage plugins in your Figma file*

2. Search for the plugin you need. For example, here we type '`Zeplin`' and select `Zeplin`.

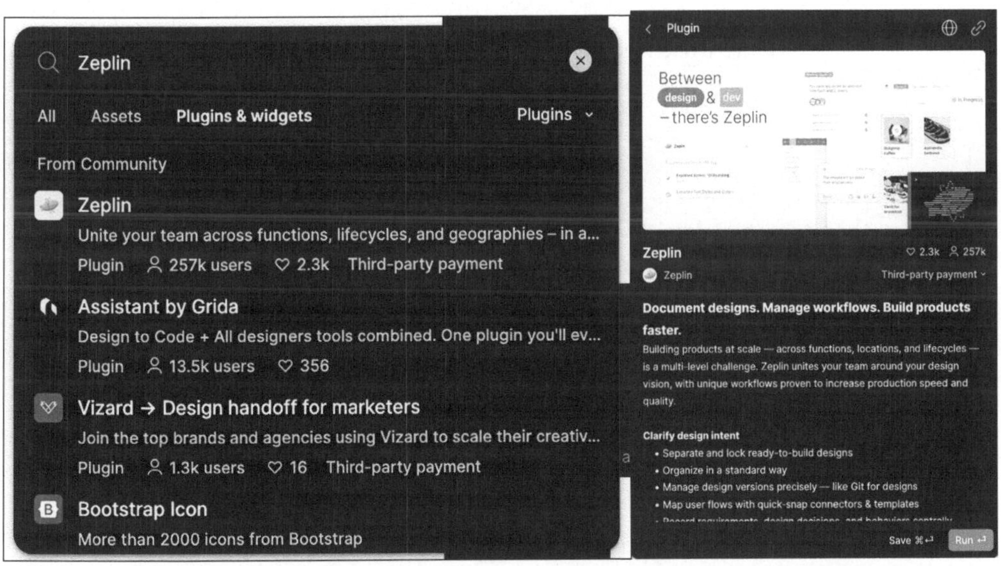

Figure 8.7: *Search and select the plugin you need, for example, Zeplin*

3. Give required permissions for the plugin to access your Figma information.

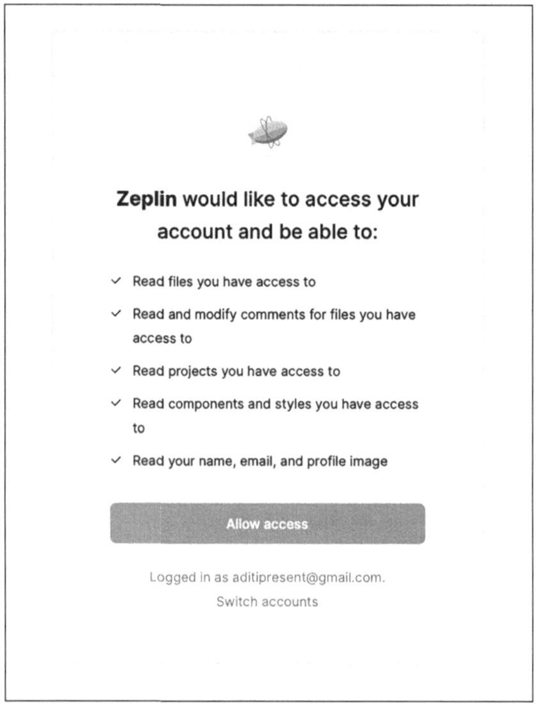

Figure 8.8: *Give required access to your Figma instance*

4. Sign in into the Zeplin instance and select your relevant role.

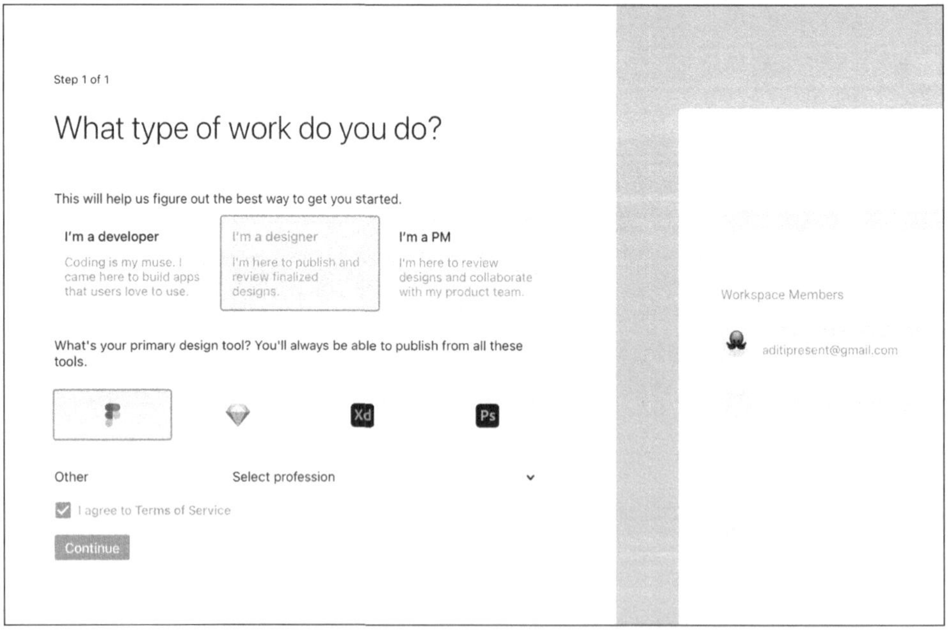

Figure 8.9: *Select your role type and other settings to get started with Zeplin*

5. Post connecting to Zeplin, return to your Figma file, select the frames (you need code snippets for) and start using the plugin.

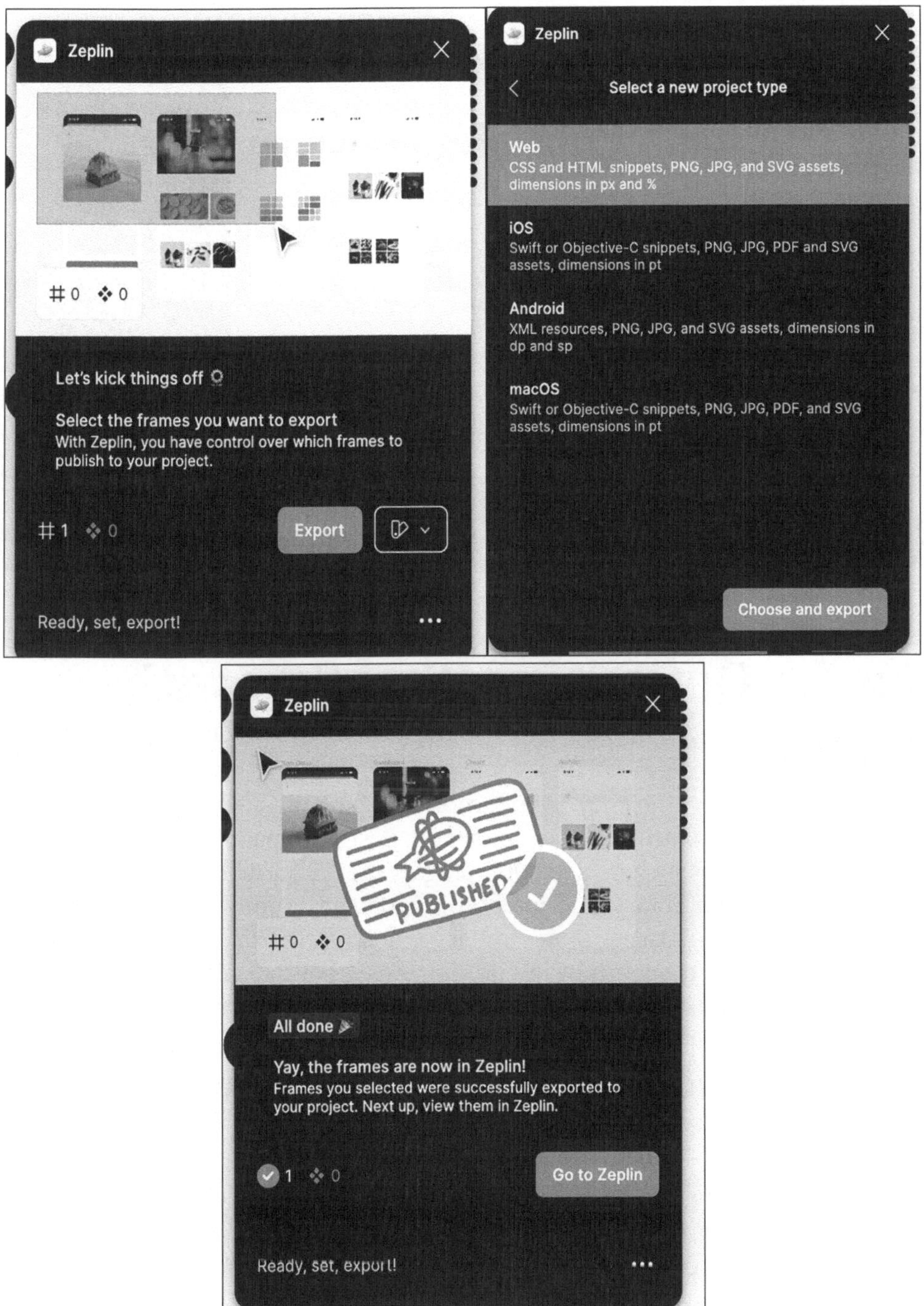

Figure 8.10: *Select your frames and the project type to enable export*

6. Once the export is completed, the Figma frames are ready in Zeplin.

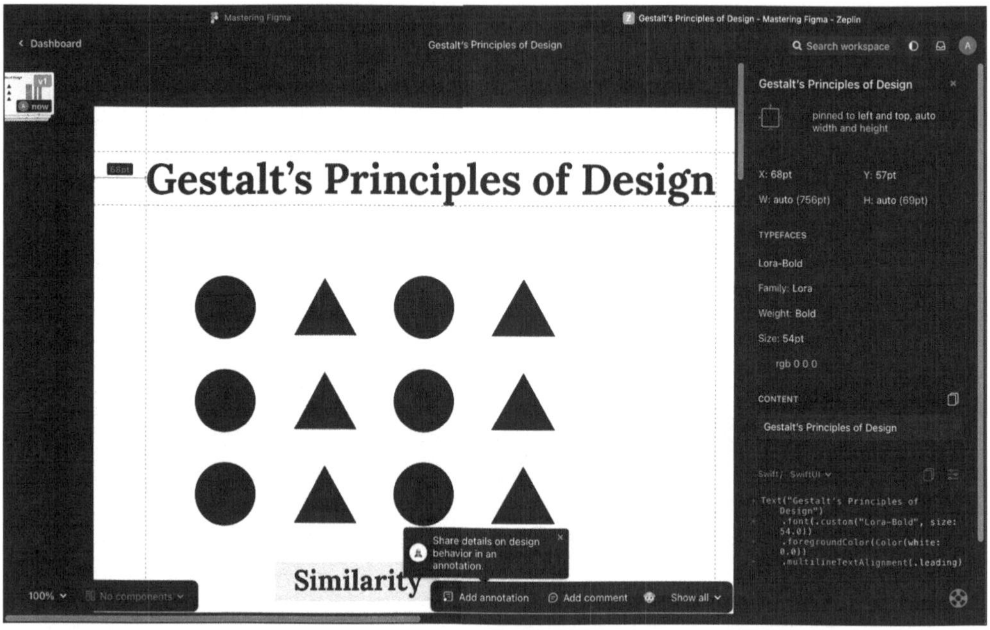

***Figure 8.11**: Figma frames in Zeplin*

Tips for Optimizing Workflow with Plugins

Maximize your design efficiency by incorporating plugins into your Figma workflow. Plugins automate repetitive tasks, enhance design capabilities, and streamline collaboration. Key tips include selecting plugins that align with your specific needs, managing your plugin library, and integrating popular options such as Content Reel for dummy text and images, Stark for accessibility checks, and Auto Layout for responsive design. By thoughtfully integrating these tools, you can significantly boost productivity, maintain design consistency, and focus more on creative tasks.

Selecting the Right Plugins for Your Workflow

With thousands of plugins available, it can be overwhelming to choose the right ones. Here are some tips for selecting plugins that will enhance your workflow:

- **Identify Your Needs:** Determine which tasks you frequently perform and find plugins that can help automate or simplify these tasks.

- **Read Reviews and Ratings:** Check the reviews and ratings of plugins to ensure they are reliable and well-supported by the developer community.
- **Test and Iterate:** Experiment with different plugins to see which ones best fit your workflow. It is advisable to try out multiple options before settling on the best one.

Best Practices for Plugin Management

Managing plugins effectively is crucial for maintaining an efficient workflow.

- **Regularly Update Plugins:** Ensure that your plugins are always up to date to take advantage of new features and bug fixes.
- **Organize Your Plugins:** Keep your plugins organized and remove any that you no longer use to avoid clutter and confusion.
- **Stay Informed:** Follow plugin developers and Figma communities to stay informed about new plugins and updates to existing ones.

Troubleshooting Plugins in Figma

Figma offers multiple ways to troubleshoot when stuck using a plugin. For details on how to troubleshoot, visit: https://toxigon.com/figma-plugin-troubleshooting.

Here are some quick tips on how to troubleshoot:

- **Plugin Not Loading:** Ensure your internet connection is stable, restart Figma, or update to the latest version. If the issue persists, reinstall the plugin as the original installation might be corrupted.
- **Error Messages:** Read the message carefully, consult plugin documentation, or search for solutions online. Contact the plugin developer if needed.
- **Slow Performance:** Clear your browser cache, close unnecessary tabs, or check your system's hardware capacity. Switching browsers may also help.
- **Incorrect Output:** Verify your input, review documentation, or test the plugin with different data. Reach out to the developer for advanced issues.

Case Study: A UX Design Team at a Tech Startup

A rapidly growing tech startup faced a common challenge: streamlining their design-to-development process. With a small, dynamic team of UX designers and developers, they needed to enhance collaboration and reduce the time spent on design revisions. The company decided to integrate Figma with Zeplin and utilize the Content Reel plugin to achieve their goals. This case study explores their journey, the solutions they implemented, and the positive outcomes they achieved.

The Challenge

The UX design team at the startup was tasked with creating user interfaces for their flagship product, a complex web application.

The team faced several challenges:

- **Inefficient Design Handoff:** The process of handing off designs to developers was time-consuming and prone to miscommunication. Designers would often spend significant time creating detailed specifications, which developers found difficult to interpret accurately.
- **Repetitive Content Generation:** Prototyping required the use of placeholder content, such as text and images. Manually generating this content was tedious and slowed down the design process.
- **Design Revisions:** Frequent design revisions were necessary due to misalignments between the design and development teams. This resulted in wasted time and effort.

The Solution

To address these challenges, the team decided to integrate Figma with Zeplin and use the Content Reel plugin.

Here is how these tools were implemented:

- **Figma-Zeplin Integration:**
    - **Seamless Handoff:** By integrating Figma with Zeplin, the team streamlined the design handoff process. Designers could export their Figma designs directly to Zeplin, where developers could access detailed specifications, assets, and code snippets.
    - **Improved Communication:** Zeplin provided a centralized platform for designers and developers to collaborate. Developers could comment directly on designs in Zeplin, asking for clarifications and providing feedback.
    - **Accurate Implementation:** The detailed specifications and measurements provided by Zeplin reduced the chances of misinterpretation, ensuring that the final product matched the design vision.
- **Content Reel Plugin:**
    - **Rapid Prototyping:** The Content Reel plugin allowed designers to quickly generate placeholder content, including text, avatars, and icons. This significantly sped up the prototyping process.
    - **Consistency:** The plugin ensured consistency in the use of placeholder content, making prototypes more realistic and easier to test with users.

- **Focus on Design:** By automating content generation, designers could focus more on the creative aspects of their work rather than repetitive tasks.

Implementation Process

The implementation process involved several steps:

1. **Training and Onboarding:**
   a. The team conducted training sessions to familiarize designers and developers with Zeplin and the Content Reel plugin.
   b. Documentation and best practices were created to ensure a smooth transition and consistent use of the tools.
2. **Workflow Integration:**
   a. The design workflow was updated to include regular exports from Figma to Zeplin. This became a standard part of the design process, ensuring that developers always had access to the latest designs.
   b. The Content Reel plugin was integrated into the design process, with designers using it to populate prototypes with realistic content.
3. **Feedback and Iteration:**
   a. The team established a feedback loop to continuously improve the use of Zeplin and Content Reel. Regular meetings were held to discuss any issues and share tips for better usage.
   b. Based on feedback, the team refined their workflows, ensuring that both tools were used to their full potential.

Outcomes

The integration of Figma with Zeplin and the use of the Content Reel plugin led to several positive outcomes:

- **Reduced Design Time:**
  - The time spent on design handoff and generating placeholder content was significantly reduced. Designers could now create prototypes faster and with greater ease.
  - Developers received more accurate and detailed specifications, reducing the need for back-and-forth communication and revisions.
- **Improved Collaboration:**
  - The integration fostered better collaboration between designers and developers. The ability to comment directly on designs in Zeplin improved communication and understanding.

    - The centralized platform for design specifications ensured that everyone was on the same page, leading to fewer misunderstandings and misalignments.
- **Higher Quality Outputs:**
    - The detailed specifications and assets provided by Zeplin ensured that the final product closely matched the design vision. This resulted in higher quality outputs and a more polished user experience.
    - The use of realistic placeholder content from Content Reel made prototypes more effective for user testing, leading to better-informed design decisions.
- **Enhanced Productivity:**
    - By automating repetitive tasks and streamlining workflows, the team's overall productivity increased. Designers had more time to focus on creative problem-solving and innovation.
    - The reduced need for design revisions and improved accuracy of implementations saved time and resources.

Summary

The UX design team at the tech startup successfully addressed their challenges by integrating Figma with Zeplin and using the Content Reel plugin. This case study demonstrates how leveraging Figma's ecosystem of plugins and external tools can streamline workflows, enhance collaboration, and improve the quality of design outputs. By adopting these tools, the team not only increased their productivity but also achieved a higher level of accuracy and consistency in their design-to-development process. This experience highlights the value of integrating plugins and external tools in modern design workflows, encouraging other teams to explore and utilize these resources.

Hands-On Exercises

These hands-on exercises provide practical experience with Figma's plugins and external tools, illustrating how they can be integrated into various stages of the design process to enhance productivity, collaboration, and the overall quality of design projects.

Exercise 1: Getting Started with Plugins

Objective: Familiarize yourself with finding, installing, and using plugins in Figma.

Search and Install Plugins:

1. Open Figma and navigate to the Community tab.
2. Search for the "`Content Reel`" plugin.
3. Click on the plugin and install it.
4. Repeat the process for the "`Unsplash`" plugin (for inserting high-quality stock images).

Using Content Reel:

1. Create a new Figma file.
2. Design a simple form with text fields for name, email, and address.
3. Use the Content Reel plugin to fill these text fields with placeholder content.
4. Adjust the placeholder content settings to see different options available in the plugin.

Using Unsplash:

1. Design a card component with an image placeholder.
2. Use the Unsplash plugin to insert a random image into the image placeholder.
3. Explore different categories of images and insert a few to see how they change the appearance of your card design.

Reflection: Note how the plugins enhance your design process by providing quick access to content and images, saving you time and effort.

Exercise 2: Streamlining Design Handoff with Zeplin

Objective: Learn how to integrate Figma with Zeplin for a smoother design handoff to developers.

Setting Up Zeplin:

1. Create an account on Zeplin (if you do not have one).
2. Install the Zeplin desktop app.

Exporting from Figma to Zeplin:

1. Open a Figma project that contains multiple frames (representing different screens of a design).
2. Select the frames you want to export.

3. Go to the `File` menu, choose "`Export`," and select "`Export to Zeplin`".
4. Follow the prompts to connect your Figma account to Zeplin and complete the export.

Exploring Zeplin:

1. In Zeplin, open the project you just exported.
2. Explore the design specs, assets, and code snippets generated by Zeplin.
3. Invite a developer to the project and ask them to review the design specs.

Adding Annotations in Zeplin:

1. Add comments and annotations to your design in Zeplin, providing additional context and instructions for the developers.
2. Practice resolving comments once they are addressed.

Reflection: Discuss with your team how Zeplin improves the clarity and efficiency of the design handoff process.

Exercise 3: Enhancing Workflow with More Plugins

Objective: Explore and utilize additional plugins to enhance your workflow in Figma.

Install the Figmotion Plugin:

1. Search for the "`Figmotion`" plugin in the Figma Community.
2. Install the plugin, which allows you to create animations directly within Figma.

Create a Simple Animation:

1. Open a new Figma file and create a basic shape (for example, a circle).
2. Open Figmotion and create a new animation.
3. Set keyframes for the circle's position, size, and color.
4. Preview the animation and make adjustments as needed.

Install the Stark Plugin:

1. Search for the "`Stark`" plugin in the Figma Community.
2. Install the plugin, which helps ensure your designs are accessible.

Check Accessibility:

1. Open a design project in Figma.
2. Use the Stark plugin to check for color contrast issues.
3. Adjust the colors in your design based on the plugin's recommendations to improve accessibility.

Explore More Plugins:

1. Browse the Figma Community for other useful plugins, such as "**`Autoflow`**" for creating user flows or "**`Map Maker`**" for generating custom maps.
2. Install and experiment with at least one additional plugin that you find interesting or useful.

Reflection: Consider how each plugin can enhance different aspects of your design workflow and discuss with your team which plugins might be adopted for regular use.

Conclusion

In this chapter, we delved into the rich ecosystem of plugins and external tools available in Figma, highlighting their critical role in enhancing design workflows and collaboration. We began by exploring the variety of plugins in Figma's ecosystem, emphasizing how they extend the platform's capabilities beyond its core functions. By integrating third-party tools, designers can streamline repetitive tasks, introduce new functionalities, and improve efficiency, ultimately allowing for more focus on creativity and problem-solving.

The practical tips provided for optimizing workflow with plugins serve as a guide for incorporating these tools effectively. We examined the process of searching, installing, and using plugins, and showcased how different plugins can be leveraged to tackle specific design challenges. From content generation to accessibility checks and animation creation, each plugin adds a unique value, empowering designers to produce higher-quality work with less effort.

Through detailed hands-on exercises, we offered practical applications of these concepts, enabling readers to gain confidence in utilizing plugins to enhance their projects. By mastering the use of plugins and external tools, designers can significantly improve their workflow, foster better collaboration with team members, and ensure that their design processes are both efficient and innovative. As you continue your journey with Figma, integrating these powerful tools will be crucial for staying ahead in the ever-evolving landscape of design technology.

Transition to the next chapter

As we conclude our exploration of integrating plugins and external tools in Figma, we have equipped ourselves with the knowledge to enhance and streamline our design workflows significantly. Plugins and third-party integrations have shown us how we can push the boundaries of what is possible in Figma, optimizing every aspect of our design process. Next, we will turn our attention to an essential aspect of modern design– responsiveness. In *Chapter 9, Designing Responsively for Multiple Devices*, we will dive into designing responsively for multiple devices. This chapter will guide you through the principles of responsive design within Figma, techniques for designing for various screen sizes and resolutions, and methods for previewing and testing your designs on different devices.

Recap of Key Points

- **Overview of Figma's Plugin Ecosystem:** We explored the diversity of plugins available in Figma's ecosystem, highlighting their potential to extend the platform's core functionalities. Plugins provide various capabilities, from enhancing productivity to introducing new design features.
- **Integrating Third-Party Tools for Enhanced Functionality:** We covered how to integrate third-party tools with Figma, emphasizing the benefits of a seamless workflow. We discussed specific plugins that help streamline tasks such as content generation, accessibility checks, and animation creation, providing practical examples of their use.
- **Optimizing Workflow with Plugins:** Practical tips were provided on how to search for, install, and effectively use plugins to optimize your design process. Strategies for selecting the right plugins for specific design challenges were highlighted, emphasizing the importance of tailoring plugin use to individual project needs.
- **Enhancing Design Workflows:** By mastering the use of plugins and external tools, designers can significantly enhance their workflows, fostering better collaboration and innovation. The integration of these tools is crucial for staying competitive and efficient in the evolving landscape of design technology.

CHAPTER 9
Designing Responsively for Multiple Devices

Introduction

In the contemporary digital landscape, users interact with websites and applications across a multitude of devices, each with different screen sizes, resolutions, and capabilities. Designing for this diversity requires a responsive approach that ensures a consistent and optimal user experience, regardless of the device used. This chapter delves into the principles and techniques of responsive design using Figma, a powerful tool that enables designers to create adaptable and flexible layouts efficiently.

Responsive design is not merely about making a website look good on both desktop and mobile devices; it is about creating a seamless user experience that adapts fluidly to the context of use. This involves understanding and implementing fluid grids, flexible layouts, and breakpoints, as well as creating reusable components and design systems that maintain consistency across various platforms.

We will explore how Figma's features–such as auto layout, constraints, and device preview–can be harnessed to design for different screen sizes and resolutions. You will learn practical techniques for ensuring that typography and spacing are responsive, creating prototypes for user testing, and integrating designs with development tools for a smooth handoff. By the end of this chapter, you will have a comprehensive understanding of how to design responsively with Figma, equipping you with the skills to tackle real-world projects and deliver exceptional user experiences across all devices.

Structure

In this chapter, we will cover the following topics:

- Principles of Responsive Design within Figma
- Benefits of Designing Responsively
- Designing for Screen Sizes and Resolutions
- Previewing Designs on Different Devices
- Tips for Using Figma to Design Successful and Responsive Apps
- Case Study
- Hands-On Exercises

Principles of Responsive Design within Figma

Mastering responsive design principles is essential for creating flexible and adaptive user interfaces that look great on any device. In this section, you will delve into the core principles of responsive design within Figma and learn how to implement fluid grids and flexible layouts using Figma's auto layout and constraints features. You will discover the importance of breakpoints and how to simulate different screen sizes to ensure your design adapts seamlessly across devices. Additionally, you can explore how to build reusable components and design systems that maintain consistency and efficiency across projects. By understanding and applying these principles, you will be able to create designs that offer a cohesive and user-friendly experience, no matter the device.

Overview of Key Concepts

- **Fluid Grid**
    - **Definition**: Uses percentages for widths so that elements scale proportionally with the screen size.
    - **Example**: A website layout where a column is set to 50% width. On a screen 800px wide, it will be 400px; on 400px, it will be 200px.
    - **Use Case**: Ensures scalability across various screen sizes without fixed dimensions.
- **Flexible Layout**
    - **Definition**: Combines fluid grids with flexible media (like images) to adapt content.
    - **Example**: A text block set at 80% width and an image set with max-width: 100% resizes gracefully without distortion or cropping.

  - **Use Case**: Great for creating layouts that maintain proportion across devices.

- **Breakpoints**
  - **Definition**: Specific screen widths where CSS rules change to adjust the design for different devices.
  - **Example**:

```
@media (max-width: 768px) {
  .header { font-size: 18px; }
}
```

    At widths below 768px, the header's font size changes.

  - **Use Case**: Allows tailored design changes for mobile, tablet, or desktop.

- **Responsive Design**
  - **Definition**: A holistic approach using fluid grids, flexible layouts, and breakpoints to create a seamless user experience.
  - **Example**: A responsive website adapts to any device by changing column layout, font sizes, or image scaling. A three-column desktop layout might convert to a single-column layout on mobile.
  - **Use Case**: Ensures a cohesive experience across devices.

Now, let us dive deep into these key concepts.

Fluid Grids and Flexible Layouts

Fluid grids and flexible layouts are the foundation of responsive design. They allow a design to adapt to different screen sizes and orientations seamlessly.

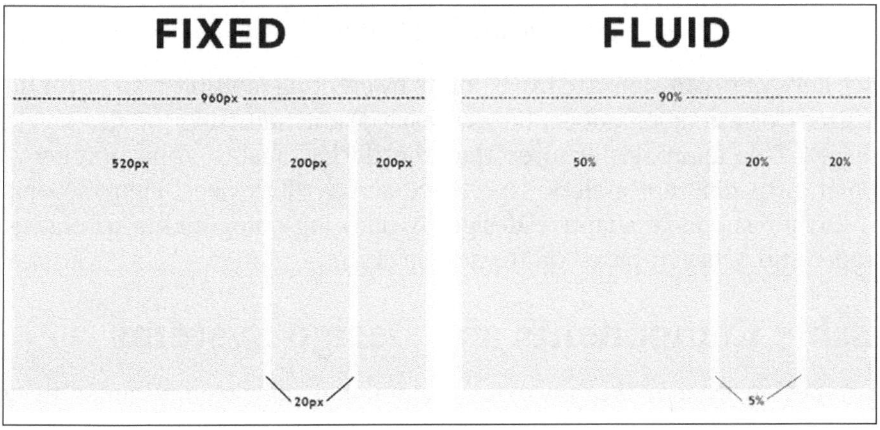

***Figure 9.1**: Image showing fixed versus fluid layout, where fixed layout gets pixel specifications and fluid grids are assigned percentages to allow for smoother content flow as the layout changes per device. Link: https://trellis.co/blog/why-fluid-responsive-design-is-best*

In Figma, designers can utilize auto layout and constraints to achieve this fluidity. Auto layout allows for dynamic resizing of components based on their content and container size, while constraints ensure that elements maintain their relative position and size within a frame. This is particularly useful for creating interfaces that need to look good on both small mobile screens and large desktop monitors.

Breakpoints and Adaptive Design

Breakpoints are specific screen widths where the design layout changes to provide an optimal user experience.

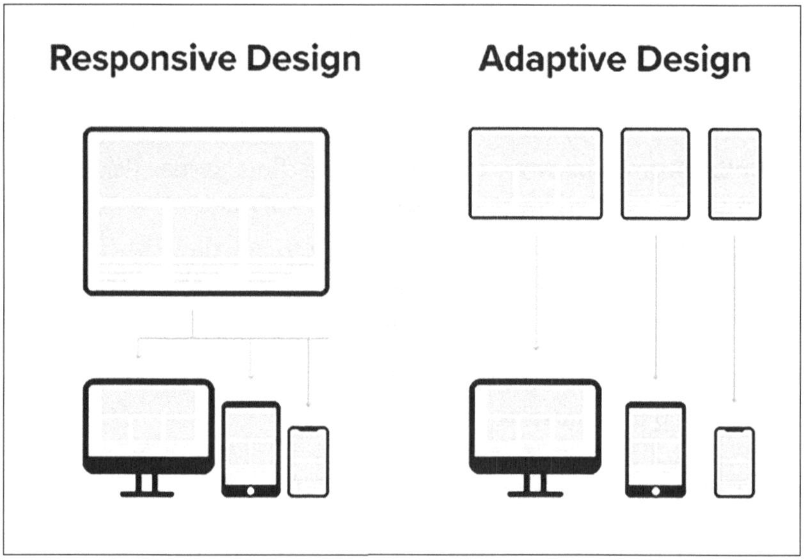

Figure 9.2: *Responsive (renders layout per device) versus adaptive design (specific design is created for every device) Link: https://bootcamp.uxdesign.cc/responsive-vs-adaptive-web-design-21117f4f267d*

In Figma, designers can simulate breakpoints by creating multiple frames for different screen sizes (for example, mobile, tablet, desktop) and adjusting the design elements accordingly. This approach ensures that the design adapts appropriately at each breakpoint, providing a seamless experience across all devices. Figma's component system further supports adaptive design by allowing components to change their appearance and behavior based on the screen size.

Reusable Components and Design Systems

A robust design system is crucial for maintaining consistency and efficiency in responsive design. In Figma, designers can create and store reusable components within a shared library, which can be easily accessed and implemented across various projects.

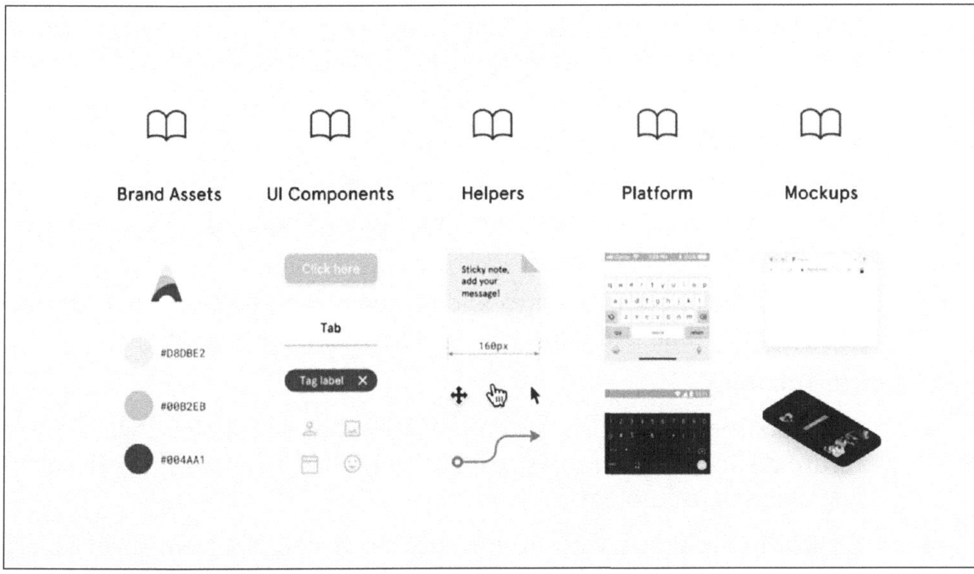

***Figure 9.3**: Types of UI design assets in Figma Link: https://www.figma.com/best-practices/components-styles-and-shared-libraries/*

These components can be configured to adapt to different screen sizes and resolutions, ensuring a consistent look and feel across all devices. Utilizing Figma's design system capabilities allows for rapid iteration and a unified design language throughout a product.

Benefits of Designing Responsively

By designing responsively, you ensure that your digital product is versatile, user-friendly, and prepared to meet the demands of an increasingly mobile audience. This approach not only enhances the user experience but also offers significant benefits in terms of reach, cost efficiency, and long-term sustainability.

- **Enhanced User Experience:**
  - **Consistency Across Devices**: Responsive design ensures that your website or application provides a consistent user experience across various devices, including desktops, tablets, and smartphones.
  - **Improved Usability**: By adapting to different screen sizes, responsive design makes navigation and interaction easier for users, reducing the need for excessive scrolling or zooming.
- **Increased Reach:**
  - **Broader Audience**: As more people access the internet from mobile devices, responsive design allows you to reach a wider audience by catering to their preferred devices.

  - **SEO Benefits**: Search engines such as Google prioritize mobile-friendly websites in their rankings. Responsive design improves your SEO, making it easier for users to find your site through search engines.

- **Cost-Effectiveness:**
  - **Single Codebase**: Maintaining a single responsive website or application is more cost-effective than developing and maintaining separate versions for different devices.
  - **Easier Maintenance**: Updates and changes need to be made only once, reducing the time and effort required for maintenance.
- **Future-Proofing:**
  - **Adaptability**: Responsive design prepares your website or application for future devices and screen sizes, ensuring that it remains functional and attractive as technology evolves.
  - **Scalability**: It allows your design to scale seamlessly from small to large screens, providing flexibility and longevity to your digital product.
- **Improved Performance:**
  - **Optimized Loading Times**: Responsive design often includes performance optimization techniques, such as using fluid grids and flexible images, which can lead to faster loading times on all devices.
  - **Resource Efficiency**: By delivering the same HTML to all devices and using CSS media queries to modify the display, responsive design can be more resource-efficient than serving different versions of a site.
- **Increased Conversion Rates:**
  - **Higher Engagement**: A better user experience leads to higher engagement, which can result in increased conversion rates, whether it is completing a purchase, signing up for a newsletter, or any other desired action.
  - **Reduced Bounce Rates**: Users are more likely to stay on a website or application that is easy to navigate and interact with, reducing bounce rates and increasing the likelihood of conversion.
- **Consistent Branding:**
  - **Unified Design Language**: Responsive design allows for a consistent design language across all devices, strengthening your brand identity and ensuring a unified look and feel.
  - **Professional Appearance**: A responsive site or app appears more professional and trustworthy, and that can enhance brand perception and customer loyalty.

- **Analytics and Reporting:**
    - **Unified Analytics**: With a single responsive design, you can consolidate analytics and reporting, making it easier to track user behavior and performance metrics across all devices.
    - **Better Insights**: Understanding how users interact with your site on different devices provides valuable insights that can inform future design and marketing strategies.

Designing for Screen Sizes and Resolutions

Creating designs that look great on every device involves understanding and accommodating various screen sizes and resolutions. In this section, we will explore how to effectively use Figma's frame presets for common devices, ensuring that your designs start with the correct dimensions. We will learn how to apply constraints and auto layout to maintain responsive and adaptable layouts. We will also discover techniques for adjusting typography and spacing to enhance readability and visual appeal across different screens. By mastering these strategies, you can ensure that your designs are optimized for any device, providing a consistent and engaging user experience from smartphones to desktops.

***Figure 9.4**: The variety of screens around us in the modern world require we design responsively*
Link: https://www.webfx.com/blog/web-design/what-is-responsive-web-design/

Types of Screen Resolution Sizes Available in Figma

Figma supports a wide range of screen resolution sizes to accommodate the diverse array of devices used today. Understanding these resolution sizes and how to design for them in Figma is crucial for creating adaptable and user-friendly interfaces across various devices and screen sizes. Following are some of the common types:

- **Mobile Resolutions:**
  - Small (320x568) for older and smaller smartphones.
  - Medium (375x667) for average smartphones such as the iPhone SE.
  - Large (414x896) for modern smartphones such as the iPhone X and newer.
- **Tablet Resolutions:**
  - Small (768x1024) for smaller tablets such as the iPad Mini in portrait mode.
  - Large (834x1112) for standard tablets such as the iPad Air in portrait mode.
  - Extra Large (1024x1366) for larger tablets such as the iPad Pro in portrait mode.
- **Desktop Resolutions:**
  - Standard (1280x800) for older or smaller laptop screens.
  - Full HD (1920x1080) for modern desktop monitors.
  - Quad HD (2560x1440) for high-resolution monitors.
  - Ultra HD (3840x2160) for 4K monitors.
- **Wide Screens and TV Resolutions:**
  - HD Ready (1280x720) for older HDTVs.
  - Full HD (1920x1080) for standard HDTVs and many monitors.
  - Ultra HD (3840x2160) for 4K TVs and monitors.
- **Custom Resolutions:**
  - Figma allows designers to create custom artboard sizes to match specific device requirements or unique project needs. This flexibility is particularly useful in designing for emerging devices or custom installations.

Designing for Multiple Viewports

Designing for multiple devices requires a thorough understanding of different viewports and screen resolutions. Viewports refer to the visible area of a web page on a device, which varies significantly between smartphones, tablets, and desktops. Screen resolution, measured in pixels, determines the level of detail a display can show. Figma provides presets for common devices, making it easier for designers to start with the correct dimensions and ensure their designs are optimized for various viewports and resolutions.

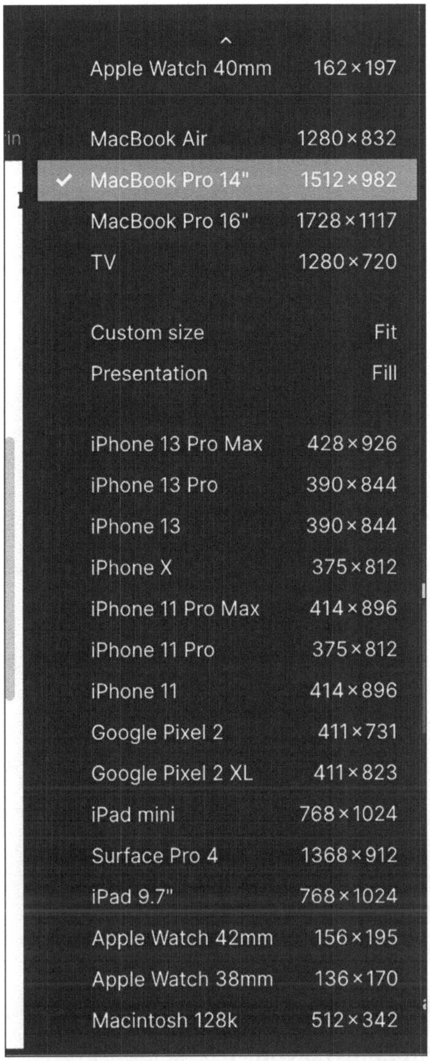

Figure 9.5: *Types of screen resolution and device types in Figma*

Using Figma's Auto Layout

Constraints in Figma allow designers to set rules for how elements should resize and reposition in response to changes in the frame size. This ensures that designs remain responsive and visually appealing across different screen sizes.

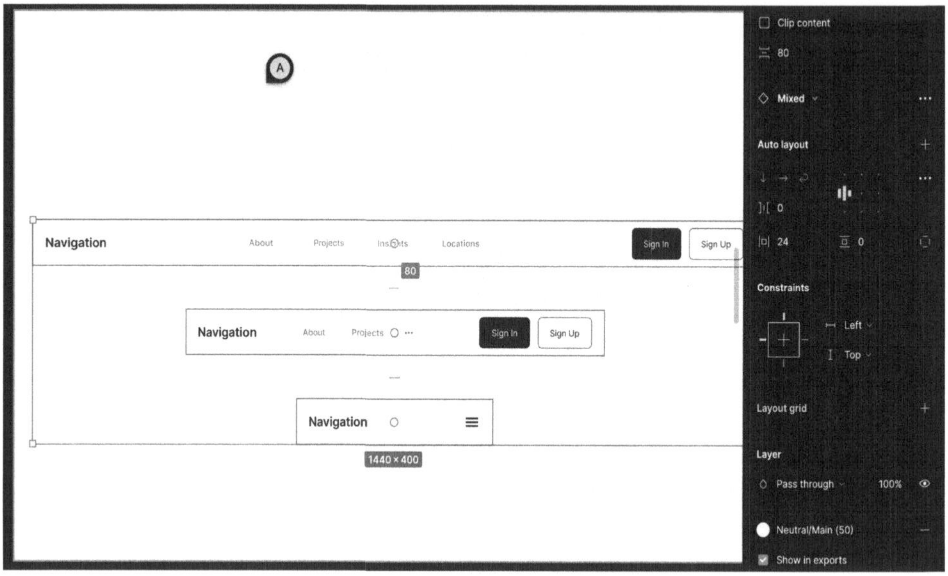

Figure 9.6: *Auto layout in Figma*

For instance, setting constraints to **`'left and right'`** for a navigation bar ensures it stretches across the screen width regardless of the device. Auto layout enhances this further by allowing designers to create frames that automatically adjust their size and position based on their content, facilitating a more flexible and responsive design.

You can add auto layout to a frame or a selection of objects. This includes:

- New or empty frames
- Frames with existing content
- Components and component sets
- Groups or other selections of layers and/or objects

There are a **few ways to add auto layout** to a selection:

- Use the keyboard shortcut ⇧ *Shift* A.
- In the right panel, click next to auto layout.
- Right-click on a frame or object and select **`Add auto layout`**.
- Once you use auto layout, nested objects will be set to auto space between, fill container, and center aligned.

When you use the **`"Suggest Auto Layout"`** feature in Figma, the tool identifies elements in a frame or component that should be arranged with auto layout. It creates multiple auto layout frames simultaneously, ensuring your design remains intact while making it responsive. This approach eliminates the manual effort of adding frames one by one, streamlining the process for efficiency.

You can access this option from a few places:

- Use the keyboard shortcut:
  - Mac: ^ *Control* ⇧ *Shift* A
  - Windows: ^ *Control* Alt ⇧ *Shift* A
- Right-click the frame or object and go to **`More layout`** options > **`Suggest auto layout`**.
- Select **`Suggest auto layout`** from the **`Actions`** menu.

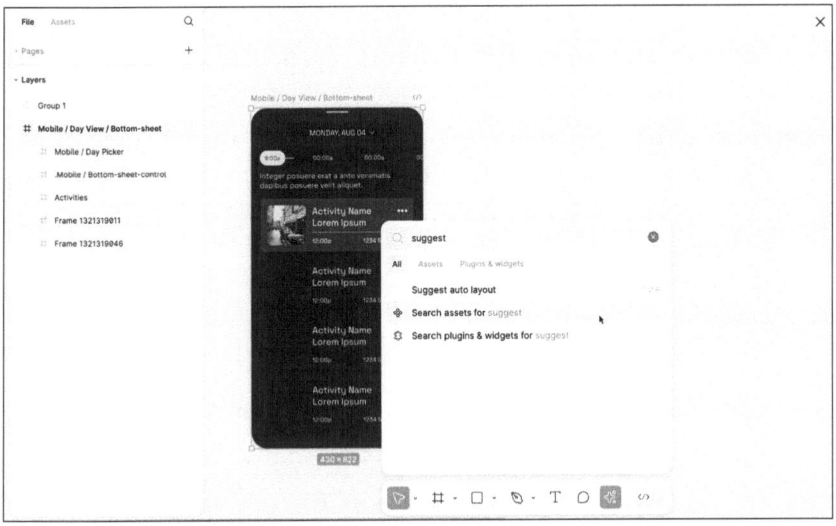

Figure 9.7: *Typeahead options when searching*

Users can choose the **`'Suggest Layout'`** feature in Figma.

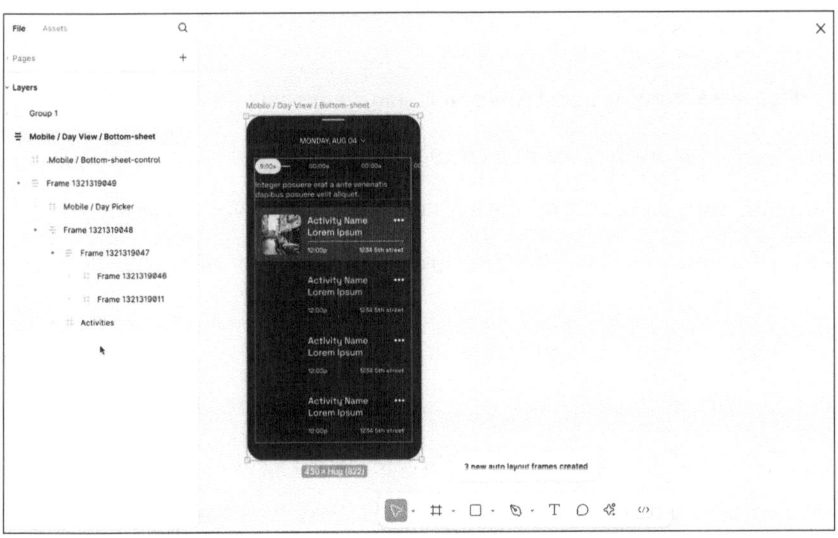

Figure 9.8: *Using 'suggest layout' feature in Figma*

You can nest an auto layout frame within another auto layout frame. This allows you to combine horizontal and vertical layouts to create complex interfaces. When you nest an auto layout frame, the nested frame will have both parent and child properties.

In the following example, there are four levels of auto layout:

- **Button**: Each button is a horizontal auto layout. This allows the button to grow and shrink as we change the label text.
- **Button Row**: We then add both buttons to another horizontal auto layout. This allows objects to respond when we make any changes to a sibling's contents.
- **Post**: We then add our buttons to a vertical auto layout with the other objects in the post. This includes a description, an image and the user's profile.
- **Timeline**: We have added three to a vertical auto layout to create our timeline. The auto layout frame is the top-level frame which sits on the canvas.

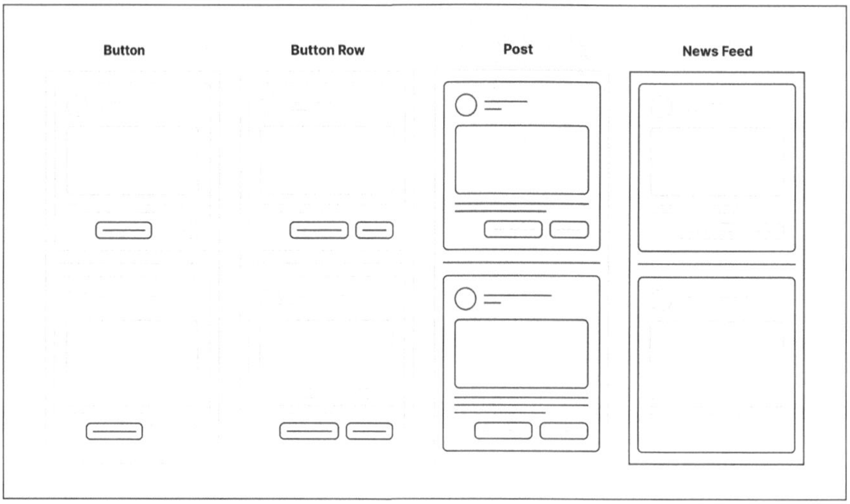

Figure 9.9*: Nesting auto layouts in Figma, image courtesy: help.figma.com*

You can nest auto layout frames in a couple of ways:

1. Drag an auto layout frame into an existing auto layout frame.
2. Create a new auto layout frame around a selection of auto layout frames (and other objects).
    a. Select the auto layout frame, and the other layers you would like to include.
    b. Use the keyboard shortcut ⇧ *Shift* A to add auto layout.
    c. Figma will create a frame around your selection and add auto layout.

When you remove auto layout, you will have access to a frame's regular properties. There are a couple of ways to remove auto layout:

1. Right-click on the frame and select **`Remove Auto Layout`**.
2. In the right panel, click the **`Next`** to Auto layout.
3. Use keyboard shortcuts:
   a. **Mac**: Option + *Shift* A
   b. **Windows**: *Alt* + *Shift* A

Setting Constraints in Figma

Constraints are critical while designing UI that needs to be utilized for viewing on multi-devices such as mobile or desktop. Constraints guide Figma's layers on how to respond (adjust their alignment) when a frame is resized. The layer to which the constraint is applied acts according to the predefined constrained manner.

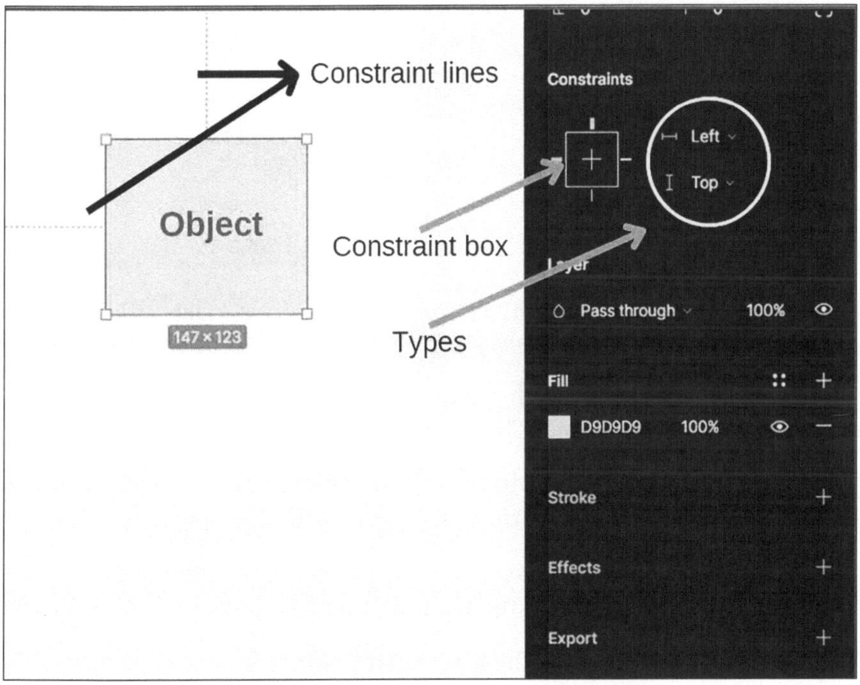

Figure 9.10: *Setting constraints in Figma*

You can set **Horizontal or Vertical constraints** to your assets.

There are five options in the horizontal alignment, which make alignment horizontally dynamic and adjustable. These are:

1. **Left**, which allows the object to be adjusted concerning the left side of the frame so if the frame is resized to the left side, then the object will flow leftward.

2. **Right**, which allows the object to be adjusted concerning the right side of the frame so if the frame is resized to the right side, then the object will flow rightwards.
3. **Left and right,** allow the object to be adjusted concerning both sides of the frame so if the frame is moved anyway along the x-axis, then to that side the object will grow in size.
4. **Center**, which allows the object to be adjusted concerning the horizontal center of the frame giving the option to have a stable object in the position it is first placed.
5. **Scale**, which allows the object's parameters (object and dimension) to be defined as a percentage of the frame's dimensions, so the object will readjust its parameters according to how the frame will be adjusted.

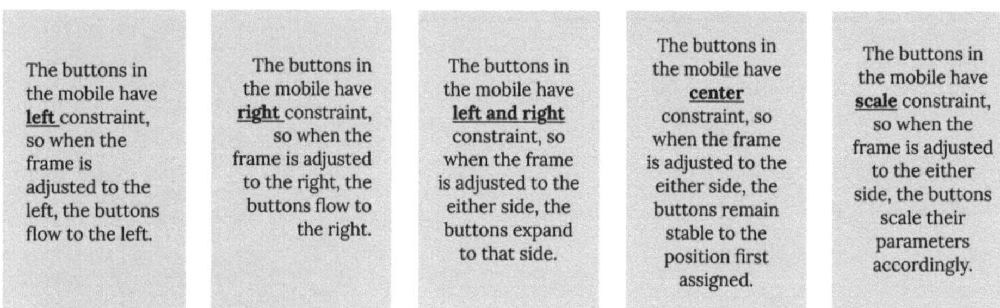

***Figure 9.11**: Types of horizontal constraints (from left to right: left, right, left and right, center, and scale). Reference: https://www.geeksforgeeks.org/constraints-in-figma/*

Similarly, there are five options in vertical alignment, which make the alignment vertically dynamic and adjustable. These are:

1. **Top**, which allows the layer to be adjusted about the top of the frame, so if the frame is resized to the top, then the object will flow upwards.
2. **Bottom**, which allows the layer to be adjusted about the bottom of the frame, so if the frame is resized to the bottom, then the object will flow downwards.
3. **Top and Bottom** maintain the layer's parameters (size and position) about the top and bottom of the frame, so if the frame is resized along the y-axis, then to that side, the object shows an increase in size.
4. **Center**, which allows the layer to be adjusted about the vertical center of the frame, so if the frame is adjusted to any side along the y-axis, the object remains stable in its determined position.
5. **Scale**, which allows the layer's parameters (size and position) to be defined as the percentage of the frame's dimension, so now the object will readjust its parameters according to how the frame will be adjusted.

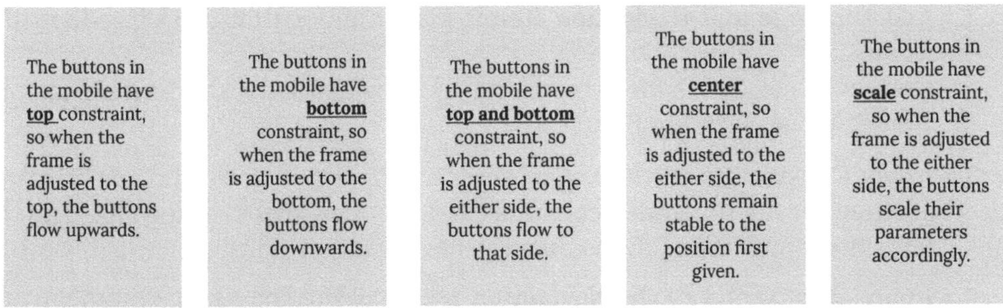

***Figure 9.12**: Types of vertical constraints (from left to right: top, bottom, top and bottom, center, and scale). Reference: https://www.geeksforgeeks.org/constraints-in-figma/*

To apply constraints:

1. Select the layer given within the frame you intend to apply constraint to.
2. Adjust the vertical and horizontal parameters that appear when the layer is selected.
3. Click on each tab of either vertical or horizontal constraint box and select the layer according to the need.

Overcoming limitations with constraints:

Constraints can be applied to any layer within a frame, but not to layers outside the frame or when the auto layout feature is enabled. You can also apply constraints to frames nested within other frames, but they cannot be applied to groups; if applied to a group, Figma will assign constraints to the individual layers within it. Constraints are only effective for rows and columns set to stretch, and do not work with other types of layouts.

Once constraints are applied, they remain fixed and will affect the design whenever a frame is resized. However, this may require some components to be adjusted. To prevent this from affecting the design, Figma offers an option to bypass constraints while resizing. On Mac, hold Command (Cmd), and on Windows, hold Control (Ctrl) to prevent components from being repositioned outside the applied constraints.

Example of using a constraint:

Scenario: You are designing a responsive website header that contains a logo on the left side and a navigation menu on the right. You want the logo to stay in place, while the navigation menu should adjust its layout and size as the screen width changes.

1. **Create the Header Frame:** Start by creating a frame that represents the header. Set its width to be variable, so it can stretch or shrink depending on the viewport size.

2. **Add the Logo and Navigation Items:** Place the logo on the left side of the frame.
   Create the navigation menu on the right side with a few text links (for example, Home, About, Services, Contact).
3. **Apply Constraints to the Logo:** Select the logo and go to the `Constraints` section. Set the Horizontal constraint to `Left`. This keeps the logo fixed on the left side of the header, even when the header is resized.
4. **Apply Constraints to the Navigation Menu:** Select the navigation menu and set the Horizontal constraint to `Right`. This ensures the menu stays aligned to the right side of the header when it stretches. For vertical alignment, you may set it to Center, so the menu stays vertically centered in the header.
5. **Test Responsiveness:** Now, resize the header frame to simulate how the layout will behave on different screen sizes: The logo should stay fixed on the left side of the header. The navigation menu should adjust its position to the right and stay centered vertically, ensuring the overall layout remains balanced.

Creating Responsive Typography and Spacing

Responsive typography involves adjusting text elements to maintain readability across different devices. This includes scaling font sizes, line heights, and adjusting letter spacing. In Figma, designers can create text styles for different breakpoints, ensuring that text remains legible on small mobile screens and large desktops alike.

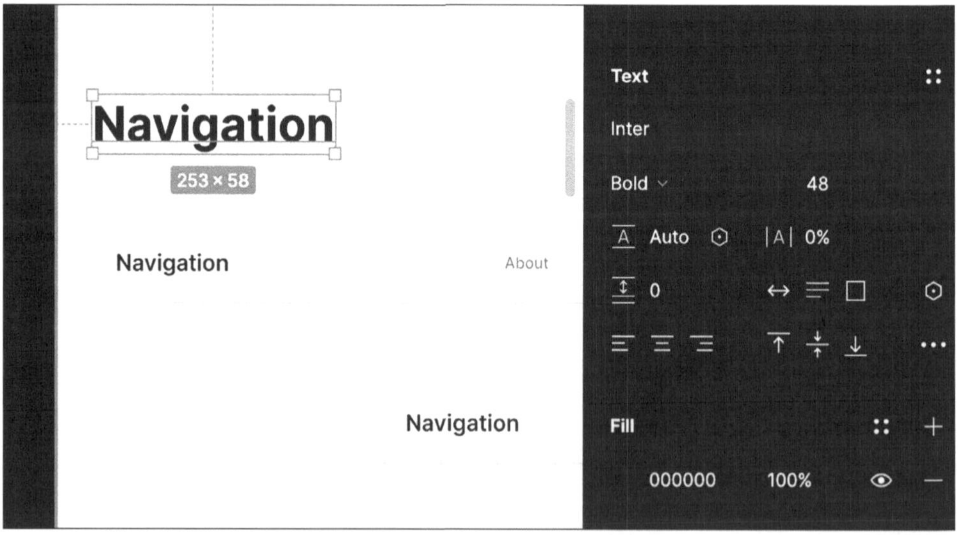

***Figure 9.13**: Typography settings in Figma*

Additionally, responsive spacing between elements ensures that the design remains balanced and aesthetically pleasing on all screen sizes. Proper use of margins, padding, and spacing helps maintain a clean and functional layout.

Previewing Designs on Different Devices

Ensuring that your design looks great on all devices is crucial for delivering a seamless user experience. In this section, you will learn how to utilize Figma's built-in device preview features to see how your designs appear on various screen sizes and resolutions. We will discover how to quickly switch between different device views, create interactive prototypes, and test them on actual devices. This hands-on approach will help you identify and fix any issues early in the design process, ensuring that your final product is optimized for mobile phones, tablets, desktops, and more. By mastering these previewing techniques, you can ensure a consistent and engaging user experience across all platforms.

Figma's Device Preview Features

Figma includes built-in device preview features that allow designers to see how their designs will appear on different devices. By selecting the appropriate frame preset and using the preview feature, designers can switch between various device views and ensure that their designs are responsive.

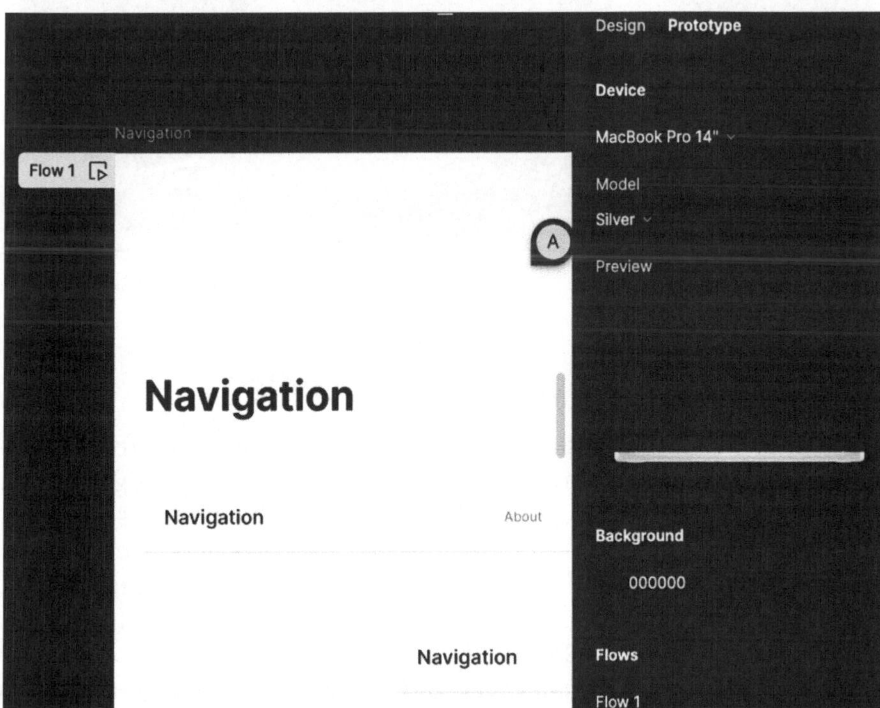

Figure 9.14: *Prototype settings in Figma*

This immediate feedback helps identify and resolve issues that may arise from different screen sizes and resolutions.

Prototyping and User Testing

Creating interactive prototypes in Figma enables designers to test their designs on actual devices. These prototypes can be shared with users or stakeholders for feedback, which is invaluable for identifying usability issues and ensuring the design works well across all devices. Testing prototypes on real devices helps uncover problems that might not be apparent in a desktop environment, such as touch target sizes on mobile screens or navigation patterns on tablets.

Figure 9.15: *In-person usability testing. Link: https://usabilitygeek.com/critical-usability-testing-mistakes-and-how-to-avoid-them/*

Integrating with Development Tools

For a smooth handoff from design to development, Figma integrates with various development tools and platforms. Designers can export their designs in multiple formats, such as CSS, SVG, or PNG, providing developers with the necessary assets and specifications. Figma's collaboration features also enable real-time communication between designers and developers, ensuring that the responsive design principles are accurately implemented. Tools such as Zeplin or Figma's own Inspect feature allow developers to extract CSS properties directly from the design files, ensuring fidelity in the final product. By adhering to these principles and leveraging Figma's extensive features, designers can create responsive designs that provide a consistent and engaging user experience across all devices. This approach not only enhances usability but also ensures that the product is accessible and enjoyable for a diverse audience.

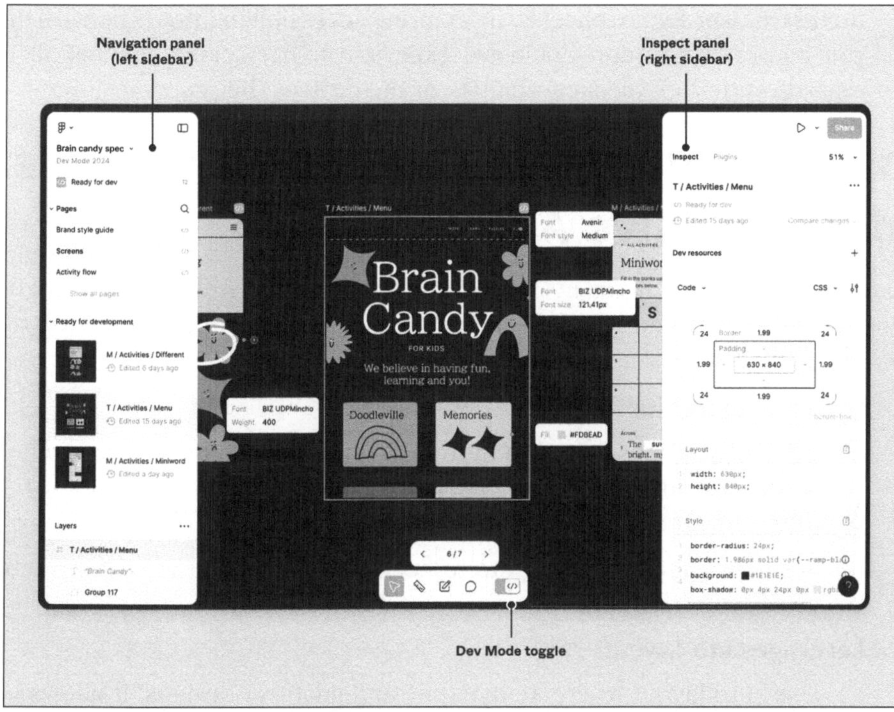

***Figure 9.16**: Dev mode in Figma. Link: https://usabilitygeek.com/critical-usability-testing-mistakes-and-how-to-avoid-them/*

Accessibility in Responsive Design

When designing a UI responsively, it is essential to consider accessibility to ensure that all users can interact with your interface, regardless of their abilities or devices.

- **Improved Navigation Across Devices:** Responsive design ensures that your UI adapts to various screen sizes, while accessibility ensures that interactive elements remain easy to navigate, whether using touch, keyboard, or screen readers.
- **Consistent Content Reflow:** As content reflows to fit different screen sizes, accessibility ensures it remains logically structured and easy to understand for all users, including those using assistive technologies.
- **Optimized Readability:** Adjusting text sizes and layouts for different devices improves readability, and incorporating accessibility best practices ensures that contrast ratios and font choices are suitable for users with visual impairments.
- **Seamless Cross-Device Interaction:** Responsive design ensures functionality across multiple devices, while accessibility ensures that these interactions remain usable by all, including those with motor or cognitive impairments.

- **Inclusive User Experience:** By integrating accessibility into responsive design, you can create a more inclusive experience that accommodates all users, regardless of their physical abilities or the devices they use.

Tips for Using Figma to Design Successful and Responsive Apps

By following the tips mentioned in this section, you can effectively use Figma to design responsive apps that offer a seamless and engaging user experience across a variety of devices and screen sizes.

- **Utilize Constraints:**
    - Use Figma's constraints to define how elements should behave when the screen size changes. This helps in maintaining the layout's integrity across different screen sizes.
    - Set constraints for elements to keep them fixed to the edges, center, or scale proportionally.
- **Leverage Auto Layout:**
    - Use auto layout to create dynamic and adaptive designs. It allows you to define padding, spacing, and alignment, which automatically adjust as the content or screen size changes.
    - This feature is particularly useful for designing lists, buttons, and other components that need to adapt to different sizes.
- **Create Multiple Frames:**
    - Design for multiple screen sizes by creating different frames for each target device. This allows you to see how your design adapts and to make necessary adjustments.
    - Start with a mobile-first approach and then scale up to tablets and desktops to ensure a seamless experience across devices.
- **Use Layout Grids:**
    - Apply layout grids to your frames to maintain consistent spacing and alignment. This is especially important for responsive design, where elements need to be flexible but orderly.
    - Use grids to guide the placement of UI elements, ensuring a balanced and visually appealing layout.
- **Prototype with Different Screen Sizes:**
    - Use Figma's prototyping features to create interactive prototypes for various screen sizes. This helps you test the user experience and make sure that the navigation and interactions work well on all devices.

  - Link frames together to simulate user flows and test how the design adapts in real time.

- **Test with Real Content:**
  - Use realistic content and data in your designs to see how they behave in different scenarios. This helps in identifying potential issues with text overflow, image scaling, and layout adjustments.
  - Utilize plugins such as Content Reel or Unsplash to fill your designs with real content easily.
- **Incorporate Responsive Design Patterns:**
  - Familiarize yourself with common responsive design patterns such as the off-canvas menu, flexible grids, and fluid typography. Incorporate these patterns into your designs to ensure they adapt gracefully.
  - Use Figma's components and variants to create reusable design patterns that can be applied across different frames and screen sizes.
- **Collaborate and Gather Feedback:**
  - Share your responsive designs with team members and stakeholders to gather feedback. Use Figma's commenting feature to discuss changes and improvements.
  - Regularly review the designs with your development team to ensure that the responsive behavior can be implemented effectively.
- **Optimize for Performance:**
  - Keep an eye on the performance of your design files, especially when working with high-resolution images and complex components. Optimize images and use vector graphics where possible to reduce file size.
  - Organize your layers and frames logically to make the design files easier to navigate and manage.
- **Stay Updated with Figma Features:**
  - Figma regularly updates its platform with new features and improvements. Stay informed about the latest updates and best practices to leverage new tools and functionalities for responsive design.
  - Follow Figma's blog, community forums, and official documentation to keep up with the latest tips and tricks.

Case Study: Designing Responsively for a Multi-Platform Banking App

A leading financial institution decided to redesign its banking app to provide a seamless user experience across multiple devices, including smartphones, tablets, and desktops.

The goal was to create a responsive design that maintained the app's functionality and aesthetic appeal, regardless of the device used. The design team chose Figma as their primary tool due to its robust features for responsive design.

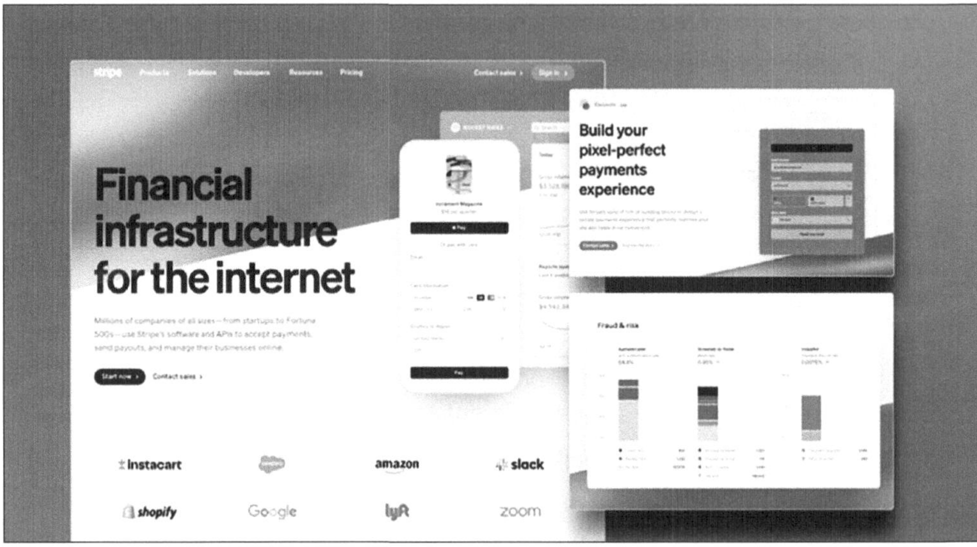

Figure 9.17: *Dev mode in Figma. Link: https://www.webstacks.com/blog/fintech-websites*

Objectives

- **Ensure Consistency:** Maintain a consistent look and feel across all devices.
- **Enhance Usability:** Improve user experience by optimizing the design for different screen sizes and resolutions.
- **Streamline Development:** Facilitate a smooth handoff to the development team with clear specifications and assets.

Implementation

- **Fluid Grids and Flexible Layouts:** The design team utilized Figma's auto layout and constraints to create a fluid grid system. This allowed components to resize and reposition dynamically based on the screen size. For example, the main navigation bar was set to stretch horizontally across the screen, ensuring it adapted seamlessly to different device widths.
- **Breakpoints and Adaptive Design:** The team identified key breakpoints for mobile, tablet, and desktop views. They created separate frames in Figma for each breakpoint and adjusted the layout accordingly. For instance, on mobile screens, the navigation menu was designed as a collapsible hamburger menu, while on larger screens, it was displayed as a horizontal bar.
- **Reusable Components and Design Systems:** To maintain consistency, the team

developed a comprehensive design system in Figma. This system included a library of reusable components, such as buttons, input fields, and icons, each designed to adapt to various screen sizes. The design system also defined color schemes, typography, and spacing guidelines, thus ensuring a unified visual language across the app.

- **Understanding Viewports and Resolutions:** The team used Figma's frame presets for common devices to start with the correct dimensions. The design was made for multiple viewports, including small mobile screens (375x667), tablets (768x1024), and desktops (1440x900). This ensured that the app was optimized for various resolutions and screen sizes from the outset.
- **Using Figma's Constraints and Auto Layout:** Constraints were applied to key elements to ensure they resized and repositioned correctly. For example, form fields and buttons were set to stretch horizontally within their parent containers. Auto layout was used for lists and grids, allowing these elements to adjust dynamically as the screen size changed.
- **Responsive Typography and Spacing:** Text styles were created for different breakpoints to ensure readability across all devices. For mobile screens, font sizes were increased slightly to improve legibility, while line heights were adjusted to enhance readability. Spacing between elements was also tailored to each device, ensuring a balanced and user-friendly layout.
- **Figma's Device Preview Features:** The team made extensive use of Figma's built-in device preview features to see how their designs would appear on different devices. This immediate feedback allowed them to identify and address any issues early in the design process.
- **Prototyping and User Testing:** Interactive prototypes were created and tested on actual devices. Users were asked to perform common tasks, such as transferring funds and checking account balances, to gather feedback on the design's usability. This testing helped identify touch target issues on mobile screens and navigation challenges on tablets.
- **Integrating with Development Tools:** Figma's integration with development tools like Zeplin facilitated a smooth handoff to the development team. Developers were provided with detailed specifications, CSS properties, and assets directly from the Figma design files. This ensured that the responsive design principles were accurately implemented in the final product.

Results

- **Consistent User Experience:** The redesigned app provided a seamless and consistent user experience across all devices. Users reported increased satisfaction and ease of use, particularly when switching between devices.
- **Improved Usability:** The app's usability improved significantly, with users

finding it easier to navigate and complete tasks on both mobile and desktop versions.

- **Efficient Development Process:** The streamlined handoff process facilitated by Figma's integrations and detailed specifications reduced development time and minimized errors, ensuring a high-quality final product.

Summary

The case study demonstrates how Figma's powerful features can be leveraged to design a responsive banking app that works effectively across multiple devices. By adhering to the principles of responsive design, utilizing Figma's constraints and auto layout, and thoroughly testing on different devices, the design team successfully created a user-friendly and visually consistent app that met the needs of a diverse user base.

Hands-On Exercises for Designing Responsively for Multiple Devices

Put your responsive design skills into practice with hands-on exercises that guide you through real-world scenarios using Figma. In this section, you will create fluid grids and flexible layouts, design for multiple breakpoints, and develop reusable components that adapt seamlessly across various devices. You will also preview and test your designs on different devices to ensure they look and function flawlessly. These practical exercises will solidify your understanding of responsive design principles, enhance your proficiency with Figma's powerful features, and prepare you to tackle design challenges with confidence.

Exercise 1: Setting Up a Fluid Grid and Flexible Layout

Objective: Create a fluid grid and flexible layout that adjusts to different screen sizes using Figma's auto layout and constraints.

Steps:

1. **Create a Frame:** Open Figma and create a new frame. Use the desktop preset (1440x900) as your starting point.

2. **Add Content:** Add a few elements such as a header, a sidebar, a main content area, and a footer.

3. **Apply Auto-Layout:** Select the main content area and apply auto-layout (Shift + A). Set the direction to vertical and spacing between items to 24px.

4. **Set Constraints:** For each element within the frame, set constraints to ensure

they resize correctly. For example, set the header and footer to stretch horizontally, and the sidebar to be fixed on the left with a flexible width.

5. **Test Resizing:** Resize the frame horizontally and vertically to see how the elements adjust. Make necessary adjustments to constraints and auto layout settings to ensure a fluid and flexible layout.

Exercise 2: Designing for Multiple Breakpoints

Objective: Create layouts for different breakpoints (mobile, tablet, desktop) and ensure that the design adapts seamlessly across all devices.

Steps:

1. **Create Multiple Frames:** Create three frames for mobile (375x667), tablet (768x1024), and desktop (1440x900) presets.
2. **Design for Mobile:** Start with the mobile frame and design a simple landing page with a header, main content area, and footer. Use a vertical layout and ensure all elements are legible and accessible.
3. **Adapt for Tablet:** Copy the mobile design to the tablet frame. Adjust the layout to make use of the extra space. For example, you might change the navigation to a horizontal bar and adjust text sizes.
4. **Adapt for Desktop:** Copy the tablet design to the desktop frame. Adjust the layout to utilize the wider screen. This might include adding more columns, increasing spacing, and enhancing visual hierarchy.
5. **Review Consistency:** Compare all three frames to ensure consistency in design and functionality. Make any necessary adjustments to maintain a coherent user experience across all breakpoints.

Exercise 3: Creating and Using Reusable Components

Objective: Develop reusable components that adapt to different screen sizes and integrate them into a design system.

Steps:

1. **Create Basic Components:** Create basic UI components such as buttons, input fields, and cards. Design these components with responsiveness in mind, ensuring they look good on various screen sizes.
2. **Define Component Properties:** Use Figma's component properties to define how these components should adapt to different screen sizes. Set constraints and auto layout settings accordingly.

3. **Build a Design System:** Organize these components into a design system. Create a Figma library and publish the components to make them available for use across multiple projects.
4. **Integrate Components:** Use the components from your design system to build a sample page. Ensure that each component adapts correctly to different screen sizes by testing in mobile, tablet, and desktop frames.
5. **Update and Iterate:** Make updates to your components as needed. See how changes in the component reflect across all instances in your design.

Exercise 4: Previewing and Testing Designs on Different Devices

Objective: Preview and test your designs on actual devices to ensure they are responsive and user-friendly.

Steps:

1. **Use Figma's Device Preview:** Select your design frame and use Figma's built-in device preview feature. Switch between different device views to see how your design adapts.
2. **Create Interactive Prototypes:** Create interactive prototypes of your design. Link different pages and interactions to simulate user flow.
3. **Share Prototypes:** Share your prototypes with team members or stakeholders and gather feedback. Use Figma's sharing features to generate a link.
4. **Test on Real Devices:** Test your prototypes on real devices (smartphones, tablets, desktops). Pay attention to touch targets, text readability, and overall usability.
5. **Iterate Based on Feedback:** Gather feedback from your testing and make necessary adjustments to improve responsiveness. Update your design system as needed.

Conclusion

Responsive design is essential in today's multi-device world, where users interact with digital products across various screen sizes and resolutions. This chapter explored the core principles of responsive design within Figma, including fluid grids, flexible layouts, breakpoints, and reusable components. We also delved into designing for different screen sizes and resolutions, utilizing Figma's constraints and auto layout features, and ensuring responsive typography and spacing.

Through practical exercises, you gained hands-on experience in creating adaptive layouts, setting up multiple breakpoints, building and using a design system, and testing your designs on real devices. These exercises highlighted the importance of fluid design principles and the capabilities of Figma in managing responsive design workflows efficiently. By adhering to the principles and techniques discussed, you can ensure that your designs provide a consistent and engaging user experience across all devices. This not only enhances usability but also broadens the accessibility and appeal of your digital products. As technology continues to evolve, mastering responsive design will remain a critical skill for any designer aiming to create versatile and user-friendly interfaces.

In summary, responsive design is not just about making your designs look good on different devices; it is also about creating a seamless and intuitive experience that adapts to the user's context. Figma's powerful tools and features support this process, enabling you to design responsively with precision and efficiency. As you continue to apply these principles in your projects, you will be well-equipped to meet the challenges of designing for a multi-device world.

Transition to the next chapter

With the completion of *Chapter 9, Designing Responsively for Multiple Devices*, you have gained essential skills in designing responsive interfaces using Figma. Now, it is time to apply these skills to real-world scenarios. *Chapter 10, Real-World Projects and Case Studies*, will focus on applying Figma skills to practical projects by managing design projects from start to finish using Figma's powerful features. We will explore real-world examples of successful designs, providing insights into best practices and innovative solutions.

Recap of Key Points

- **Principles of Responsive Design within Figma**: Use auto layout and constraints to create designs that adapt to different screen sizes. Implement different layouts for various screen sizes by using frames to simulate breakpoints.
- **Designing for Various Screen Sizes and Resolutions**: Use Figma's frame presets for different devices to start with correct dimensions. Apply constraints and auto layout to ensure elements resize and reposition appropriately across different screen sizes. Adjust text sizes, line heights, and spacing to ensure readability and aesthetic balance on all devices.
- **Previewing and Testing Designs on Different Devices:** Utilize built-in preview features to see how designs look on different devices. Create interactive prototypes and test them on actual devices to gather feedback and identify usability issues. Use Figma's integration with development tools for a smooth handoff, providing developers with clear specifications and assets.

CHAPTER 10
Real-World Projects and Case Studies

Introduction

This chapter delves into the practical application of Figma skills through real-world projects and case studies that you can curate into portfolio projects. It provides readers with insights into how Figma is used in professional design contexts and offers guidance on applying Figma techniques to their own projects. The chapter begins by highlighting ways to showcase your work such as case studies featuring successful designs created with Figma. Readers gain valuable insights into the design process, from initial concept development to final execution, through detailed analysis of these real-world examples.

The chapter also offers practical tips and strategies for building a professional design portfolio using Figma projects. Readers learn how to curate and showcase their work effectively, highlighting their skills and expertise to potential employers or clients. By exploring real-world projects and case studies, the readers gain a deeper understanding of how Figma can be leveraged to solve design challenges and create impactful designs. This chapter is designed to serve as inspiration for the readers to apply their newfound Figma skills to their own projects and build a strong portfolio of work.

Structure

In this chapter, we will cover the following topics:

- Ways to Showcase Your Work
- Case Studies Showcasing Successful Designs
- The Evaluation Rubric of a Design Case Study
- Selected Examples of Good UX Design
- Tips for Building a Professional Design Portfolio

- Follow Along and Build a Case Study
- Solving Design Challenges with Figma
- Applying Figma Techniques to Your Projects

Ways to Showcase Your Work

You can use a variety of ways to communicate the process and impact you have created with your Figma portfolio projects. To help you with your journey and choosing the right medium to showcase your work, the table that follows outlines the audience, purpose, and content across a case study, a real-world project, and a portfolio project. Throughout this chapter, we may use these terms interchangeably.

A **case study** is a detailed, narrative-focused analysis of a specific design project or process.

- **Purpose**: To illustrate the designer's problem-solving skills, decision-making, and the impact of their work.
- **Structure**: Typically includes the problem statement, research and insights, design process, outcomes, and reflections.
- **Focus**: Communicating the thought process, challenges faced, and lessons learned, often with a storytelling approach.

Real-world projects are design initiatives that address actual business or user needs in practical, non-theoretical scenarios.

- **Purpose**: To solve real problems, create tangible value, and meet client, stakeholder, or user requirements.
- **Scope**: May involve collaboration with teams, deadlines, and constraints such as budget or technical limitations.
- **Examples**: Corporate product designs, client-based assignments, or contributions to commercial or nonprofit initiatives.

Portfolio projects are curated examples of a designer's work intended to showcase their skills, expertise, and creativity to potential employers, clients, or collaborators.

- **Purpose**: To demonstrate the breadth and depth of design capabilities and build credibility.
- **Source**: Can include real-world projects, case studies, or speculative work (self-initiated or conceptual designs).
- **Presentation**: Often tailored to highlight specific strengths, aligning with the designer's goals or the audience's interests.

Aspect	Case Studies	Real-World Projects	Portfolio Projects
Audience	Design reviewers, peers, hiring managers	Clients, end-users, and stakeholders	Employers, clients, and collaborators
Purpose	To explain a design process and insights	To address practical, real-world problems	To showcase expertise and versatility
Content	Focused on narrative and process	Deliverables for real scenarios	Highlighted examples of best work

***Table 10.1**: Ways to showcase your work with respective audience, purpose, and content*

Case Studies Showcasing Successful Designs

Finding inspiration from case studies is crucial for learning Figma because it provides practical, real-world examples of how the tool is used by professionals to solve design challenges. Here are some reasons why this is important:

- **Understanding Application in Real-World Contexts:**
  - **Practical Insights**: Case studies showcase how Figma is applied in various industries and projects, providing practical insights that go beyond theoretical knowledge.
  - **Problem-Solving Techniques**: They demonstrate how designers use Figma to address specific design problems, offering solutions and techniques that can be applied to similar challenges.
- **Learning Best Practices:**
  - **Effective Use of Features**: By analyzing case studies, learners can see how advanced features of Figma, such as blending modes, effects, and typography tools, are effectively utilized in professional projects.
  - **Workflow Optimization**: Case studies often highlight efficient workflows and strategies for collaboration, helping learners to adopt best practices in their own design processes.
- **Gaining Inspiration and Ideas:**
  - **Creative Inspiration**: Seeing the innovative designs and creative solutions in case studies can spark new ideas and inspire learners to experiment with different design approaches in Figma.
  - **Expanding Skill Set**: Exposure to a variety of design styles and techniques helps learners expand their skill set and adapt new methods to their projects.

- **Building Confidence:**
  - **Real-World Validation**: Understanding how successful designers use Figma builds confidence in learners, showing them that they can achieve similar results by applying what they have learned.
  - **Step-by-Step Guidance**: Detailed breakdowns of design processes provide step-by-step guidance, making it easier for learners to replicate and understand complex techniques.
- **Networking and Community Engagement:**
  - **Connecting with Designers:** Case studies often highlight the work of specific designers or teams, providing opportunities to connect with them and learn more about their experiences and insights.
  - **Participating in Discussions**: Engaging with case studies can lead to participation in discussions and fora, fostering a sense of community and shared learning among Figma users.
- **Benchmarking and Self-Assessment:**
  - **Setting Standards**: By studying high-quality case studies, learners can set benchmarks for their work and strive to meet or exceed industry standards.
  - **Identifying Strengths and Weaknesses**: Comparing their work to professional case studies helps learners identify areas for improvement and focus their learning efforts on specific skills.

Exploring Case Studies

Case studies showcasing successful designs can be found in various online platforms and resources. Here are some notable sources where designers and design enthusiasts can explore in-depth analyses of successful design projects:

Figma Community:

- Link: https://www.figma.com/community
- Figma itself has a vibrant community where designers share their projects and case studies. Browsing the Figma community can provide direct insights into how professionals and enthusiasts are using Figma to create impactful designs.

Design Blogs and Websites:

- Websites such as Medium, Smashing Magazine, and Awwwards often feature detailed case studies on various design projects. These platforms provide comprehensive breakdowns of design processes, challenges, and solutions.
- Medium–UX Case Studies, link: https://medium.com/tag/ux-casestudies

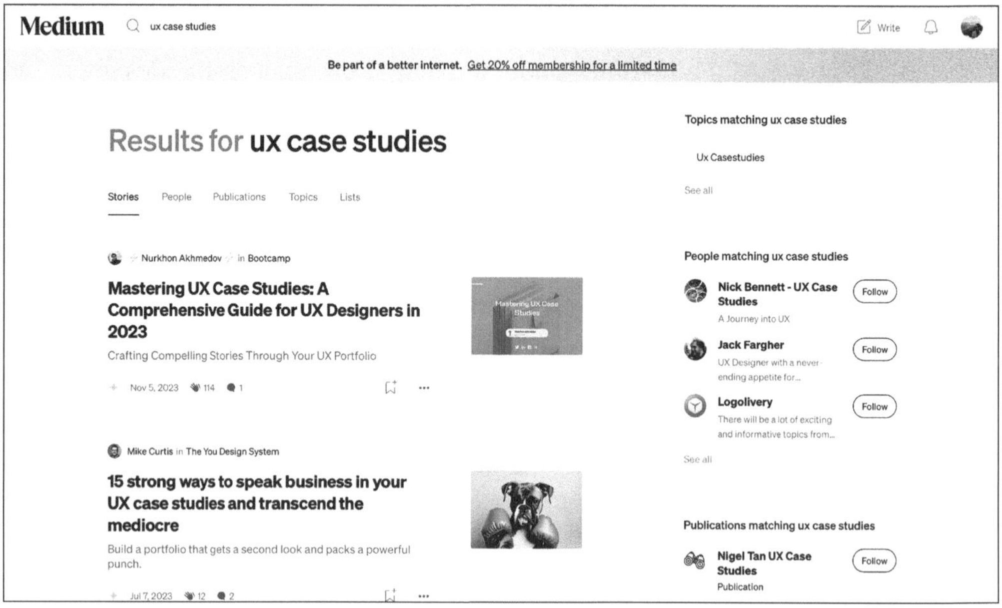

Figure 10.1: *Medium UX case studies*

- Smashing Magazine, link: https://www.smashingmagazine.com

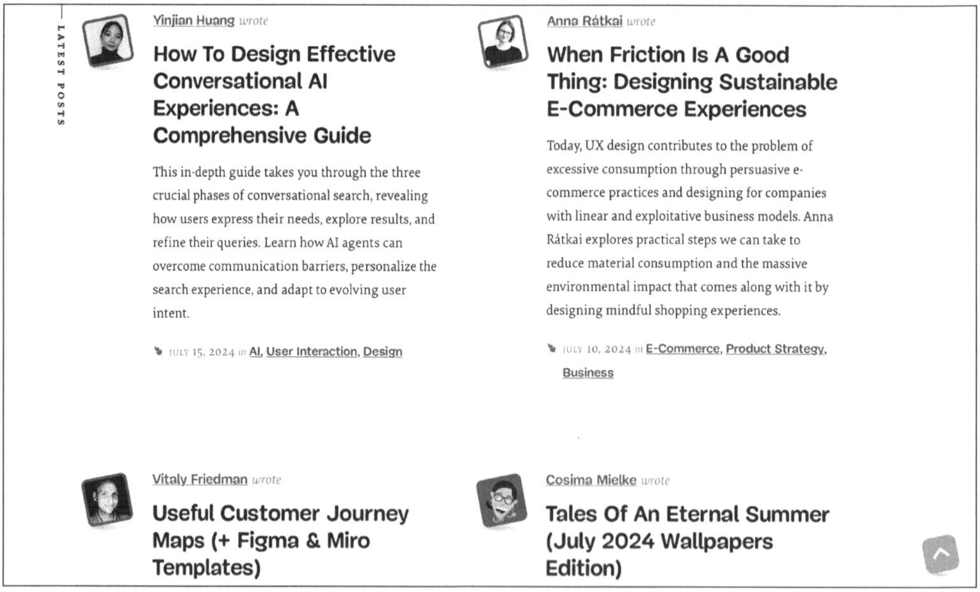

Figure 10.2: *Smashing Magazine*

- Awwwards, link: https://www.awwwards.com

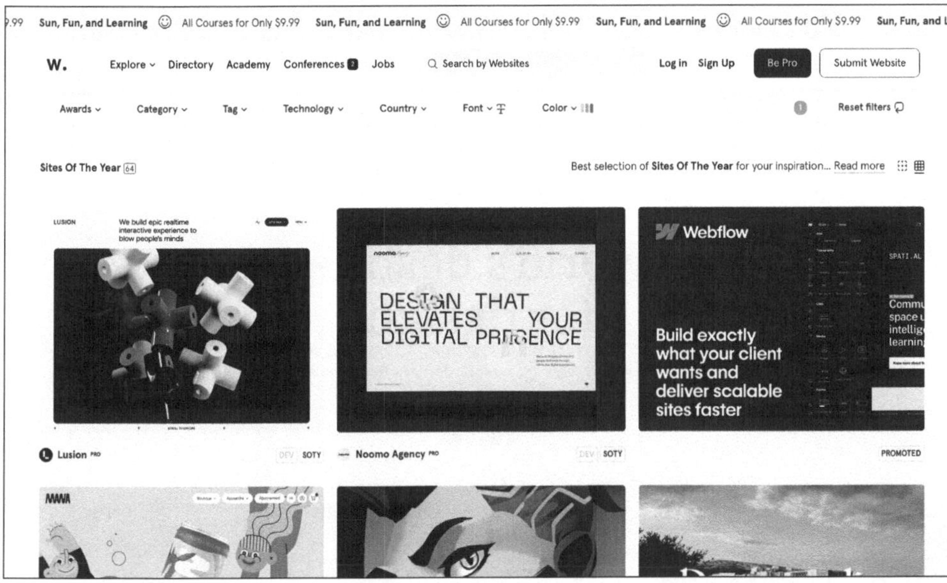

Figure 10.3: *Awwards website*

Design Portfolios and Personal Websites:

- Many designers showcase their work and case studies on personal websites and portfolios. Platforms such as Behance and Dribbble are great places to explore these portfolios and gain insights into different design approaches and methodologies.
- Behance, link: https://www.behance.net

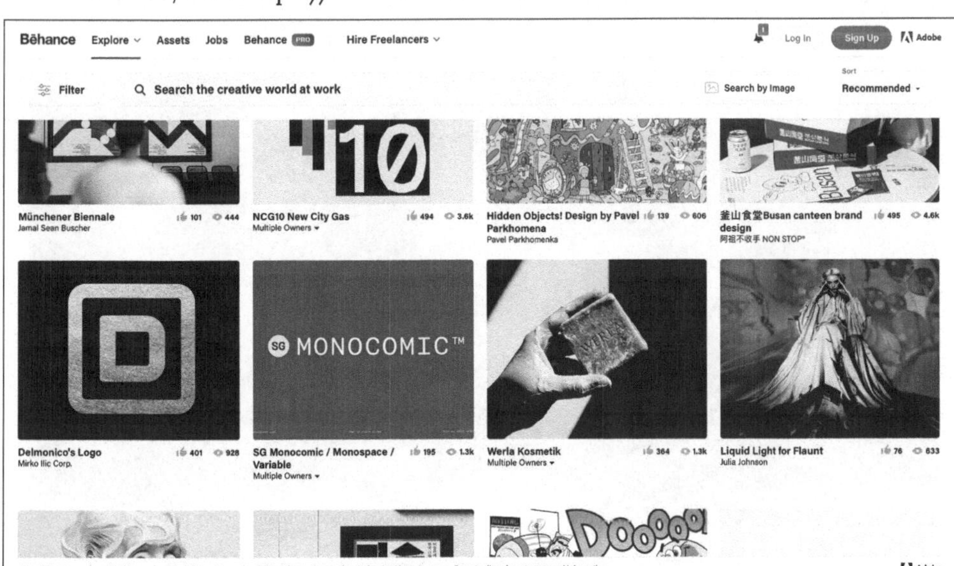

Figure 10.4: *Behance website*

- Dribbble, link: https://dribbble.com

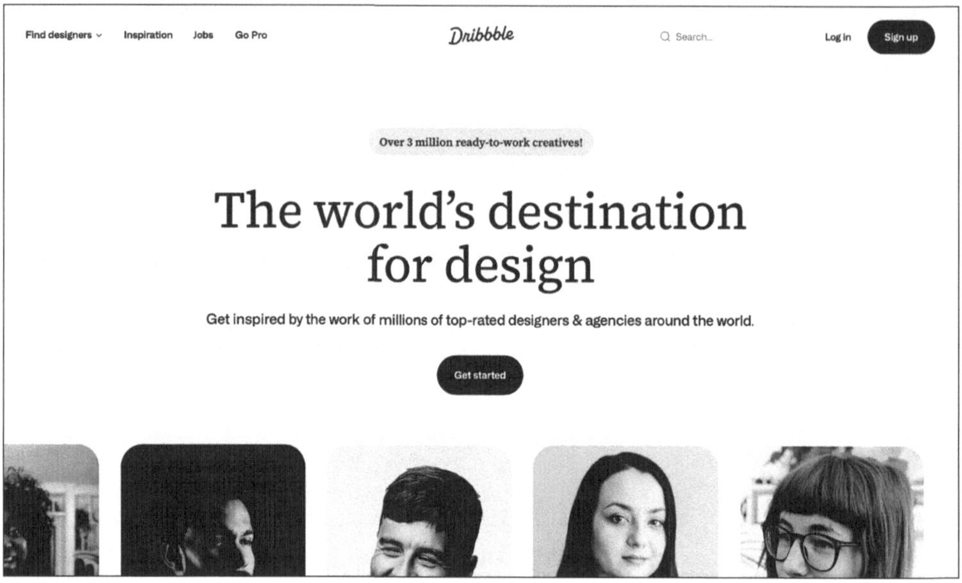

Figure 10.5: *Dribble website*

Company Blogs and Design Agencies:

- Leading design agencies and tech companies often publish case studies on their blogs, highlighting their work with clients. These case studies offer valuable insights into professional design processes and client interactions.
- IDEO, link: https://www.ideo.com/

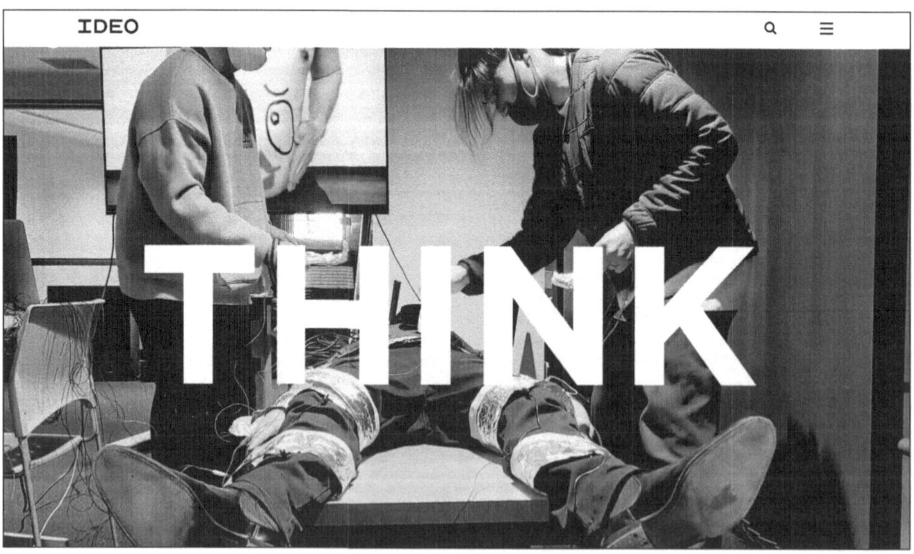

Figure 10.6: *IDEO website*

- Nielsen Norman Group, link: https://www.nngroup.com/

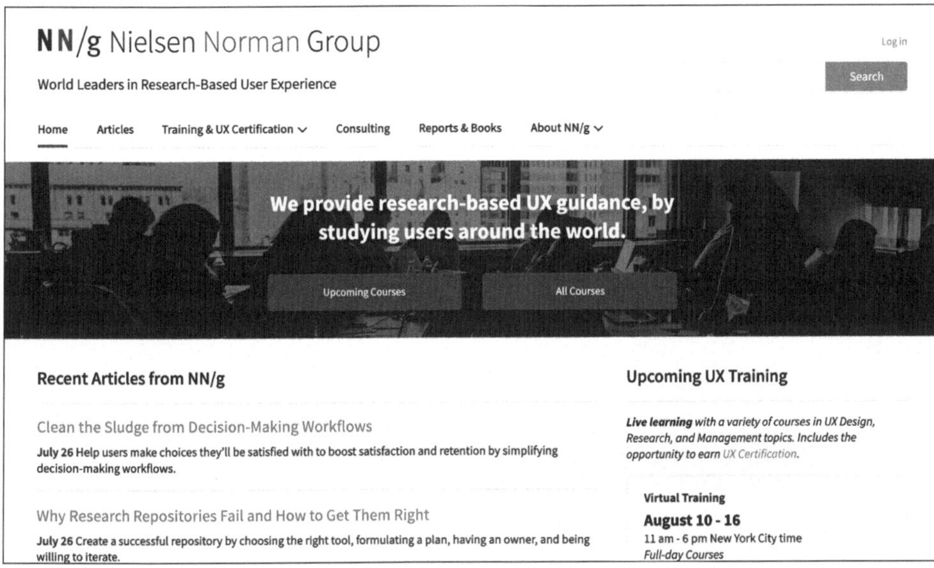

Figure 10.7: *NNG website*

Design Conferences and Webinars:

- Attending design conferences, webinars, and workshops can provide access to case studies presented by industry experts. These events often feature talks and presentations on successful design projects.
- UXDX, link: https://uxdx.com

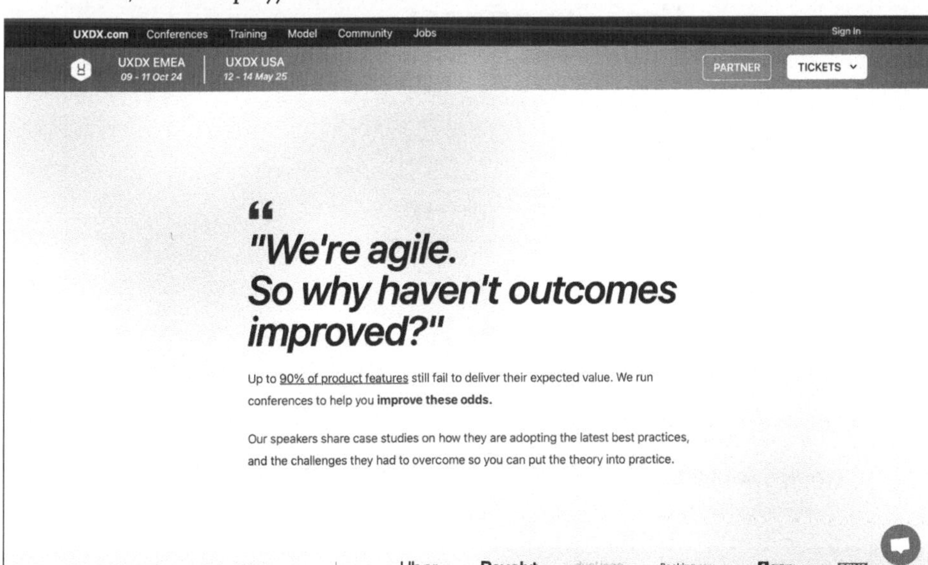

Figure 10.8: *UXDX website*

- Interaction Design Association (IxDA), link: https://ixda.org

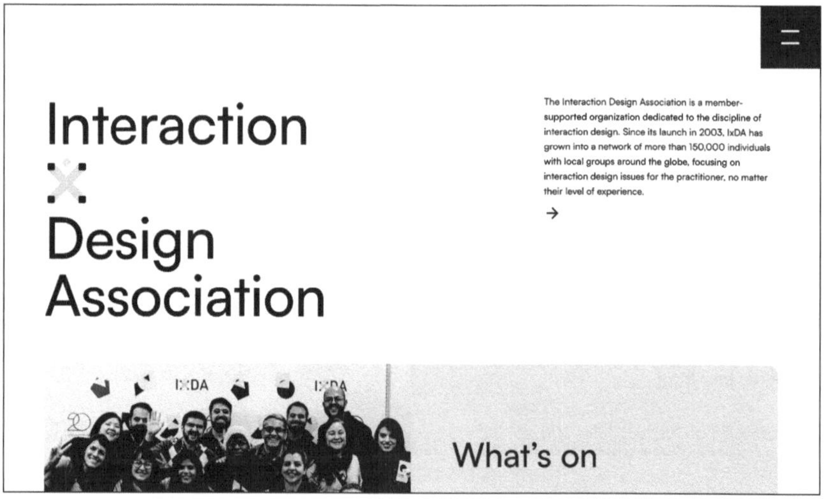

***Figure 10.9**: IxDA website*

Academic Journals and Publications:

- For more scholarly case studies, academic journals and publications on design and human-computer interaction (HCI) can be valuable resources. These journals often feature research-based case studies with in-depth analysis.
- Journal of Usability Studies, link: https://uxpajournal.org

***Figure 10.10**: Journal of UX website*

YouTube and Online Courses:

- Many designers and educators share their case studies and design processes on YouTube and through online courses. Platforms such as Coursera, Udemy, and LinkedIn Learning also offer courses that include case studies.

The Evaluation Rubric of a Design Case Study

Evaluating a good design case study involves examining several key criteria to ensure it effectively communicates the designer's process, skills, and impact. The following table provides a rubric of the evaluation criteria detailing when a case study exceeds, meets, or does not meet the bar for a hiring manager. Self-evaluate your work against this table before your next UX portfolio walkthrough to improve your chances of landing the job.

Key Points	Exceeds the Bar	Meets the Bar	Does Not Meet the Bar
Clarity and Structure			
Clear Objective: Starts with a clear problem statement, goals, and intended impact.	Objective is exceptionally detailed and tied to user and business outcomes.	Objective is stated but lacks depth or clear connection to user/business impact.	Objective is vague or missing entirely.
Logical Flow: Follows a logical narrative structure: problem, research, ideation, design, implementation, results, and reflections.	Narrative is seamless, intuitive, and supported with strong transitions and context.	Narrative follows structure but may lack fluidity or minor sections are unclear.	Narrative is disorganized or incomplete.
Readable Layout: Uses headings, bullet points, and visual aids to enhance readability and support the narrative.	Layout is highly organized, with engaging visuals that enhance understanding.	Layout is readable but may be overly dense or lack strong visual support.	Layout is cluttered or lacks proper formatting and visuals.

Research and Insights			
User Research: Demonstrates understanding of target audiences through personas, journeys, and empathy maps.	User research is thorough, detailed, and directly informs design choices.	User research is evident but lacks depth or direct connection to design decisions.	Little to no user research is shown, or it feels superficial.
Problem Definition: Clearly defines problems based on user research and identifies pain points and needs.	Problem definition is insightful, detailed, and aligns strongly with research findings.	Problem is defined but lacks clarity or depth in alignment with research.	Problem is poorly defined or not aligned with research findings.
Insightful Analysis: Derives actionable insights from research, including competitive analysis or user feedback.	Insights are innovative and lead to impactful design directions.	Insights are present but may be basic or lack innovation.	Insights are unclear, unoriginal, or absent.
Design Process			
Ideation: Showcases brainstorming and generation of diverse ideas.	Explores a wide range of creative ideas and justifies the selected solution.	Shows some ideation with a few ideas considered.	Limited or no ideation is evident.
Design Decisions: Explains reasoning behind choices in colors, typography, layout, and interactions.	Decisions are deeply reasoned and supported by research or data.	Decisions are stated but not fully justified.	Decisions are arbitrary or lack explanation.
Prototyping and Testing: Highlights usability testing, feedback incorporation, and iteration process.	Detailed documentation of testing with clear examples of how feedback shaped iterations.	Testing is mentioned but lacks detail or depth of feedback incorporation.	Prototyping or testing is absent or superficial.

Iterations: Displays various design versions and improvements based on testing.	Iterations show significant progression with clear rationale for changes.	Iterations are present but lack depth or clear progression.	Iterations are minimal or absent.
Visual and Interactive Elements			
High-Quality Visuals: Includes high-resolution images, wireframes, mockups, and prototypes.	Visuals are polished, compelling, and effectively communicate design details.	Visuals are clear but lack polish or completeness.	Visuals are missing, low quality, or unclear.
Interactive Prototypes: Provides links to interactive prototypes showcasing functionality.	Prototypes are fully functional and demonstrate advanced interactivity.	Prototypes are functional but basic or limited in scope.	Prototypes are not included or are non-functional.
Design Consistency: Maintains a cohesive visual style aligned with brand or project requirements.	Design is highly consistent and demonstrates strong brand alignment.	Design is consistent but with minor deviations.	Design lacks consistency or brand alignment.
Results and Impact			
Metrics and Outcomes: Highlights measurable outcomes such as user engagement, conversion rates, or satisfaction scores.	Metrics are detailed and show significant impact backed by data.	Metrics are included but may lack depth or clear impact.	Metrics are vague or absent.
Feedback: Includes stakeholder or user feedback to validate success.	Feedback is comprehensive and showcases user or stakeholder satisfaction.	Feedback is included but minimal or lacks detail.	Feedback is missing or irrelevant.
Reflection: Reflects on lessons learned, challenges faced, and potential future improvements.	Reflection is deep, thoughtful, and provides actionable insights for future work.	Reflection is present but superficial or lacks actionable insights.	Reflection is absent or uninformative.

Personal Contribution			
Role and Responsibilities: Clearly articulates the designer's specific contributions.	Role is clearly defined with substantial individual contributions showcased.	Role is mentioned but lacks specificity or detail.	Roles and responsibilities are unclear or absent.
Collaboration: Details collaboration with team members, such as developers and product managers.	Collaboration is detailed, showing strong teamwork and synergy.	Collaboration is mentioned but lacks detail or emphasis.	Collaboration is missing or downplayed.
Communication and Storytelling			
Engaging Narrative: Presents a compelling story about the project journey.	Narrative is highly engaging and emotionally connects the reader with the project.	Narrative is clear but may lack engagement or flow.	Narrative is disjointed or uninspiring.
Professional Tone: Maintains a professional tone, free of jargon and grammatical errors.	Tone is polished, professional, and easy to understand for diverse audiences.	Tone is professional but may include minor errors or unclear phrasing.	Tone is unprofessional or includes multiple errors.
Cohesiveness: Ensures all elements of the case study work together seamlessly.	Case study feels unified, with all elements reinforcing the main narrative effectively.	Case study is cohesive but with some inconsistencies or gaps.	Case study feels fragmented or disconnected.
Aesthetics: Demonstrates visually appealing and polished design that reflects the designer's attention to detail.	Aesthetic is visually striking, refined, and aligned with best design principles.	Aesthetic is acceptable but lacks refinement or originality.	Aesthetic is poorly executed or visually unappealing.

Table 10.2: *Evaluation rubric for a portfolio review*

Selected Examples of Good UX Design

Following is a curated list of case studies that fair well on the rubric of what makes a good UX design. Please visit the links provided on a computer and add your thoughts to why or why not you like the example as a portfolio.

Study Hall Design:

https://studyhall.design

Figure 10.11: *Study Hall Design website*

Using the rubric from the previous section, what do you like about it?

Using the rubric from the previous section, what can be improved?

Fan Study By Spotify:

https://fanstudy.byspotify.com

Figure 10.12: *Study Hall Design website*

Using the rubric from the previous section, what do you like about it?

Using the rubric from the previous section, what can be improved?

UI/UX Design by Ana for a Mobile App:

https://www.uiuxbyana.com/privileeapp

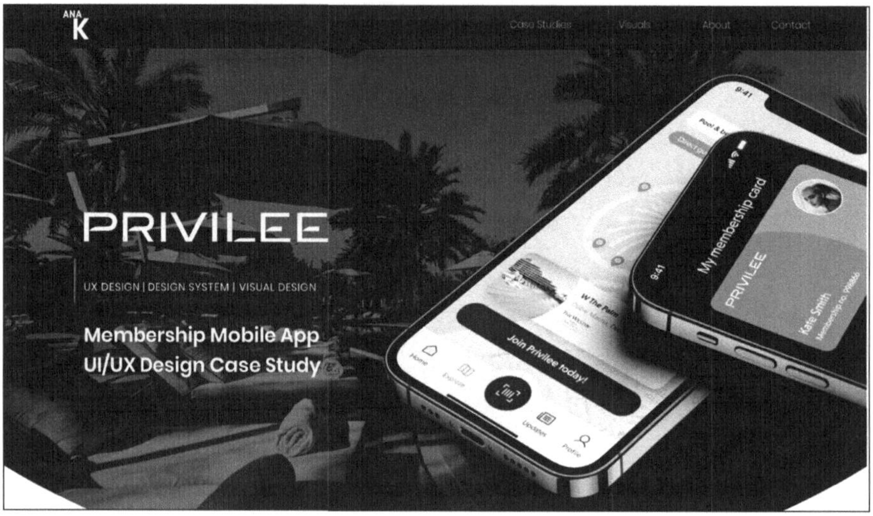

Figure 10.13: *Case study for mobile app design*

Using the rubric from the previous section, what do you like about it?

Using the rubric from the previous section, what can be improved?

Pencil and Paper strategy for Dashboard Design:

https://www.pencilandpaper.io/services/data-dashboard

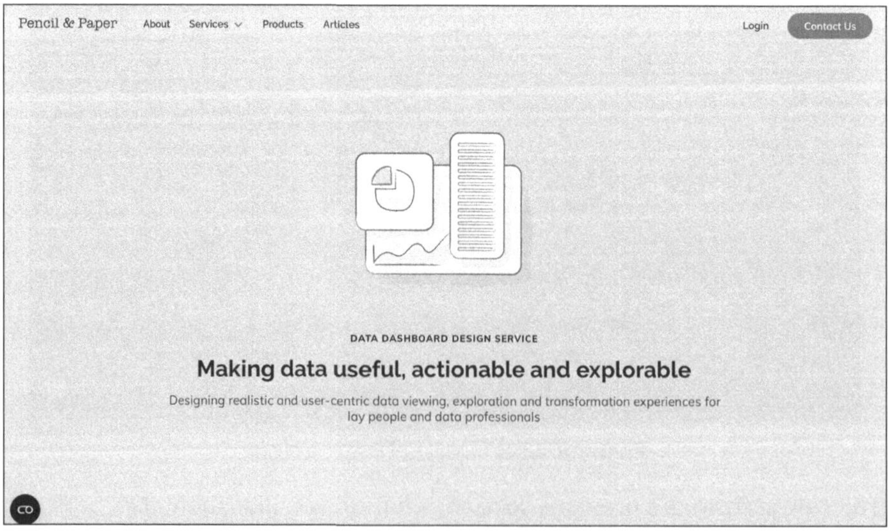

Figure 10.14: *Case study for process that the agency applies to creating dashboard designs*

Using the rubric from the previous section, what do you like about it?

Using the rubric from the previous section, what can be improved?

Hello Monday

https://www.hellomonday.com

Figure 10.15: *Hello Monday website hosts multiple case studies*

Using the rubric from the previous section, what do you like about it?

Using the rubric from the previous section, what can be improved?

Tips for Building a Professional Design Portfolio

By curating a diverse range of projects, highlighting your design decisions and problem-solving abilities, and presenting your work effectively, you can create a professional design portfolio that showcases your skills and makes a strong impression on potential employers or clients. Here are some tips to ensure your portfolio stands out:

Selecting Projects that Showcase a Range of Skills:

- **Diversity of Work**: Include a variety of projects that demonstrate different aspects of your design skills. This could be a mix of UI/UX design, web and mobile interfaces, branding, and illustration.
- **Depth and Breadth**: Show both the breadth of your skills by including different

types of projects, and the depth by featuring comprehensive case studies of significant projects.

- **Technical Skills**: Highlight projects that required technical prowess, such as complex interactions, animations, or advanced use of Figma features like auto layout and interactive components.
- **Soft Skills**: Include projects that demonstrate your soft skills, such as collaboration on team projects or your ability to adapt to client feedback.

Highlighting Key Design Decisions and Problem-Solving Abilities:

- **Design Rationale**: For each project, clearly articulate the design decisions you made and the rationale behind them. Explain why you chose certain colors, typography, layout structures, and how these choices contributed to the project's goals.
- **Challenges and Solutions**: Highlight specific challenges you faced during the project and how you overcame them. This shows to potential employers or clients your problem-solving skills and resilience.
- **Impact and Results**: Whenever possible, include metrics or feedback that demonstrate the success of your designs. This could be user engagement statistics, client testimonials, or improved usability scores.

Once you have curated your best projects, the next step is to present them in a way that is both visually appealing and easy to navigate.

Using Figma to Create a Cohesive Portfolio Layout:

- **Consistent Layout**: Design a portfolio layout in Figma that is consistent across all projects. Use a grid system to ensure that alignment and spacing are uniform, creating a clean and professional look.
- **Interactive Elements**: Take advantage of Figma's interactive components to make your portfolio more engaging. This could include clickable prototypes that allow viewers to interact with your designs or hover states that reveal additional information.
- **Responsive Design**: Ensure your portfolio looks great on all devices by designing with responsive principles in mind. Use Figma's constraints and auto layout features to adapt your layout for different screen sizes.
- **Accessibility**: Pay close attention to accessibility guidelines and ensure legibility with readable font sizes, color contrast ratios, alt text for imagery, visual hierarchy with labels (screen reader), and rem values to scale the design. Use typography, color, and spacing to create a visual hierarchy that guides viewers through your portfolio. Important information should be prominent and easy to read.

Adding Annotations and Descriptions to Provide Context:

- **Descriptive Text**: Include clear and concise descriptions for each project. Explain the project's goals, your role, the tools you used, and the outcome.
- **Annotations**: Use annotations to highlight specific parts of your designs. This can help viewers understand the functionality and thought process behind your work. Figma's comment feature can be useful here, allowing you to add notes directly on your designs.

Tips for Presenting Your Portfolio to Potential Employers or Clients:

- **Tailor Your Portfolio**: Customize your portfolio for each job application or client pitch. Highlight the projects and skills that are most relevant to the position or client needs.
- **Professional Presentation**: When presenting your portfolio, whether in person or virtually, be prepared to walk through your designs and explain your thought process. Practice delivering a clear and confident presentation.
- **Online Presence**: Ensure your portfolio is accessible online. Use platforms like Figma's prototype sharing feature or create a personal website. Make it easy for potential employers or clients to view your work without requiring downloads or additional software.
- **Feedback and Iteration**: Regularly update your portfolio based on feedback from peers, mentors, and industry professionals. Continuously iterate on your portfolio to keep it current and reflective of your best work.

Follow Along and Build a Case Study

Use the following prompts to generate your very own case study. The exercise will typically take you about 40 hours to generate materials and 80 hours to curate a case study.

Phase 1: Project Kickoff and Discovery

Objective: Understand the current user experience and identify areas for improvement.

Develop a redesign plan using Figma to streamline the design process and facilitate collaboration.

Interview question examples:

- Warm-up questions such as name and role.
- How would you describe your role?
- Please walk me through the process of completing Task A.
- What do you dislike/like about the process today?

Redesign plan example:

- **Discovery**: Interview users groups A and B.
- **Define**: Present findings to design team, synthesize, and define the problem.
- **Design**: Figma prototyping low-fidelity.
- **Deliver**: Deliver to Dev.

Actions:

- Conduct user research through surveys, interviews, and usability testing of the existing app. Tip: Record all sessions.
- Analyze feedback to identify key pain points and areas for enhancement.
- Create a detailed project plan, including a timeline, task allocation, and milestones. You will most likely use Jira for project planning.

Findings:

Users reported difficulty in navigating the complex interface and finding specific features.

The existing design must be updated and aligned with modern UI/UX standards.

Tip: *Take screenshots of UI steps and place them in Figma to reference and/or create a process flow.*

There was a need for a more intuitive and visually appealing design to increase user satisfaction and efficiency.

Objective: Create wireframes to visualize the new structure and layout of the desktop app.

Use Figma's collaborative features to involve stakeholders in the design process.

Actions:

- Develop low-fidelity wireframes for key screens and user flows using Figma.
- Hold collaborative design workshops with stakeholders to gather feedback and refine wireframes.
- Used Figma's commenting feature to document feedback and design decisions.
- Grouping text or auto layout for process flow: You may also group text and shapes to create process flows that outline the current and target states before low fidelity. Or you can use auto layout to allow for automatic formatting.
    - **Step 1**: Create text.
    - **Step 2**: Click "*Shift*"+"A".
    - **Step 3**: Select a fill color.

- **Step 4**: Create a few boxes and "*Shift*"+ "A" to auto layout the process flow.

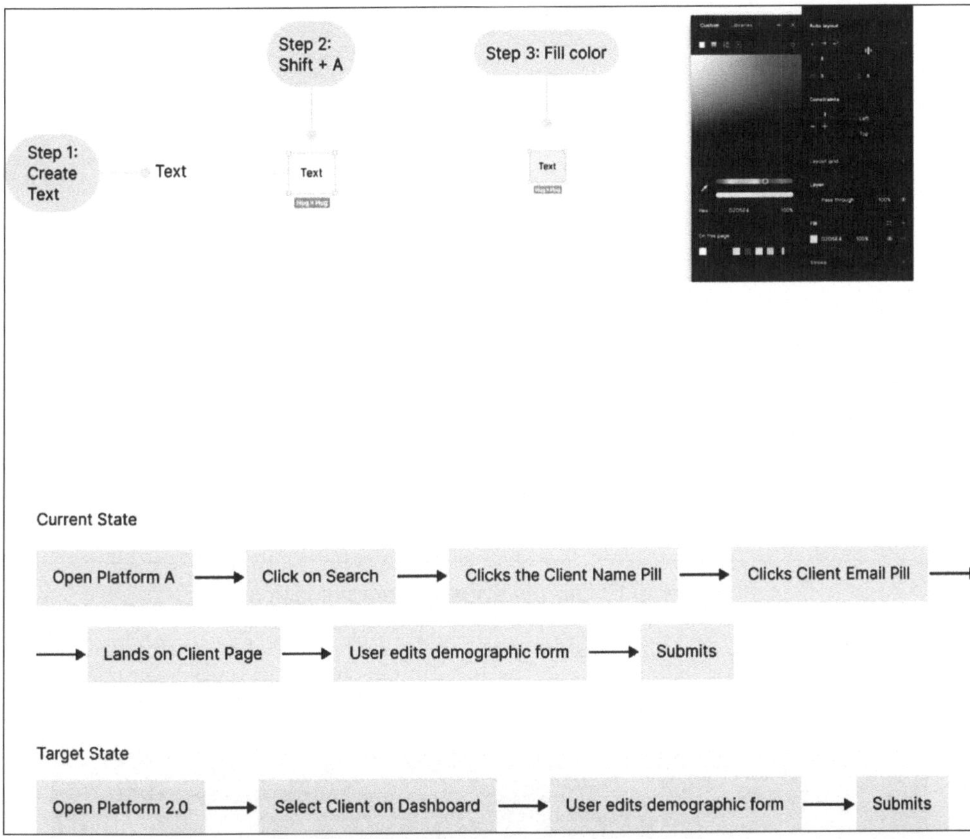

Figure 10.16: *Creating user flows in Figma*

- Present these flows to your stakeholders.
- **Low-fidelity:** See if you have an available low-fi asset kit by your team. You can create shapes within a frame to represent low fi.

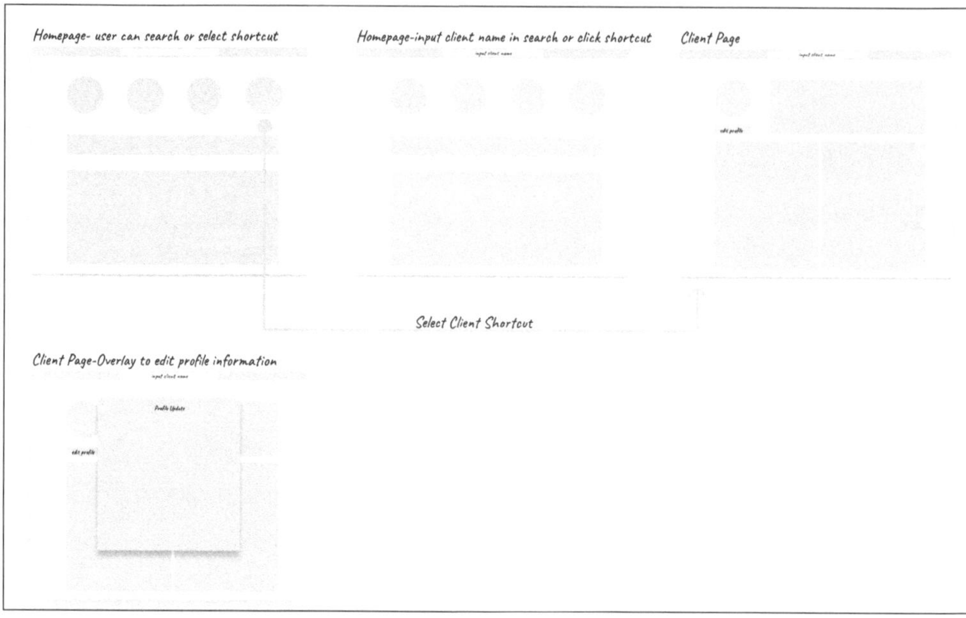

Figure 10.17: *Low fidelity wireframes in Figma*

Comments: Your team and stakeholders can make comments for feedback. Press "C" or select the comment bubble. Tag people by clicking "@" + "name". Select anywhere in the wireframe to comment.

Figure 10.18: *Commenting in Figma*

Phase 3: Designing Solutions

Objective: Develop high-fidelity designs to showcase the visual style and detailed UI elements. Create interactive prototypes to test user flows and gather feedback.

Actions:

- Design high-fidelity mockups using Figma, incorporating modern UI principles and the company's branding guidelines.
- Apply advanced design techniques such as blending modes, effects, and advanced typography to enhance the visual appeal.

Outcome:

- The high-fidelity designs received positive feedback for their modern look and improved usability.

- Interactive prototypes helped stakeholders visualize the final product and provided a basis for user testing.

Workflow Steps:

- **Step 1:** Lay out the frames in the desired order. You will want to create a frame to start prototyping and grouping elements. Ensure you review any existing design systems that you may leverage.
- **Step 2:** Go to prototype mode.

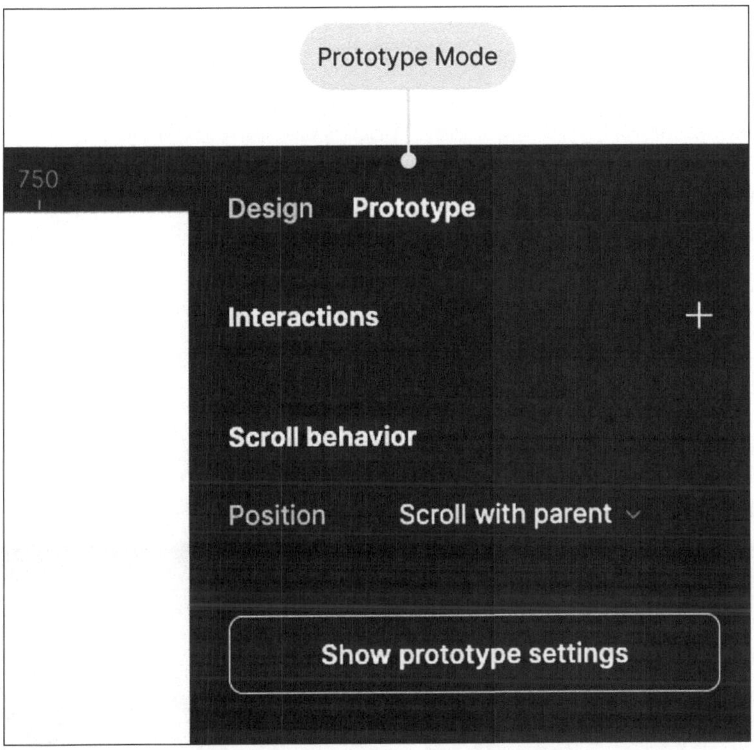

Figure 10.19: *Prototype mode in Figma*

- **Step 3**: Select the element you want to prototype. In this use-case, we want to select Disney and update their profile.
- **Step 4**: Pull the line to your desired destination.

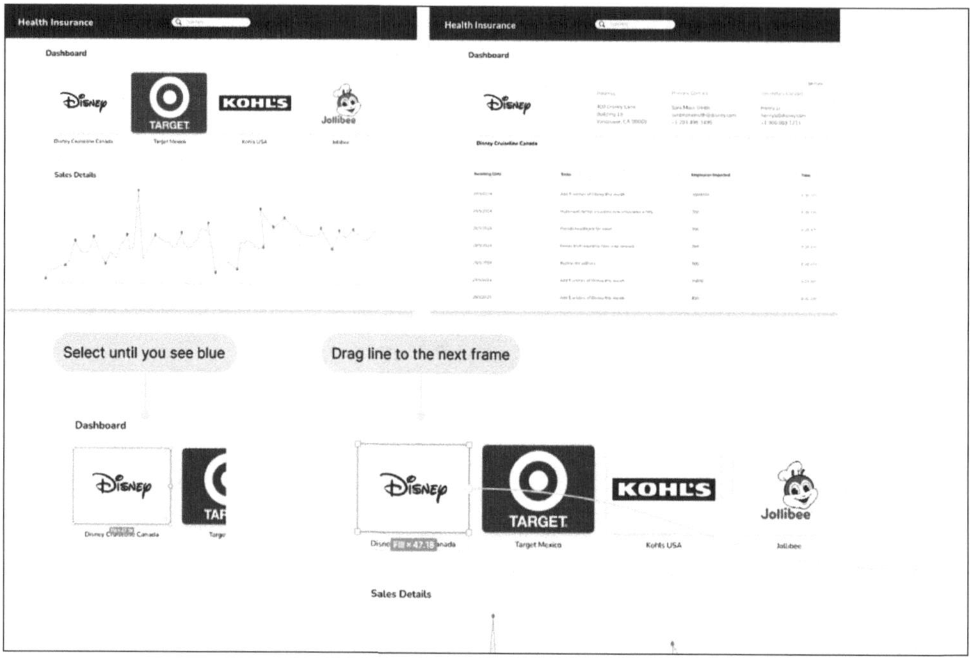

Figure 10.20: *Creating visual design frames in Figma*

- **Step 5:** Preview the prototype by selecting the play button. Or select "*Shift*" + "*Spacebar*" to preview. Ensure that you name the flows so that in the prototype mode, you can select flows there.

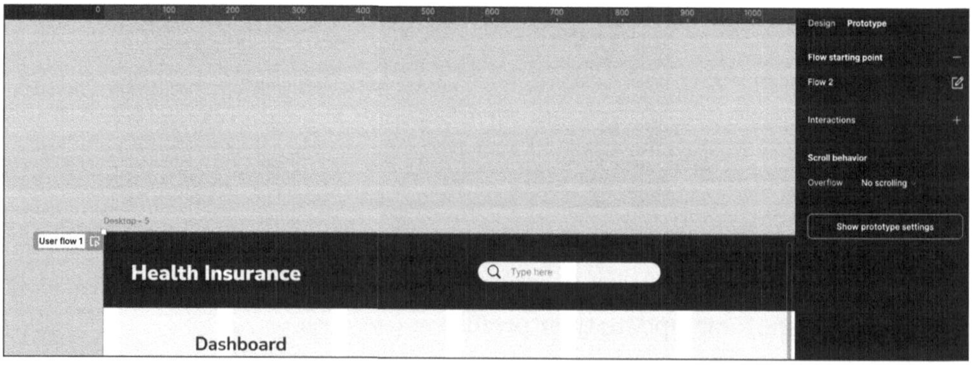

Figure 10.21: *Naming a flow in Figma*

- **Special Effects:** May not be used for enterprise design due to existing design systems and existing logos. You may play around with the objects to add visual appeal. Select the layer that reads, "**`Pass through`**." There are overlapping layers to understand the results.

Figure 10.22: *Special effects in Figma*

- **Typography:** For typography, modify the size, kerning, and leading. Try it: Add text and use the typography setting to turn it into all caps. Play with adding bullet points or numbered lists.

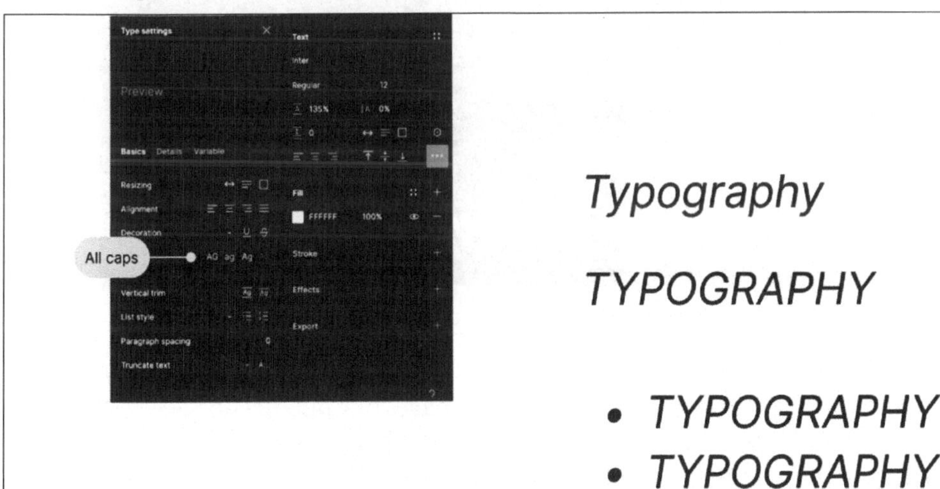

Figure 10.23: *Typography in Figma*

Phase 4: Evaluation of Design Solutions

Objectives: Validate the new design through extensive user testing and gather actionable feedback. Iterate on the design based on user feedback to ensure optimal usability.

Actions:

- Conducted usability testing sessions with current users of the desktop app, using the interactive prototypes created in Figma.
- Collected quantitative and qualitative data on user interactions and pain points.
- Used Figma's version control and comment resolution features to manage iterations and document changes.

Outcome:

- User testing revealed areas where the design could be further improved, such as simplifying certain workflows and enhancing accessibility features.
- Iterative design refinements led to a more intuitive and efficient user experience.

To review, when you select the play button, you will be taken to a prototype page after you complete the prototyping. Allow the usability testing to take place here. You can then document the areas where the users have had issues.

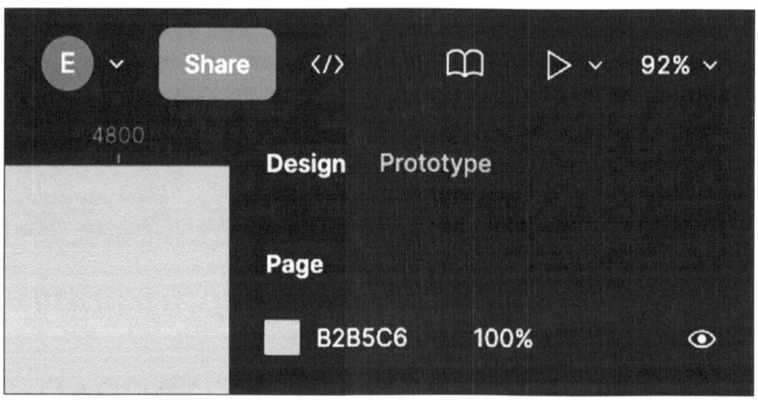

Figure 10.24: *Prototype play button in Figma*

When you have multiple flows, ensure to version up and date the flows. You may divide the wireframes by pages. Add a blank page, but put dashes "---". The page will create a line divider to help with organizing the pages. Section off each of the flows by selecting the section tool. That will make it easier to move around the flows.

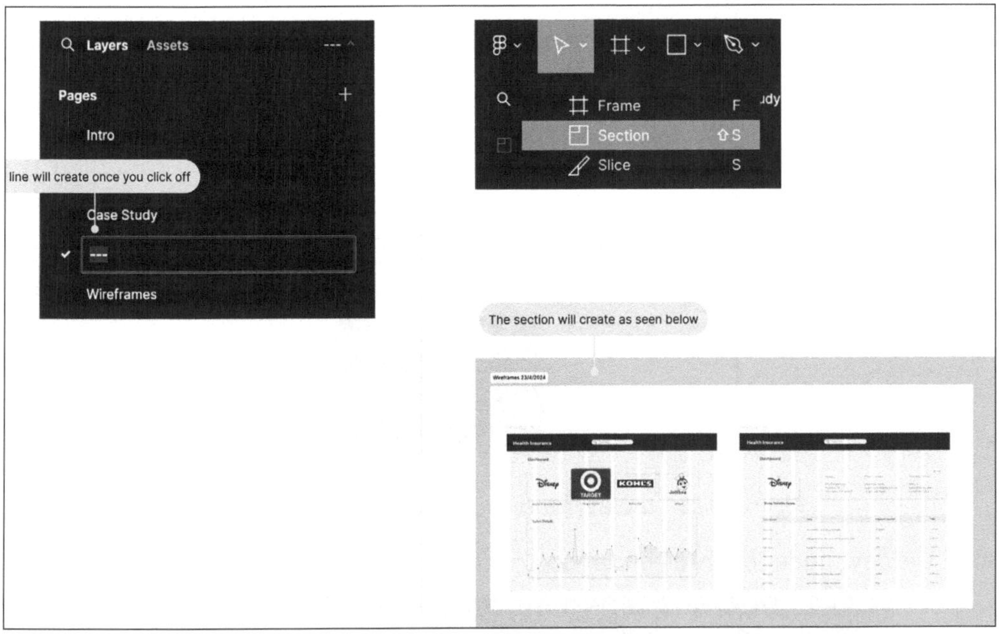

Figure 10.25: Creating sections in Figma

Phase 5: Development Handoff

Objectives: Finalize the design and prepare for development handoff. Ensure seamless communication between the design and development teams.

Actions:

- Finalized high-fidelity designs and created a comprehensive style guide in Figma, detailing components, typography, and color schemes.
- Used Figma's export features to generate assets and specifications for developers.
- Held handoff meetings to ensure that developers understood the design and could implement it accurately.

Outcome:

- The development team successfully implemented the new design, thanks to the detailed documentation and assets provided.
- The redesigned desktop app launched with improved usability, modern aesthetics, and positive user feedback.

Select the section frame and click on the label. You will select "`ready for dev`." That way, the dev team knows which flows are free.

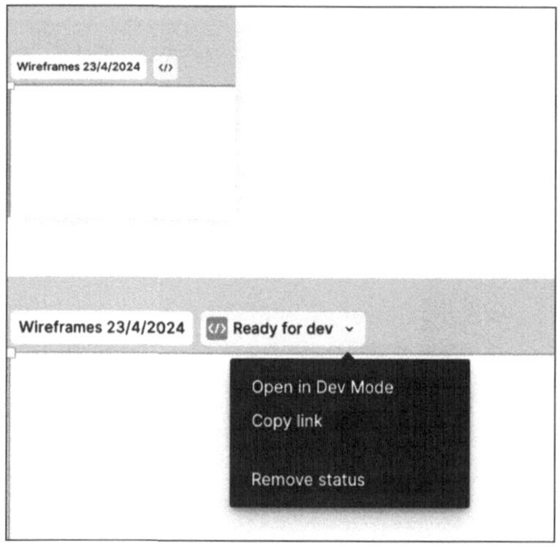

Figure 10.26: *Labeling the section as ready for development*

Go in the dev mode to write comments for the dev team.

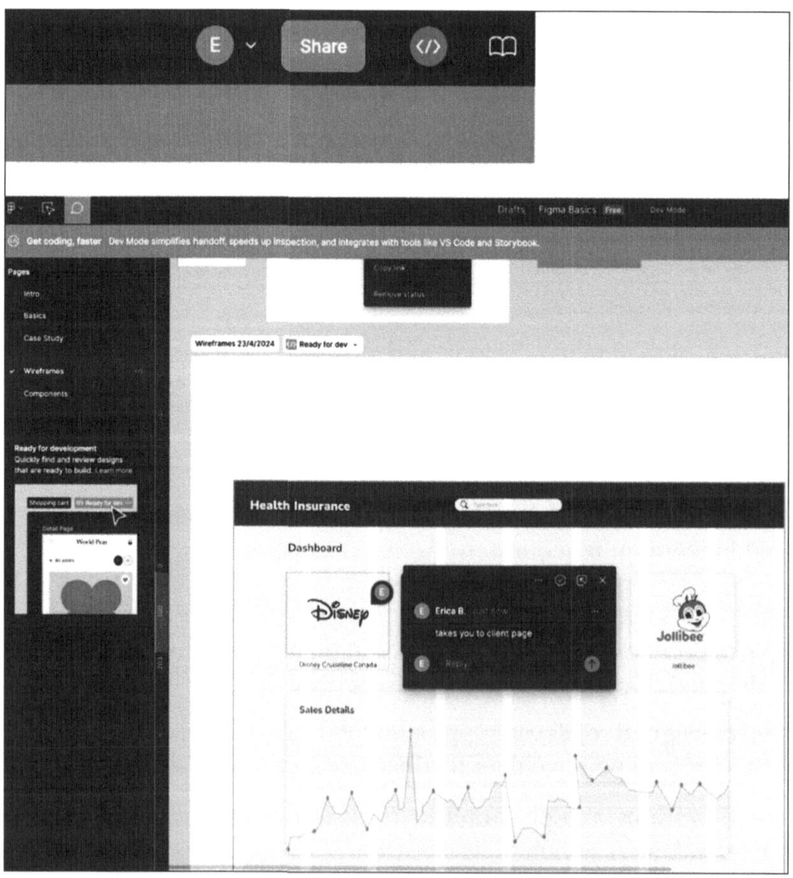

Figure 10.27: *Example of leaving comments for developers*

Solving Design Challenges with Figma

- **Leveraging Figma's Real-Time Collaboration Features:** Figma stands out in the design industry for its robust real-time collaboration capabilities, which are crucial for modern design workflows. By allowing multiple team members to work on the same design file simultaneously, Figma eliminates the bottlenecks associated with traditional design tools where files need to be passed back and forth. This feature ensures that everyone is working with the most up-to-date version of the design, significantly reducing the chances of miscommunication and outdated revisions. Real-time collaboration fosters a more dynamic and interactive environment where ideas can be shared, refined, and implemented instantly.
- **Effective Communication and Feedback Loops:** Effective communication is essential for successful design projects, and Figma excels in facilitating this through its built-in commenting and annotation features. Team members and stakeholders can leave comments directly on specific design elements, making feedback precise and actionable. This streamlines the review process and ensures that all feedback is consolidated in one place. Figma's ability to resolve comments once they are addressed keeps the design process organized and transparent. Additionally, integrating video conferencing tools with Figma can further enhance communication by allowing live discussions and immediate feedback during design reviews.
- **Responsive Design:** Designing for multiple devices requires a responsive design approach, and Figma provides the tools needed to create adaptable layouts. With features like auto layout and constraints, designers can build designs that automatically adjust to different screen sizes and orientations. Auto layout allows designers to create components that resize and reflow content based on the screen size, ensuring a consistent and user-friendly experience across devices. Constraints enable designers to define how elements should behave when the screen size changes, providing precise control over the layout's responsiveness.
- **Using Auto Layout and Constraints:** Auto layout and constraints are powerful tools in Figma for creating responsive designs. Auto layout helps in organizing and maintaining the spatial relationships between different design elements, making it easier to scale and adapt designs to various screen sizes. Constraints allow designers to set rules for how elements should resize or reposition relative to their containers or other elements. By combining auto layout with constraints, designers can ensure that their designs are flexible and adaptable, providing a seamless experience across different devices and screen resolutions.

- **Prototyping and Testing:** Prototyping is an integral part of the design process, allowing designers to create interactive versions of their designs that can be tested on real devices. Figma's prototyping features enable designers to link different screens and create transitions, mimicking the flow of a real application or website. This is essential for testing and refining user interactions and navigation. By conducting thorough prototyping and testing, designers can identify and address usability issues early in the design process, leading to more user-friendly and effective designs.

Conducting User Testing and Iterating Based on Feedback: Creating interactive prototypes in Figma is a straightforward process that brings designs to life, allowing designers and stakeholders to experience and evaluate the functionality of the design. Interactive prototypes are invaluable for conducting user testing, as they provide a realistic representation of the final product. User testing involves observing real users as they interact with the prototype to identify pain points, usability issues, and areas for improvement. Figma's prototyping capabilities make it easy to simulate complex interactions and gather meaningful feedback.

Based on the feedback from user testing, designers can iterate on their designs to enhance usability and address any identified issues. This iterative process involves making adjustments to the design, updating the prototype, and conducting further testing until the design meets the desired user experience and functionality goals. By continuously refining the design based on user feedback, designers can ensure that the final product is intuitive, efficient, and meets the needs of the target audience.

Applying Figma Techniques to Your Projects

By applying these Figma techniques to your own projects, you can ensure that your design process is organized, efficient, and effective. Whether you are just starting a new project or looking to enhance an existing one, leveraging Figma's advanced features and continuously improving your skills will enable you to create exceptional designs that stand out and meet the needs of your users.

1. **Getting Started with Your Own Projects**

    a. **Identifying Project Goals and User Needs:** The first step in any design project is to clearly define the goals and understand the needs of the users. Start by identifying what you want to achieve with your project. Are you designing a website, a mobile app, or a desktop application? What are the primary objectives of your design? Understanding the end goals will guide your design decisions throughout the project. Equally important is understanding the needs and behaviors of your target users. Conduct user research, create user personas, and gather feedback to gain insights into what your users expect and need from your design. This foundational understanding will ensure that your design solutions are user-centric and aligned with your project goals.

   b. **Planning Your Design Process:** Effective planning is essential for a successful design project. Begin by outlining the key stages of your design process, from initial concept development to final execution. Break down the project into manageable tasks and set realistic timelines for each phase. Create a project roadmap that includes milestones and deadlines to keep your project on track. Consider using project management tools to organize your tasks and collaborate with team members. Planning your design process helps you stay organized, manage your time efficiently, and ensure that all aspects of the project are addressed systematically.

2. **Using Figma's Advanced Features**

   a. **Implementing Blending Modes, Effects, and Advanced Typography:** Figma offers a range of advanced features that can elevate the quality of your designs. Blending modes allow you to create visually stunning effects by controlling how layers interact with each other. Experiment with different blending modes to achieve unique visual outcomes and enhance the overall aesthetics of your design. Effects such as shadows, gradients, and blurs add depth and dimension to your design elements, making them more engaging and realistic. Advanced typography techniques, including kerning, leading, and text effects, enable you to create visually appealing and readable text treatments. Mastering these advanced features will give you greater control over your designs and allow you to create sophisticated and polished results.

   b. **Utilizing Plugins to Enhance Workflow and Capabilities:** Figma's plugin ecosystem offers a wealth of tools that can enhance your workflow and expand the capabilities of the platform. Plugins can automate repetitive tasks, integrate with other tools, and provide additional functionality that is not available natively in Figma. For example, you can use plugins to generate placeholder content, create complex animations, or import data from external sources. Explore the Figma Community to discover and install plugins that can streamline your design process and help you achieve your project goals more efficiently. Incorporating plugins into your workflow allows you to work smarter, not harder, and focus more on the creative aspects of your design.

3. **Continuous Learning and Improvement**

   a. **Staying Updated with Figma's Latest Features and Updates:** Figma is continually evolving, with regular updates and new features being introduced to enhance its capabilities. Staying updated with these changes is crucial for maximizing your efficiency and effectiveness as a designer. Follow Figma's official blog, join design communities, and participate in webinars and workshops to stay informed about the latest features and best practices. Experiment with new tools and techniques to expand your skill set and incorporate them into your projects. Continuous learning and improvement will keep you at the forefront of design innovation and enable you to deliver cutting-edge solutions that meet the ever-changing demands of the industry.

Conclusion

In this chapter, we have explored how to apply Figma techniques to your own projects, focusing on essential steps such as identifying project goals, understanding user needs, and planning your design process. We delved into the use of Figma's advanced features, including blending modes, effects, and advanced typography, as well as the integration of plugins to enhance your workflow and capabilities. Finally, we emphasized the importance of continuous learning and staying updated with Figma's latest features to keep your skills sharp and relevant.

Now, it is time to put these insights and techniques into practice. Take what you have learned and apply it to your real-world projects. By doing so, you will not only refine your skills but also create designs that are both user-centric and visually compelling. Experiment with different features, explore new plugins, and keep pushing the boundaries of what you can achieve with Figma.

Building a strong portfolio with Figma projects is crucial for showcasing your skills and expertise to potential employers or clients. A well-curated portfolio demonstrates your ability to tackle diverse design challenges, make informed design decisions, and create impactful solutions. As you continue to grow as a designer, remember that your portfolio is a living document that should evolve with your skills and experiences. Keep updating it with your best work, and let it be a testament to your growth in the field of design.

Recap of Key Points

- **Effective Use of Figma in Professional Contexts:** Understanding how Figma is employed by professionals to create and manage design projects from start to finish, highlighting its practical application in real-world scenarios.
- **Evaluation and Presentation of Design Case Studies:** Learning to assess design case studies using a structured rubric that emphasizes clarity, problem-solving, and user-centric approaches, and understanding how to present these effectively in a portfolio.
- **Strategies for Building a Strong Design Portfolio:** Tips on selecting and curating projects that showcase a diverse range of skills and key design decisions and using Figma to create a cohesive and visually appealing portfolio layout.

- **Solving Design Challenges with Figma:** Leveraging Figma's real-time collaboration, responsive design capabilities, and interactive prototyping to address and solve complex design challenges effectively.
- **Applying Advanced Figma Techniques:** Integrating advanced Figma features such as blending modes, effects, and typography into your own projects, and utilizing plugins to enhance functionality and streamline the design workflow.

Index

D

H

I

R

U